MW00426547

To ~~Pat Naidt~~

~~Keep up your~~

~~critical thinking!~~

~~Always~~

Practical Pacifism

PRACTICAL PACIFISM

Andrew Fiala

Algora Publishing
New York

© 2004 by Algora Publishing.
All Rights Reserved
www.algora.com

No portion of this book (beyond what is permitted by
Sections 107 or 108 of the United States Copyright Act of 1976)
may be reproduced by any process, stored in a retrieval system,
or transmitted in any form, or by any means, without the
express written permission of the publisher.
ISBN: 0-87586-290-x (softcover)
ISBN: 0-87586-291-8 (hardcover)
ISBN: 0-87586-292-6 (ebook)

Library of Congress Cataloging-in-Publication Data

Fiala, Andrew G. (Andrew Gordon), 1966-
  Practical pacifism / Andrew Fiala.
     p. cm.
  Includes bibliographical references and index.
  ISBN 0-87586-290-X (pbk. : alk. paper) — ISBN 0-87586-291-8 (hard cover :
alk. paper) — ISBN 0-87586-292-6 (ebook)
  1. Pacifism. 2. Just war doctrine. 3. Terrorism. I. Title.

  JZ5566.4.F53 2004
  303.6'6—dc22
                        2004006343

Printed in the United States

For my sons, with hope for a better world

Acknowledgements

I first presented the general idea of practical pacifism in a short article, "Practical Pacifism and the War on Terror," in *The Humanist* (vol. 62, no. 6, November/December 2002). Two chapters of the book are versions of articles that have been published elsewhere. A version of Chapter 4 was published in *Logos: A Journal of Catholic Thought and Culture* (vol. 7, no. 2, Spring 2004) and a version of Chapter 6 was published in *Essays in Philosophy* (vol. 3, March 2003; www.humboldt.edu/-essays/); they are reprinted here with permission.

My thoughts have developed in conversation with many other individuals. I would like to thank especially Derek Jeffreys, Hye-Kyung Kim, Rob Metcalf, John Lachs, and of course Julaine, Gordon, and Valerie Fiala.

TABLE OF CONTENTS

PREFACE

Practical pacifism is not absolute pacifism; it does not reject violence in all cases. Rather, it develops out of the idea that sometimes war may be justified, even as it questions whether any given war is in fact a just one.

This book attempts to articulate a certain uneasiness about the justification of war. Most of us do not know whether the wars that are fought in our names are justifiable. Most of us do not have access to intelligence information and classified documents that might help us understand the wars we fight. Moreover, history shows us that governments and the media present us with biased, incomplete, or false information about the wars we fight, the causes of these wars, and the way they are fought. War is so horrible that we should resist engaging in it until we are certain that it is necessary and justifiable; but in most cases, we simply cannot make that determination. Therefore, the thesis of practical pacifism is that we should be reluctant to consent to war, in most cases.

I came to this argument as I reflected on the events of the last several years — the attacks of September 11, the US declaration of war on terrorism, the invasion of Afghanistan, and the invasion of Iraq. The more I thought about these events, the more I realized that I lacked the sorts of information I would need to make good judgments about them. The skeptical standpoint of practical pacifism can be derived from the history of warfare as well as from current events. Citizens have often been manipulated into supporting wars that were neither necessary nor just. This Socratic insight into our pervasive ignorance

1

about the justification of war left me feeling uneasy about the military actions that Americans and our allies have all been asked to support in the last few years.

We must be honest about our ignorance. We often cannot say with certainty whether a war is just or unjust. This acknowledgement of ignorance should make us more careful in our judgments about war. Recent events show us, however, how reckless people can be. In the prelude to the invasion of Iraq, many controversial claims were made on both the pro-war and anti-war sides. Critical thinkers need to learn to see through the unfounded claims and hyperbolic rhetoric made by those on all sides of such debates. The first step toward making a better world is to learn to ask critical questions — even of oneself — in pursuit of the truth.

But we must still decide, and act, even when we are uncertain. The main question this book asks is: What should citizens of democracies do when they realize their own lack of certainty about the wars they are asked to support? Typically, we are told that we should stifle our doubts and trust our leaders. This response effectively asks us to give up our responsibility and judgment. But this abdication of responsibility is unacceptable: when one's country goes to war, one needs to know that the war is a just one. Especially in a democracy, where we are asked to consent to war, we must be certain that the sacrifices and suffering that will be caused are justified. Until it can be adequately proved that a specific war is justifiable, we should continue to question and resist.

The notion that we might support a war assumes that war can be just — that good reasons for going to war sometimes exist, and that war can be waged justly. The long tradition of thought about war and its justifications, known as "just war" thinking, is the jumping off point for the argument of practical pacifism.

Once we understand the notion of just war, we must then seek to understand the details of the war we are asked to support. Unfortunately, we often discover our own ignorance as we pursue knowledge about actual wars. This is especially true for those of us — ordinary citizens — who are not privy to governmental secrets, proposed battle plans, and other details. A bit of self-awareness shows us that much of the information we have about proposed wars comes through the filters of the government and the media, which have their own goals. An analysis of history shows us that the information provided to citizens about war is often false or incomplete. Moreover, as we reflect on psychology we realize that during times of crisis citizens tend to become more credulous and trusting of authority. All of this serves as a reminder that we must

2

remain committed to questioning ourselves about whether any given war is justified.

If we have reason to doubt that our information is inadequate to enable us to decide whether an actual war is just, then we are left with the task of questioning and resisting. Citizens should educate themselves about just war theory and about the history of warfare, as well as learning more about the nature of U.S. military power in the context of world politics. Citizens can work for justice by continuing to ask critical question both of those in power and of themselves.

There is a healthy division and tension in democracies. Citizens who lack specialized information and training are allowed to ask critical questions of the experts and the authorities. This tension is healthy because it helps keep those in power "honest," reminding them of their obligation to analyze situations both rationally and morally on behalf of the people they represent. This tension ought to put a brake on the drive for war. Debate forces us all to reflect on the moral requirements for war. Citizens of the global superpower have a unique responsibility to ensure that this power is used justly, to demand that their leaders live up to the standards of just war theory and that they prove that proposed uses of military force are justified.

I developed this thesis in reflecting on current events. Much of the book was written during the lead up to the invasion of Iraq in 2003 and during the immediate aftermath of the war. This war shows us quite clearly the problem that leads to practical pacifism. The US government made arguments before the United Nations and before the American people about the necessity and justification of the war. These arguments were said to be based upon intelligence assessments about, for example, the possibility that Iraq possessed weapons of mass destruction. Ordinary citizens had no way of knowing whether these assessments were accurate. The fear of terrorism, combined with a tendency to trust the government, led people to support the invasion of Iraq as part of the government's broad war on terrorism. (Ironically, the level of our fear of terrorism, too, is largely a reaction to government reports whose merit we cannot assess.) One year after the invasion, it is acknowledged that the threat from Iraq was exaggerated and deception may have been involved in the arguments that were made to support the war. Government efforts to convince citizens that war is needed can lead to manipulation and deception. Citizens who lack knowledge tend to trust the authorities, rather than question them. Thus citizens must be empowered with a healthy skepticism toward authority.

In the 21st century, we can expect that military power will be used to fight preemptive wars and wars of humanitarian intervention. But to decide whether such wars are justified requires a much more complicated process than the wars traditionally described by just war theory. The idea of preemption (first-strike) requires us to assess threats before they materialize. And humanitarian intervention requires that we make historical and political judgments about the long-term costs and benefits of violating a nation's sovereignty — not to mention destroying cities and killing people — in the name of human rights. Ordinary citizens usually lack the detailed technical knowledge required to make sound judgments in both of these cases. Thus, citizens should be committed to the sort of practical pacifism described here: we should continue to question and resist in the hope that military force that is used in our names will in fact be just.

Chapter 1. Practical Pacifism

> All history is the decline of war, though the slow decline...
> Emerson[1]

Are we making progress toward peace? Liberal political thinkers since Kant have argued that the advance of democracy and the spread of the idea of human rights would lead to the diminution of war.[2] Since Jane Addams, liberals, feminists, and others have argued that the empowerment of women and other oppressed groups, along with the cultivation of compassion, would lead us beyond the war system.[3] And Americans such as Emerson have argued that Americans have a unique opportunity and responsibility to move beyond what he called, as long ago as 1838, "the war-establishment."[4] Following Kant and Emerson, some argue that the creation of international bodies dedicated to peace, such as the United Nations, as well as the spread of economic and cultural globalization, will lead us beyond war.[5] And finally, others argue that the direct and immediate visual impression of war that is made possible by media

---

1. Ralph Waldo Emerson, "War" (an address to the Boston Peace Society from 1838) in *The Complete Writings of Ralph Waldo Emerson* (New York: William Wise and Co., 1929), II: 1142.

2. Kant, *Perpetual Peace* in *Kant: Political Writings* (Cambridge: Cambridge University Press, 1991); Michael Doyle, *Ways of War and Peace* (New York: Norton, 1997); John Rawls, *The Law of Peoples* (Harvard University Press, 1999).

3. Jane Addams, *The Long Road of Woman's Memory* (New York: Macmillan, 1916; BoondocksNet Edition, 2000). Also, see essays in Adrienne Harris and Ynestra King, eds., *Rocking the Ship of State: Toward a Feminist Peace Politics* (Boulder: Westview Press, 1989) and Betty Reardon, *Sexism and the War System* (New York: Teacher's College Press, 1985).

4. Emerson, "War," II: 1143.

technologies will make us more compassionate and aware of the suffering that is caused by war.[6]

Unfortunately, despite advances, war persists. We are still deciding what sorts of national and international institutions we want to create and how we want to empower them. And nation-states are still run by elites who are committed to the idea of military power. Indeed, the most dangerous and most overlooked irony of recent political history is the fact that the state that most vehemently declares itself to be a democracy — i.e., the United States — is also the most powerful and militaristic state in history. The last century saw the United States make a remarkable transformation from an isolated republic to a warfare state with global imperial commitments.[7] It is not too much to conclude that citizens of the United States have a unique responsibility and opportunity to use democracy to end war. Emerson held out the hope for an American continent populated by diverse immigrants and inspired by a creative impulse to overcome the stagnant traditions of European feudalism. This progressive vision was to include the dawning of a new maturity in which the war-establishment would be overcome. Unfortunately, this hope seems to have faded in light of the creation of the modern American military state. Nonetheless, America continues to occupy a unique place in history; not, as in Emerson's time, because of the freshness of our nation, but because of the immensity of our power. Now is the time to learn to use this power responsibly.

Despite our formal freedom, we citizens of democracies have not yet overcome the alienation and apathy that are created by the mass societies in which we live.[8] As Emerson so famously pointed out, we lack self-reliance. Self-reliance is antithetical to mass societies and militaristic states. But self-reliance is essential to the cause of peace. Emerson put it as follows.

---

5. See Boutros Boutros-Ghali, *An Agenda for Peace*, second edition (New York: United Nations, 1995). Kant makes this argument in *Perpetual Peace*; Emerson makes it in "War." For a discussion of the empowerment of the United Nations for humanitarian and peace-keeping missions, see Kofi A. Annan, "Two Concepts of Sovereignty," *The Economist*, September 18, 1999. For a discussion of globalization, see Peter Singer, *One World* (New Haven: Yale University Press, 2002), especially Chapters 1 and 4; for a discussion of the ways in which globalization is linked to the escalation of war, see Samuel Huntington, *The Clash of Civilizations* (New York: Simon and Schuster, 1996), Chapter 10.

6. See Michael Ignatieff, *The Warrior's Honor* (New York: Henry Holt, 1997). A similar argument is made by John Lachs, "Both Better and Better Off," *Journal of Speculative Philosophy* 15: 3, 2001, reprinted in *A Community of Individuals* (New York: Routledge, 2003).

7. For a history of this, see Peter Manicas, *War and Democracy* (Cambridge, MA: Blackwell, 1989), Chapters 13 and Epilogue. For a recent discussion of the American Empire, see Michael Ignatieff, "The Burden," *New York Times Magazine*, January 5, 2003.

8. See, for example, Jean Bethke Elshtain, *Democracy on Trial* (New York: Basic Books, 1995).

If peace is to be maintained, it must be by brave men, who have come up to the same height as the hero, namely, the will to carry their life in their hand, and stake it at any instant for their principle, but who have gone one step beyond the hero, and will not seek another man's life — men who have, by their intellectual insight or else by their moral elevation, attained such a perception of their own intrinsic worth that they do not think property or their own body a sufficient good to be saved by such dereliction of principle as treating a man like a sheep.[9]

True "warriors" for peace are sustained by courage and self-reliance to stand up for justice while criticizing militarism in the face of a pervasive military establishment. This responsibility for courage, self-reliance, and for the earnest pursuit of critical inquiry into the ideology that supports the military state rests equally upon all citizens. Unfortunately, despite our culture of self-reliance, the citizens of the United States have failed to question the development in the United States of the warfare state, with its massive nuclear arsenal, its standing army, its global military deployments, and its routine employment of military force throughout the world. Perhaps we are not yet, as Emerson thought, fully self-reliant. We have not yet realized either the full potential of democracy or the meaning of cosmopolitan citizenship. And we have ignored the facts and dangers of militarism. So, as we educate ourselves about militarism, we must take upon ourselves the duties of individual responsibility. The irony of the newly global era is that individual responsibility is still the center of human progress. But now is the time for us to empower ourselves to ensure that progress is made. As Jonathan Glover states, "because we live in the first period of history in which there is such full awareness of cruelty and killing as they happen, our response is particularly important."[10] In this new era, no one can feign ignorance about political violence: we see it every day on the television. Despite this immediate experience of political violence, peace still requires education of the human spirit such that each human being recognizes his/her own responsibility for ending the violence which we all witness. Liberal institutions are essential for any lasting peace because they are founded on the twin ideas that all human beings are worthy of respect and that each of us is morally responsible for the violence committed in our names. Violence should be anathema to liberalism

---

9. Emerson, "War," II: 1147.

10. Jonathan Glover, *Humanity: A Moral History of the 20th Century* (New Haven: Yale University Press, 1999), 42.

because violence violates the autonomy of its victims: violence is, by definition, something done against the will of the victim.[11]

Those who are committed to peace and to democracy believe that human beings can be trusted to create for ourselves solutions to our problems. However, we are also suspicious of the machinations of power. My effort in the present book is to clarify the way in which melioristic hope and critical suspicion are linked. Those who believe in the possibility of nonviolent action are distrustful of political power, while hopeful that democratic international institutions can bring about the peace we seek. In the long run, however, the real solution to the problem of war is education and citizen empowerment. An educated global citizenry will be able to resist imperial and militaristic power, while reconstructing both national and international cultures along more pacific lines. This means that the most "practical" part of "practical pacifism" is its commitment to vigorous education about the horrors of war, about the undemocratic nature of militarism, and about possibilities for peace. I should note, however, that this book is not a practical manual for nonviolent social reform. Instead, it is a philosophical argument detailing practical reasons why we should choose peace over war.

The practical form of pacifism I defend runs counter to a more religiously or metaphysically grounded form of pacifism — what I call absolute pacifism. The certainty and dedication to peace that is provided by more absolute forms of pacifism is inspirational. However, religious belief can also lead to violence when its commitments to eschatological absolutes becomes fanatical. For pacifism to be broadly effective, it must be articulated and defended from a humanistic and *moral* standpoint that transcends religious sectarianism. This is not to say that Gandhi, Martin Luther King, Jr., or other religious pacifists are closed-minded or intolerant. Rather, for pacifism to become practical, it must be defended and adopted by way of some form of "overlapping consensus": different individuals must come to see, from within their diverse world-views, that a practical commitment to peace is reasonable. This approach, which relies upon the pragmatic development of a moral consensus, has been defended by liberal philosophers such as John Rawls and even by the Pope.[12] Pope John Paul II said, in response to the problem of terrorism: "The various Christian confessions, as well as the world's great religions, need to work together to eliminate the social

---

11. The question of the definition of violence and its connection to political institutions will be discussed extensively in Chapter 5.

and cultural causes of terrorism. They can do this by teaching the greatness and dignity of the human person, and by spreading *a clearer sense of the oneness of the human family*. This is a specific area of ecumenical and inter-religious dialogue and cooperation, a pressing service which religion can offer to world peace."[13] This approach to peace aims beyond religion toward a moral consensus that is developed pragmatically through dialogue aimed at overlapping consensus.

Some might argue that religion and its hope that peace can be accomplished is necessary to motivate us to work for peace. Gandhi writes, optimistically: "If we turn our eyes to the time of which history has any record down to our own time, we shall find that man has been steadily progressing towards nonviolence."[14] However Gandhi's approach is grounded in a religious world-view that not all share. And like other religious pacifists, his hope is ultimately directed toward a realm that transcends the ordinary realm of human politics. And yet, Gandhi also bases his optimism on facts about this world. He thought that the large scope of history showed that human beings were progressing beyond violence. Gandhi noted that we are no longer cannibals and that we are making progress in respecting the sanctity of life. Moreover, Gandhi recognized, as early as 1940, that we were developing toward a truly international civilization. Gandhi's practical successes can show us that nonviolence is in fact a viable political policy. However, Gandhi's approach is ultimately a spiritual one. One wonders whether nonviolence can be grounded in a more pragmatic and humanistic approach to politics. Gandhi's spiritualism is in fact explicitly linked to his optimism. He claimed, for example, that the evolution of the human spirit provided the best reason to hope for progress toward peace: "Man as animal is violent, but as Spirit is nonviolent. The moment he awakes to the Spirit within he cannot remain violent. Either he progresses towards ahimsa or rushes to his doom."[15] Although Gandhi develops his idea of ahimsa (nonviolence) from within Indian religious thought, his basic ideas have

---

12. The idea of an overlapping consensus has been defended most vigorously by John Rawls in his *Political Liberalism* (New York: Columbia University Press, 1995). It is interesting to note that the idea of an overlapping consensus about international law was defended by Jacques Maritain — who writes from within the Catholic faith tradition — in his *Man and the State* (Chicago: University of Chicago Press, 1951).

13. Pope John Paul II, "No Peace Without Justice, No Justice Without Forgiveness," January 1, 2002, for a celebration of the World Day of Peace, section 12 (http://www.vatican.va/holy_father/john_paul_ii/messages/peace/documents/hf_jp-ii_mes_20011211_xxxv-world-day-for-peace_en.html).

14. Mohandas Gandhi, "Is Non-Violence Impossible," in *Non-Violence in Peace and War — 1920-1942* (New York: Garland Publishing, 1972), 310.

15. Gandhi, "Is Non-Violence Impossible," 311.

much in common with Christianity and with certain parts of Western liberalism: a commitment to ecumenical, tolerant, and peaceful coexistence. It is this ethical commitment that I want to examine, while divorcing it from a religious metaphysics.

The pragmatist approach to peace is uniquely American. Since it is the unique responsibility and opportunity of citizens of the United States to work toward peace, it is fitting that we consider a uniquely American approach to pacifism, as found in the work of important American philosophers such as Emerson, Thoreau, James, Addams, Dewey, and others.[16] The American pragmatist approach begins with a basic empirical insight into the horror and waste of war. It is also founded upon the idea that our institutions and cultures can be subject to intelligent human control. Although religious belief lay just below the surface in the writing and thinking of Emerson, this religious belief is understood from the direction of a theory of moral development. Emerson writes that war is a product of the infancy of humankind. We begin as aggressive warriors. We learn, eventually, to avoid aggression. The final progress will be toward a willingness to avoid violence even to the point of self-sacrifice. Emerson tells us that the "higher man" "sacrifices himself, and accepts with alacrity wearisome tasks of denial and charity; but, being attacked he bears it and turns the other cheek, as one engaged, throughout his being, no longer in the service of an individual but to the common soul of all men."[17] Emerson expresses

---

16. I should note that there has been quite a bit of discussion about whether American pragmatists must be committed to peace. I discuss some of this literature in Chapter 8. There is also discussion about whether pragmatism possesses the moral resources necessary to effectively resist violence. Louis Menand's book, *The Metaphysical Club* (New York: Farrar, Strauss, and Giroux, 2001), puts this in stark relief by contrasting the nonviolent commitment and social activism of absolutists such as Gandhi and King to the pragmatic pacifism and social activism of Dewey and Oliver Wendell Holmes. Menand acknowledges that pragmatism is linked to democracy, tolerance, and nonviolence. "Pragmatism was designed to make it harder for people to be driven to violence by their beliefs" (*The Metaphysical Club*, p. 440). But he questions whether the pragmatic approach is sufficient to cultivate a commitment either to liberty or to nonviolence. "Martin Luther King, Jr., was not a pragmatist, a relativist, or a pluralist, and it is a question whether the movement he led could have accomplished what it did if its inspirations had come from Dewey and Holmes rather than Reinhold Niebuhr and Mahatma Gandhi" (*The Metaphysical Club*, p. 441). For a critical discussion of Menand's view of pragmatism, see Cheyney Ryan's discussion as presented at the 2003 meeting of the Society for the Advancement of American Philosophy, available on line at http://www.american-philosophy.org/ 2003_conference/2003_papers/tp-7.htm. The deeper problem seems to be that since pragmatists are not committed to moral absolutes, they can be accused of supporting a crass consequentialism in which "the end justifies the means." As I shall argue in what follows, a more robust understanding of pragmatism, following Dewey, emphasizes the interdependence of means and ends that rejects such crass consequentialism. For further discussion of my own pragmatic pluralistic method, see the Appendix to Chapter 1.

10

a moral enthusiasm for pacifism that he was later to exchange for a more realistic approach to the question of political violence. Emerson eventually supported the use of violence in the cause of abolition: he supported John Brown, for example, and the Union cause in the Civil War. Nonetheless, Emerson expresses a hope for a world beyond war in which individuals would evolve the moral capacity to resist the temptation for violence. His later support for the use of violence in pursuit of a just cause shows us that a fundamental commitment to pacifism can be conjoined with a recognition of certain practical situations when violence reluctantly can be employed. It is this practical approach to violence (as opposed to its absolute prohibition) that is the unique contribution of American philosophy.

This is not to say, however, that American pragmatism uses a crass means-end calculus in considerations of the use of violence. Indeed, the tradition of American philosophers that I have in mind was almost always reluctant to justify violence, even while admitting that in rare cases violence could be justified. One of the practical points made in this tradition is that one must properly understand war and the war-system in order to be able to resist it. Following Emerson, William James, America's most famous pragmatist, also struggled with the practical question of war and peace. Almost 100 years ago, in 1906, he delivered his oft-cited essay, "The Moral Equivalent of War." In it he analyzed the virtues of the war system. But he concluded with the following:

> The fatalistic view of the war function is to me nonsense, for I know that war-making is due to definite motives and subject to prudential checks and reasonable criticisms, just like any other form of enterprise. And when whole nations are the armies, and the science of destruction vies in intellectual refinement with the science of production, I see that war becomes absurd and impossible from its own monstrosity. Extravagant ambitions will have to be replaced by reasonable claims, and nations must make common cause against them.[18]

James is hopeful that reasonableness can prevail even in the realm of national and international politics, that eventually we will fully understand the horror and absurdity of war, and that we will consciously choose to get beyond our bellicose presuppositions. This idea is grounded in a melioristic commitment

17. Emerson, "War," II: 1144.
18. William James, "The Moral Equivalent of War," available online: (http://www.emory.edu/EDUCATION/mfp/moral.html).

to the idea that since politics and culture are produced by humans, we can intelligently alter them. Jane Addams, another American pragmatist (who won the Nobel Peace Prize in 1931), expressed a similar spirit of hope. Like James, Addams believed that the idea of peace must be more than simple opposition to war. It must also include a commitment to democracy and to larger projects of social justice. In an address delivered in 1899, "Democracy or Militarism," she writes that peace is "no longer merely absence of war, but the unfolding of life processes which are making for a common development."[19] Addams' hope for peace is linked explicitly to a pragmatic recognition that humanity is developing a form of moral conscience that points beyond war. Her hope extends directly to the empowerment produced by democracy: she hopes that when women and the oppressed masses who have long silently suffered the horrors of war are empowered, war will come to an end. She writes, "There are indications that the human consciousness is reaching the same stage of sensitiveness in regard to war as that which has been attained in regard to human sacrifice. In this moment of almost universal warfare there is evinced a widespread moral abhorrence against war, as if its very existence were more than human nature could endure. Citizens of every nation are expressing this moral compunction, which they find in sharp conflict with current conceptions of patriotic duty."[20] This idea of widespread abhorrence against war, even in the midst of war, echoes Gandhi's idea about spiritual progress. The problem is how to mobilize this moral sentiment so that we can actually end war.

Addams hints at the problem when she notes that abhorrence to war seems to run counter to our patriotic duty. Nation states are founded on force. When we question the war-system, we question the legitimacy of the warfare state. This is why pacifism is radical and why pacifists are viewed as subversive. Unfortunately, most of us do not want to rock the ship of state and so we acquiesce to the inevitability of the nation state's commitment to military power. But this quiet complacency can be combated through education about the basic ideas of democracy. Again, the classic American philosophers are useful in this regard. Thoreau, for example, famously opposed militarism and preached civil disobedience to the militaristic state. His basic anarchism — his declaration of "war on the State" — is based upon his commitment, following Emerson, to

---

19. Jane Addams, "Democracy or Militarism" from BoondocksNet Edition, 2000 (http://www.boondocksnet.com/ai/ailtexts/addams.html).

20. Jane Addams, *The Long Road of Woman's Memory* (New York: Macmillan, 1916; BoondocksNet Edition, 2000).

the sanctity or sovereignty of the individual. "There will never be a really free and enlightened State until the State comes to recognize the individual as a higher and independent power, from which all its own power and authority are derived, and treats him accordingly."[21] We must work to educate people about this democratic conception of the limits of state power. And we must continually point out the contradiction found in the fact that the greatest "democracy" on earth is also the greatest military power.

This is not to say that pacifists must be anarchists. Nor is it to say that American pragmatists must be pacifists. Dewey, for example, was focused on the intelligent reform of national institutions. He was committed to the idea behind international institutions dedicated to democracy. And he at one time — during debates about American involvement in World War I — supported the idea that war can spread both peace and democracy. Nonetheless, Dewey became more and more committed to the idea that "democratic ends demand democratic methods for their realization."[22] Dewey's ambivalence about the relationship between democracy and violence is significant because it opens us onto the practical problem of pacifism. Is it possible that peace can be enacted by means of violence? There is no easy answer to this question. Occasionally it might be necessary to use violence in defense of freedom. Some cases seem obvious: it might be justified to use violence to defend my family from an invader. However, the question becomes quite complicated when it is directed to national and international politics. At issue, here, is a question of the burden of proof: can we be sure that any use of violence is in fact justified? I will discuss this in what follows as the question of whether ordinary citizens of mass societies can be sure that the use of military violence is justified in light of just war criteria. My answer is that, in most cases, citizens simply cannot know that the use of violence is justified. And so, since violence is prima facie bad, citizens should resist the drive to war. This is the way in which democracy will put a brake upon the war system.

Unfortunately, the world is a complicated place and this task is not as straightforward as it might seem. Absolute pacifists can argue that all use of violence is unjustified. But a more pragmatic approach must be willing to look at

---

21. Thoreau, "Civil Disobedience" in Henry David Thoreau, *Walden and Other Writings* (New York: Modern Library, 2000), 693.

22. John Dewey, "Democratic Ends Need Democratic Methods for their Realization," in *John Dewey, Later Works* (Carbondale: Southern Illinois University Press, 1981), 14: 367-368. I discuss Dewey and the relation between pragmatism and pacifism in more detail in Chapter 8.

the complexity of each case in light of the complexity of the ends we pursue and the means we employ. The complexity of the problem of war becomes apparent if we consider the problem of peace-keeping and humanitarian intervention, both of which are uses of military force which aim at protecting the innocent and fostering democracy. Kofi Annan, the Secretary General of the United Nations, has defended such uses of force in defense of the sovereignty of the individual and in defense of a diminished idea of state sovereignty. The idea of individual sovereignty is an idea with which Emerson and Thoreau would agree. However, Annan uses this idea to defend the United Nations' role in using force. Military force might be needed to defend human rights and to end atrocities.

> State sovereignty, in its most basic sense, is being redefined — not least by the forces of globalization and international cooperation. States are now widely understood to be instruments at the service of their peoples, and not vice versa. At the same time, individual sovereignty — by which I mean the fundamental freedom of each individual, enshrined in the charter of the UN and subsequent international treaties — has been enhanced by a renewed and spreading consciousness of individual rights.[23]

Annan assumes that the use of military force can be justified when it is aimed at humanitarian ends. I must admit that I am sympathetic to this idea, an idea that is derived from an interpretation of the idea of "just cause" found in the theory of justice in war. The pragmatic problem is how to ensure that the use of military force does not become unjust. My own suggestion in what follows is that citizen empowerment is necessary. Citizens should be committed to pacifism and should set up a high burden of proof for those who would argue that military force is necessary. On some regrettable occasions, military force may be justified. But citizens should resist the idea that military force is necessary until such necessity has been proven to them beyond the shadow of a doubt. Moreover, as even Annan recognizes, we must recognize that there are many kinds of intervention other than military intervention. Practical pacifism must be committed — as James, Addams, and Dewey were — to the vigorous and intelligent application of peaceful democratic means of problem solving.

---

23. Kofi A. Annan, "Two Concepts of Sovereignty."

THE CURRENT PROBLEM

The corpses produced by violence and war piled much higher after Gandhi, Addams, and James dreamed of peace. And there were moments during the late 20th century when it did indeed seem as though we were rapidly approaching midnight on the doomsday clock. What is more dispiriting: methods of war continue to be employed even by liberal states. Kant had dared to hope, over two hundred years ago, that liberal states would not go to war with one another. But it may still be the case, as John Rawls — America's preeminent contemporary Kantian — has outlined, that liberal regimes can and will go to war against non-liberal regimes. Indeed, the wars engaged in by the United States under the rubric of the "war on terrorism" have been wars justified on this basis. We are fighting rogue states and terrorists. So, while some may claim that there has been progress toward a world beyond war, this progress reaches its limit when liberalism confronts its other. Of course, we must be careful about such dichotomizing. One wonders whether, in fact, current war making is really a matter of liberalism vs. its other or whether it is an ongoing process of militarism and imperialism.

Before turning to this vexing question, let's begin with the facts. It is hard to deny that the 20th century was a century of violence. In the 20th century, there were 187 million deaths caused by wars.[24] This mind-boggling number can be made concrete by realizing that if you counted corpses at a rate of one corpse per second, it would take six years of non-stop counting for you to count all of the dead. In the 21st century, things seem to be moving in an equally lethal direction. The terrorist attacks of September 11, 2001 and the subsequent "war on terrorism" makes it appear as if the body count will continue to grow. A cynic might conclude that we are not making progress toward peace. Despite an apparent world-wide revival of religious belief in the last decades, it appears as if the great spiritual awakening that Gandhi celebrated has yet to come — if only because some parts of that religious revival are themselves violent and fanatical. Despite the fact that some parts of the world have experienced progress toward the creation of more liberal institutions, liberal states themselves still feel the need to employ the means of war. Indeed, some have argued that the conflicts of the 21st century will be spiritual conflicts, driven by religious fanaticism and by

---

24. See Eric Hobsbawm, "War and Peace in the 20th Century," *London Review of Books*, February 21, 2002.

the clash between liberalism and its other. It might rather be the case, as Samuel Huntington has argued, that we have yet to work our way beyond the great clash between civilizations.[25]

Cynics might argue that those who tout the spread of democracy and the growth of an international civilization based on respect for human rights are either naïvely utopian or secretly imperialistic. Huntington's analysis may itself serve the interests of imperialistic American ideology by tacitly defending the imperialistic ambitions of those who would use the idea of "disseminating liberal values" as cover for the pursuit of political hegemony. Indeed, recent events (i.e., the breakdown of international institutions in light of the US-led war against Iraq) serve to give us further reasons to despair about peace. In 1995, then Secretary General of the UN, Boutros Boutros-Ghali, issued a report about the role that the United Nations might play in a world of peace. He emphasized collegiality on the UN Security Council, as well as democratic representation, democratic deliberation, and consensus within the "family of nations." Boutros-Ghali wrote, "A genuine sense of consensus deriving from shared interests must govern its [the Security Council's] work, not the threat of the veto or the power of any group of nations." He concluded that "the powerful must resist the dual but opposite calls of unilateralism and isolationism, if the United Nations is to succeed."[26] In 1995, as we sighed in relief at the end of the Cold War, these claims gave us reason to hope. Now, a mere eight years later, as we witness the unilateralism of the United States, it appears that the United Nations as a peace-making institution is foundering.

In a different century, Thoreau and James were worried about American imperialism as seen in the Mexican-American war or in the war in the Philippines. The worry about imperialism continues. Noam Chomsky has written at length about the growth of a form of American imperialism that is both undemocratic and violent. From Chomsky's perspective, one of the chief problems is that citizens lack education about the imperial ambitions and violent methods of our government. And so, a genuinely democratic opposition to imperialism cannot find traction. Within the United States, the public is kept in ignorance and isolation by subtle forms of thought control, while violence and terrorism are used as means of direct action abroad. If Chomsky is right, then even those of us who are sympathetic to his analysis are merely alienated and

---

25. Samuel Huntington, *The Clash of Civilizations*; on the religious revival, see pp. 95-101
26. Boutros Boutros-Ghali, *An Agenda for Peace*, 70.

disgruntled, without access to a practical remedy. Despite this dark outlook, even Chomsky has emphasized the necessity of hope. "If you assume that there's no hope, you guarantee there will be no hope. If you assume that there is an instinct for freedom, there are opportunities to change things."[27] This idea — the idea of the necessity of assuming hope — is fundamental for those who would work for peace. As I will argue in subsequent chapters, this hope is a pragmatic need: we must hope in order to act. Nonetheless, hope must be tempered with a careful analysis of reality. Chomsky, despite the occasional excesses of his anti-Imperialist zeal, is right about the fact that citizens are alienated: it seems that the institutional cards are stacked against empowering citizens to work for peace. At best this leaves us with profound ambivalence. We hope and work for a world beyond war, while recognizing that the war-system is firmly entrenched in institutions of war and in our bellicose traditions and cultures.

The human condition is tragically ambiguous: to be human is to be caught up in an ongoing conflict of values. We crave peace; and yet we are prone to violence. We long for progress and historical certainty; and yet human beings are individuals and human history is the product of the choices of individuals. This means that, ultimately, ideas about progress and about general spiritual renewal must focus on the choices and thought processes of individual human beings. This is true even if cultures and institutions are poised against us; in fact, in such circumstances, individual commitment, responsibility, and action are indispensable. Our responsibility is radical: each individual must at each and every moment confront the rival possibilities of violence and of peace in all that we do. We should be careful of metaphysical sleight-of-hand attempts to paint an overly optimistic view of human progress; but we should likewise be careful of similar deceptions that encourage us to dwell in doom and despair. Ethical and political thinking is often side-tracked by our tendency to look for trans-historical absolutes. The fact of the matter is that both optimism and pessimism about history fail to recognize that at each and every moment, the future is undecided. It is up to each one of us, as individuals, to choose what course the future will take.

Religious or metaphysical optimism tends to undermine the urgency of action by hiding uncertainty beneath the palliative belief that this is the best of all possible worlds. Pessimism does the same, but for the pessimist the "cure" is

---

27. Noam Chomsky, "Noise: Noam Chomsky Interview," February 1997, *Netizen* (http://hotwired.lycos.com/netizen/netizenaudio/transcripts/index41.html).

melancholy and despair. In large doses, hope and despair both have a narcotic effect: they take action out of our hands by making the result inevitable — one way or another. Nonetheless, optimists and pessimists do offer suggestions about how to create peace. Optimistic approaches to peace can be found in the West in Christianity and Marxism. Christians follow Jesus in claiming that peace can result from religious renewal. Materialists and Marxists claim that peace will only result from substantive equality that promotes human flourishing. More pessimistic Western political theorists, such as Machiavelli and Hobbes, maintain that the idea that peace can prevail is a naïve utopian illusion made doubtful by the idea that human beings are basically greedy and self-interested. The solution from this perspective is a strong central authority with the power to maintain peace by force. The Hobbesian approach corresponds to a certain Christian idea about human sinfulness and links to contemporary theories about a biological bias toward violence. The difficulties of these various approaches are obvious. Faith in God does not stop violence in this world. The Marxist revolution, like the Machiavellian Prince, is inherently violent. And the Hobbesian state, at best, concentrates violence in nation states that are themselves always at risk of war.

My own approach to peace is practical, humanistic, liberal, and melioristic. I have faith in the capacity for human development without divine intervention or total revolution. I am skeptical about grand pronouncements about the course of history, believing instead that the future course of history is always open and that it is our individual responsibility to create the future for ourselves, one person at a time. As I will argue in the chapters that follow, personal responsibility and critical resistance to violence are grounded on a basic commitment to philosophical self-consciousness. Although my approach is not religious, it is spiritual in a philosophical sense: the spirit to be developed is the spirit of rationality and self-consciousness. I conceive of philosophy as a method of modesty, tolerance, and reflection. I shall argue in these pages that this method can be the root of peace. Modesty about knowledge claims and about moral certainty leads to reluctance to use violence. Tolerance grows from self-conscious modesty and respect for autonomy. Philosophical reflection on the human condition — our fragility, our ignorance, and our tendency to succumb to easy answers and vicious ideas — supports modesty and tolerance, and ultimately leads to peace.

This type of philosophical self-consciousness is best nurtured by liberal institutions and a liberal education. However, this is not a panacea.

Philosophical self-consciousness shows us that there are no panaceas. We must continually strive to educate ourselves and others, recognizing that failure is a possibility. Nonetheless, we must have the melioristic faith that education can be effective, for without such faith, it is easy to succumb to the quietism of despair. This humanistic faith is not an abstract form of spiritualism. Rather, it recognizes that education is directed toward human beings who have bodies and inherit cultures. Education toward philosophical self-consciousness requires a healthy and functioning body and it can only develop from within one's own tradition and culture. Most importantly, this project must be put into practice. We must confront militaristic institutions however and wherever we can. The strategies for action must be guided by a pragmatic recognition that differing circumstances require different methods. However, such a form of pragmatism must not become a Machiavellian form of pragmatics where the end justifies the means. Rather, in the spirit of Dewey, we should recognize that means and ends are interdependent. Indeed, the pragmatism I have in mind is committed to democracy and nonviolence as both a means and end. Progress toward peace will be facilitated by peaceful means, such as education, that are employed with vigor and intelligence and which are disseminated as broadly as possible.

PRACTICAL PACIFISM

I call the approach I defend "practical pacifism." Practical pacifism is a theory that admits that war might be justifiable, while doubting whether any finite human being can know for sure that any particular war is in fact justifiable. This approach is an interpretation of the just war theory that focuses on the epistemological problem of determining the justification of war in practice. Although the just war theory allows for the use of violence, I interpret the just war theory as sharing with pacifism the basic idea that violence is to be avoided.[28] In just war thinking, violence should only be used as a last resort and only when it is morally justified. The problem that leads to practical pacifism is that it is often very difficult, in practice, for average citizens to decide whether any given war is in fact justified.[29] This is especially true in the complex cases

---

28. For a discussion of the affinity between just war theory and pacifism, see Richard Miller, *Interpretation of Conflict* (Chicago: University of Chicago, 1991). For a rival interpretation that emphasizes justice over peace, see George Weigel, "The Just War Tradition and the World after September 11," *Logos*, 5:3 (Summer 2002).

that afflict us today: Afghanistan, Iraq, North Korea, etc. In such cases our leaders often must decide to use violence under conditions of uncertainty. Ordinary citizens, who do not have access to our leaders' information or expertise, are even more uncertain about the justification of violence. Unless we blindly trust our leaders to make infallible judgments based upon pure motives, the rational response for citizens of democracies is to resist war.

Commonsense usually tells us that we are justified in resorting to violence in self-defense when there is no other option, when there is a true risk to life or limb, and when the violence used in self-defense is proportional to the violence we are resisting. However, this paradigm case is quite rare, in practice: it is often difficult to be sure that there are no other options and that we are in fact at risk. Moreover, the question of proportionality is a vexing one because violence is unpredictable — it is often impossible to say, in advance, whether violence will lead to escalation, whom it will directly affect, or what other kinds of damage it will do. With regard to political acts of violence such as war, matters become even more convoluted. Practical pacifism holds that since violence is something to be avoided, we should be reluctant to use it (or support its use) when we are unsure that it is necessary or justified.

Practical pacifism is a decidedly humanistic approach: it argues for erring on the side of peace, based upon arguments located firmly within human experience. Experience tells us, for example, that citizens of mass societies, who lack access to information and power, usually do not know whether acts of war committed by their governments are justifiable. This is true despite the fact that we have broad access to the media: we are often manipulated by a jingoistic press into patriotic support for war. Since acts of war are among the most horrible things that can be done by human beings, the highest level of certainty should be required for us to say that such a horror is justified. Without such certainty, citizens should resist their leaders' claims about the justification of any particular war. Although this approach has some affinities with anarchism, practical pacifism is not an explicitly anti-government approach. Rather, it is an approach that ought to be taken by rational citizens of advanced democracies who understand their own limitations and who understand the irrational nature of patriotism. Indeed if we are the least bit sympathetic to Chomsky's argument that consent is usually "manufactured" by state propaganda, then we should be

---

29. This basic idea has been defended by Paul J. Griffiths in "Just War: An Exchange," in *First Things*, no. 122, pp. 31-33. Also see George Weigel's critical response in the same issue of *First Things*.

quite skeptical of the claims that are made in support of all kinds of state violence. At least, we should admit that in most cases we simply do not know if the use of military force is justifiable. Therefore, if we agree that war is a horrible last resort, the rational strategy is for citizens to question and resist those in power who advocate the use of military force.

Thoreau made a similar argument in his essay "Civil Disobedience." Following Emerson's lead, Thoreau maintains that human beings are perverted by an alienating society, with militarism as one of the main purveyors of alienation. "The mass of men serve the state thus, not as men mainly, but as machines, with their bodies. They are the standing army, and the militia, jailors, constables, posse comitatus, etc."[30] Thoreau goes on to say that "a very few, as heroes, patriots, martyrs, reformers in the great sense, and men, serve the state with their consciences also, and so necessarily resist it for the most part; and they are commonly treated as enemies by it."[31] Self-reliant individuals ought to resist immoral actions that the government does "in their names." The true patriot and the moral hero is the one who is committed to doing right and is willing to question and resist his government when he is not convinced that his government is doing right. Military actions are supported by our tax dollars and by our tacit consent. Anyone committed to peace should find it difficult to authorize the use of war and should demand that a strong case be made justifying its use. Most of us have been taught to trust the government and to comply with its foreign policy decision. This is ironic given that our culture also fosters suspicion and distrust of politicians. American patriotism has come to mean that although we can disagree with our political leaders and critique and deflate them at home, we need to show a unified front to the rest of the world.

Now, I am not suggesting that all of our leaders are corrupt or untrustworthy. Nor do I follow Chomsky in claiming that most of us are gullible dupes. However, I am suggesting that perhaps we trust our leaders' judgment a bit too much when it comes to the all-important question of using military violence. Moreover, and this is the important point, when it comes to complex foreign policy decisions in today's global context, we often simply do not know whether we should support our leaders or not. Our leaders have more information than we do: indeed, they have access to secret information that we do not have access to. And in foreign policy, it is even more likely that an

---

30. Henry David Thoreau, "Civil Disobedience," in *Walden and Other Writings* (New York: Modern Library, 2000), 669-670.
31. Henry David Thoreau, "Civil Disobedience," in *Walden and Other Writings*, 670.

intellectual and ideological elite controls public opinion, because most of us simply do not have the requisite expertise.[32] The rational position is for us to question and resist, if we are interested in certainty with regard to the use of violence. This is especially true if we are suspicious of our leaders' moral integrity or the purity of their motives. As Thoreau said, in the context of the Mexican-American War (which he viewed as a war of conquest and empire), we should let our lives be a "counter-friction to the machine."

A practical pacifist might admit that some forms of military force are defensible. National self-defense seems an obvious case. Moreover, it might be possible to justify military intervention that is aimed at protecting human rights, keeping the peace, or creating stability. The difficulty confronted by the practical pacifist is the realization that often citizens do not know and cannot know whether their political and military leaders are motivated by a good faith attempt to follow the principles of the just war doctrine that allow such military solutions.[33] We certainly hope that our leaders are interested in justice. However, experience teaches us that our leaders are often motivated by other purposes. We must be suspicious of the Machiavellian logic of politics and of the strategies and goals of military realists. History gives us good reason to be suspicious of our leaders: the MAD-ness of the Cold War and the apocalyptic concerns of the Domino Theory, the deceit and destruction in Vietnam, the boondoggle of the Star Wars missile defense, etc. In addition, with regard to complex global issues such as those reflected in Afghanistan and Iraq, we often simply do not have enough information to know that war is justifiable.

It is important to note that practical pacifism is not committed to peace based upon religious claims about the transcendent value of nonviolence. The greatest advocates of nonviolence — Jesus, Gandhi, Martin Luther King, the Dalai Lama — have been motivated by religious insight. The religious approach is important and inspirational. However, the religious perspective puts pacifism together with an idea about the transcendent justification of suffering: we can afford to turn the other cheek because submission to evil will be rewarded in the next life. Such an approach can inspire and we can admire the dedication and faith of religious pacifists. However, a practical commitment to pacifism does not rely upon a transcendent metaphysics or religious ideas. Rather, the

---

32. See G. William Domhoff, *Who Rules America?* (Mountain View: Mayfield, 1998), Chapter 5.

33. This thesis has strong affinities with a position defended recently by Paul Griffiths in Paul J. Griffiths, "Just War: An Exchange" (with a reply by George Weigel), in *First Things*, no. 122 (April 2002), pp. 31-36.

practical pacifist recognizes the horror of suffering and the finality of death. Suffering and death should be avoided, not celebrated. This is why we have a right to use to force to defend ourselves and others. However, the motivating tension of the just war tradition is the recognition of the terrible tragedy of causing death even for the "just" purpose of preventing death. I put "just" in quotes because the deaths caused in a "just" war are better described as "unfortunate but allowable" — to call them "just" goes too far in the direction of making war seem like a good and noble thing. The practical pacifist assumes that even if some forms of violence (including war) are permissible, human fallibility makes it unlikely that we can be absolutely certain about the justification of violence. Moreover, the alienation and hyper-mediation of contemporary society make it highly unlikely that citizens of complex modern societies can know whether any proposed war is in fact justified. Finally, the advanced destructive power of modern warfare makes it more likely that the violence of war will exceed justifiable limits.

THE AMERICAN EMPIRE AND HUMANITARIAN INTERVENTION

Current events put war and the political use of violence in the headlines. Citizens of the United States have a unique responsibility to think critically about political violence, since the United States as "the sole superpower" or "global empire" is in a unique position to employ and control violence.[34] We have been aware of the problem of the military-industrial complex for several decades. While the development of the "American Empire" is leading us away from the ideals of the early republic, it is important for citizens of the United States (and her allies) to think carefully about the ways in which violence is used in our names. Although some might celebrate our triumphant power, this power brings with it immense responsibility. If we truly want an empire, we must realize that an empire requires a strong standing military force, a secretive and cumbersome bureaucracy, and a willingness to use military force. Under these conditions, I will argue that it is our duty to be extremely reluctant to support military action undertaken "on our behalf." Indeed, given the massive size of the American Empire, it is increasingly difficult to imagine conditions under which

---

34. Michael Ignatieff, "The Burden," *New York Times Magazine*, January 5, 2003.

we could say that US military action is undertaken on behalf of the interests of the citizens of the United States.

To see this, we must consider a paradigm case in which military action would be justifiable from the perspective of most citizens in the democracy. The paradigm for a just war is a defensive war to repel invaders. The just war tradition maintains that states are entitled to defend their sovereignty and territorial integrity. Moreover, it is easy to imagine that the vast majority of the citizens of the United States would concur that it is appropriate to use military force to repel invaders crossing into the States, say, from Canada. The commonsense point is that individual citizens would take up arms themselves to repel invaders who posed a threat to their lives, property, and way of life.

It is a long way from this paradigm to the types of warfare our forces are currently practicing. Most often, these efforts are described as peace-keeping and humanitarian intervention. Clearly these are not activities aimed merely at self-defense. It is further still to problematic cases such as the US invasion of Iraq in order to effect "regime change." I am not arguing that peace-keeping and humanitarian intervention are immoral and that we should not support these efforts. Rather, I am pointing out that the task of justifying these actions is far more complex than the paradigm case of self-defense. One of the main difficulties in thinking about non-defensive wars is that such wars are almost never undertaken with pure intentions. Michael Walzer, America's most important recent defender of the idea of justice in war, has indicated that "humanitarian intervention" is almost always undertaken with "mixed motives." Walzer concludes that the fact of mixed motives "is not necessarily an argument against humanitarian intervention...but it is a reason to be skeptical."[35] Walzer goes on to say that "humanitarian intervention is justified when it is a response to acts 'that shock the moral conscience of mankind.'"

I agree with this, in principle. The difficulty is that in practice, one wonders whether our political and military leaders are motivated by the same moral indignation or whether they are simply seeking to expand their power. I believe we have a responsibility to be highly skeptical of our leaders and their motives when it comes to the use of non-defensive military force. The burden of proof rests upon them to prove that the violence they intend is undertaken for the

35. Michael Walzer, *Just and Unjust Wars* (New York: Basic Books, 1977), 102. Walzer has revisited the argument about humanitarian intervention in "The Argument about Humanitarian Intervention," *Dissent*, Winter 2002. For an alternative perspective, see Chomsky, "Humanitarian Intervention" *Boston Review*, December 1993/January 1994.

right reason. While "right intention" is one of the criteria of just war thinking, one might argue that the motive does not matter, as long as suffering is prevented. The difficulty with such an approach is that without the right intention, we cannot be certain that our leaders will be properly restrained by a respect for the other principles of just war thinking. And, in fact, we cannot be certain that "humanitarian intervention" is not a smokescreen hiding imperial ambitions or a mere demonstration of power. As Duane L. Cady has recently concluded:

> Pacifists object to using allegations of moral wrong as excuses for violence, especially when nonviolent alternatives get ignored or dismissed. Pacifists are not opposed to intervention per se. But they are cautious, wary, suspicious of intervention, because genuine peace must be built from within... Where intervention is warranted, pacifists seek methods of nonviolent and thus more genuinely humanitarian intervention. This is the pacifist commitment to positive peace, something mass violence can never create.[36]

I agree with much of what Cady says; however, I am open to the possibility that occasionally military force might be necessary to protect innocent lives and ensure peace. It is hard to imagine Hitler closing the concentration camps without the war. Nonetheless, the practical point is that since war is such a horrible last resort, we must set the burden of proof very high when we are asked to justify intervention.

The issue of humanitarian intervention requires a complex justification that must appeal to many unknown factors. Are there other approaches that would work as well as military intervention? Are we truly using military power to ensure justice and protect peace or are such claims smokescreens that hide the pursuit of power and profit? Are our leaders' intentions pure? Can we be sure that the suffering caused by our military actions will be less than the suffering that military action was supposed to prevent? Can we truly accept the inevitable violation of innocent life that will occur with military action? Are those who would suffer under our military power willing to take the risk? What is the effect of military action on global stability? And what will be the effect of military service on the lives and psyches of our soldiers and their families? My

---

36. Duane L. Cady, "Pacifist Perspectives on Humanitarian Intervention," in Cady and Robert L. Phillips, *Humanitarian Intervention: Just War and Pacifism* (Lanham, Maryland: Rowman and Littlefield, 1996), 60.

basic thesis is that it is very difficult for us to have definitive answers to any of these questions. And since the use of violence is to be avoided if possible, we should resist it if we are unsure about its justification.

Military intervention for peacekeeping or to protect human rights can be a noble thing. However, the task of justification is complex. In our highly differentiated society, most of us do not have access to the information that would allow us to form a complete idea of whether or not the use of military force is justified. Perhaps our leaders have better knowledge than we do: they have access to classified intelligence about both the proposed places of intervention and about potential battle plans. However, history shows us that often the motives of the government are far from pure. We must remember that military adventures are more often undertaken in the name of self-interest than they are undertaken for moral purposes. And self-interest does not only mean the interest of the nation as a whole. It also means the interest of the ruling party or class that is seeking either to consolidate its power through war-patriotism or to use military power to advance business or other interests.

I am worried about the long-term health of our democracy, if the United States were to continue to develop into a global empire. However, I am not claiming that the US government is not legitimate or that its use of force is never justified. Nor am I advocating anarchy and rebellion. Rather, I am indicating an important tension in democracy: citizens do not have access to the same information as their leaders and thus have reason to resist when their leaders advocate actions — such as the use of military force — that are prima facie morally questionable. To deny this is to claim that we should blindly trust our leaders to always do the right thing. Our leaders are mere mortals, with judgment every bit as fallible as our own and with interests that can often run counter to an interest in either democracy or justice. They need to be reminded of the gravity of their decisions vis-à-vis the use of violence and they need to be reminded that their power ultimately rests in the hands of the people.

INDIVIDUAL RESPONSIBILITY IN THE AGE OF TERRORISM

Violence is a perennial problem. We should not be surprised by the current episodes of terrorism and war. However, we are in a new era. This new era began with the development of tools, sped up with the industrial revolution, and now in the nuclear age has advanced to create a qualitative difference in the use of violence. Sociobiologists have made convincing arguments to the effect that our early ancestors were aggressive and violent. However, with the advent of new and better methods of destruction, violence has become an even more important problem. Mechanized modern warfare leads to a significant problem for the issue of justifying war, since bombing and other dislocations caused by modern war violate the basic idea that innocent people should not be made to suffer.[37] The nuclear age and the MAD-ness of deterrent strategy led many proponents of just war thinking to reconsider the just war theory.[38] The indiscriminate destructive power of nuclear weapons and the potential for escalation during the Cold War made war inconceivable to people committed to basic non-violent assumptions. Furthermore, the events of September 11 make us even more aware of the massive destructive force that can be mobilized by a small group of people. The possible conjunction of terrorism and nuclear, chemical, and biological weapons gives us all a reason to be afraid in what might be called "the age of terrorism."

In today's world, each one of us has the capacity to destroy on a massive scale. The destructive capacity of humanity was recognized during the Cold War and we came to understand the fact that some nations possessed the means of total annihilation. Unfortunately, weapons of mass destruction that were invented and deployed by governments may now become available to individuals and groups. Although statistical analysis demonstrates the relative insignificance of terrorism, we know that terrorists possess more and better instruments of destruction.[39] The bombing of the Oklahoma City Federal Building by Timothy McVeigh and the destruction of the World Trade Center buildings by al-Qaeda terrorists still made use of conventional means: bombs and fires. Although the World Trade Center attack demonstrates the massive destruction that is achievable even by conventional means, we can easily imagine the exponential increase in destruction possible for those who might possess chemical, biological, or nuclear weapons. It is clear that individuals and small groups can destroy on a massive scale.

---

37. Robert Holmes concludes from this that modern warfare is thus "presumptively wrong" [Robert L. Holmes, *On War and Morality* (Princeton: Princeton University Press, 1989), 189].

38. See essays by Gerald Dworkin, "Nuclear Intentions," Robert W. Tucker, "Morality and Deterrence," Theodore Roszak, "A Just War Analysis of Two Types of Deterrence," as well as others collected in *Nuclear Deterrence: Ethics and Strategy* ed. by Russell Hardin, John J. Mearsheimer, Gerald Dworkin, and Robert E. Goodin (Chicago: University of Chicago Press, 1985).

39. Roger D. Congleton, "Terrorism, Interest-Group Politics, and Public Policy," *The Independent Review* 8:1 (Summer 2002).

The dislocations produced by the use of weapons of mass destruction could serve to completely undermine the status quo of political, economic, and social organization. One has only to imagine the global implications of the use of a single nuclear weapon in a center of power such as New York, London, or Tokyo. We have seen hints about the possible dislocations produced by acts of terrorism in the reaction to the events of September 11: airlines were shut down, the US economy faltered, billions of dollars and millions of human hours were spent in response. And none of this considers the most palpable effect on the victims, their families, and on our confidence in our own safety. Weapons of mass destruction make possible a much wider dislocation, disruption, and destruction. The use of biological weapons could in fact unleash a plague of global proportions.; the long-term results of nuclear or chemical contamination are truly frightening. This is a qualitative change from the destructive abilities of our primate ancestors, brought about by the cumulative application of social intelligence. Although I hope and believe that the nightmare scenarios of terrorists with weapons of mass destruction will not come true, we must use social intelligence now to solve this problem.

The long run solution to the problem rests with individuals, who must cultivate a tendency to tolerance and peace within themselves. This spiritual change is facilitated not by police but by moral teachers. One might argue, of course, that the means of destruction are themselves to blame. We should certainly restrict access to the materials and information necessary to produce such weapons. However, we also need to focus on the moral question of violence in general. If we seriously admit the potentially catastrophic use of violence envisioned, we will see that the most important challenge is to mobilize spiritual and ethical resources against violence. Spiritual reform provides the only possible long-term solution to our present situation. Institutional safeguards are obviously important for controlling the means of terrorism and war. But moral education is essential for preventing individual humans from becoming terrorists in the first place.

Perhaps the most important institutional step would be for militaristic states to scale back their militarism. Most practically, the world's stockpiles of weapons of mass destruction should be destroyed before they are used by terrorists who steal them or by states who view them as either a necessary part of deterrent strategy or more insidiously as retaliatory weapons. This may be a politically naïve goal. At the very least, we need radical safeguards to keep these volatile materials from falling into the hands of irresponsible parties. And we must make it clear that we will not tolerate the use of such weapons by our own government. The US has held a policy of "strategic ambiguity" regarding the use of nuclear weapons in response to nuclear, chemical, or biological attacks, in order to accentuate the deterrent effect of our nuclear arsenal. More recently, the Bush Administration has upped the ante in terms of the use of nuclear weapons by intimating that the US might use nuclear weapons in response to other strategic threats and by calling for the development of new and improved nuclear weapons. This and other recent events represent a continued US commitment to militarism that we must challenge.[40]

To challenge militarism, individuals must take action. Such action begins with education about the facts of militarism. One hopes that education will lead citizens to realize that the continued stockpiling of weapons of mass destruction is immoral and indeed incomprehensible. Admittedly, there might be strategic knowledge about the complexities of deterrent strategy that citizens lack. But these weapons will be used in our names. Thus we have a responsibility to educate ourselves while continually challenging the militarist status quo. Such challenges will not be effective, however, unless the individuals who work in our institutions are also responsible as individuals and educated about the folly of militarism. In other words, the real focus is the question of personal responsibility, ethics, and the recognition of our collective responsibility to end militarism. We are at an unprecedented moment in human history at which personal responsibility must be emphasized. We now possess the destructive power of the ancient gods. This awesome power makes us all radically equal in terms of our susceptibility to violence. And it makes it imperative that we each assume responsibility, now, for ending violence and the war system.

The conclusion is that we should acknowledge the conjunction of responsibility and power. There is no responsibility without power and with power comes increased responsibility. The solution to violence is not to acquiesce to the elites who would employ military force in our names. Rather, we must assert our responsibility for violence by resisting those who absurdly advocate militarism in defense of democracy.

---

40. See discussion of the new (2002) US Nuclear Posture Review by the Union of Concerned Scientists at their website: http://www.ucsusa.org/index.cfm. The Review of the Nuclear Posture is at http://www.ucsusa.org/publication.cfm?publicationID=402.

CHAPTER 1 APPENDIX: FOR PHILOSOPHERS ONLY
Method and Practical Moral Argumentation

Before I argue further, I would like to clarify my methodological presuppositions. This discussion is probably only of interest to philosophers who are trained to ask about these sorts of things. Non-philosophers may safely skip these few pages.

My approach is pragmatic, pluralistic, and humanistic. This self-description locates my thesis within a complex and contentious philosophical discourse about epistemology, ontology, and the logic of moral claims. I will avoid an extended meta-theoretical discussion in what follows in order to focus on the substantive account of practical pacifism. Nonetheless, it is important to clarify a couple of points about how I intend to proceed.

First, I begin by recognizing a certain sort of Socratic fallibilism. I am reluctant to make claims about absolute knowledge. I realize that my own theory has flaws and that objections might be raised. I acknowledge even that I might be wrong. However, I do think that the account I will develop is a very good one. I hope that the account I give is true in a rich sense of this term, although I am doubtful about whether this account "corresponds" to something like a Platonic idea. Nonetheless, I do hope that my account has "objective" significance, by which I mean that it appeals to reasons that I hope others might find compelling.

One of the outstanding difficulties of moral argumentation is the fact that different individuals find different reasons to be compelling. This problem can be developed into a critical perspective known as relativism. I do not want to get sidetracked into arguments about relativism. However, I must state that I do in fact believe that there are certain things that all human beings must accept as true based upon something like what Santayana called "animal faith."[41] Although we can be skeptical about everything, including even our own bodily existence, if we are to survive in this world we must believe certain things about the world of medium-sized objects. Although there are multiple interpretations of the metaphysical reality that supports the objects of experience, we must accept certain basic commonsense truths about the world that sustains our bodies. Such truths include claims like, "Explosive devices can be used destroy things," "No human being can live without a beating heart," and "Most human beings need to love and be loved." These claims are known by way of empirical research and inductive generalization. Moreover, I accept as basic the claim that all human subjects have unique access to their own experience. Martha Nussbaum has used this claim and others to develop a set of generalizations about human experience that can be agreed to by members of diverse cultures. With Nussbaum, I agree that there are certain features of experience that are common to all human beings.[42]

One might object that if I do not claim to have access to a transcendental absolute, my approach slips toward relativism. One might claim, for example, that the claim that I do not have infallible knowledge self-referentially undermines itself. I understand this objection and even agree with it, as far as it goes. But, I must insist that I am in fact certain about some things. I know, for example, that I do not have infallible knowledge about complicated moral and political questions. I know that I do not know whether I am absolutely right about my own moral evaluations, even though I am reasonably certain that many of my moral evaluations are true. However, from this bit of Socratic wisdom, what follows is only the certainty that I must continue to think, argue, and listen. As I shall argue in Chapter 10, it might be the case that the best hope for peace is to develop this self-consciously fallibilistic approach to moral argumentation.

Fallibilism is not, however, relativism. Although I doubt whether any human beings can possess absolute truth by access to the mind of God or to the realm of Platonic Ideas, I do not doubt that there is a common world to which

---

41. George Santayana, *Skepticism and Animal Faith* (New York: Dover, 1955).
42. Nussbaum calls this the "capabilities approach." See Martha C. Nussbaum, *Women and Human Development* (Cambridge: Cambridge University Press, 2000) and also her discussion in "Aristotle, Politics, and Human Capabilities," *Ethics* III (October 2000), 102-140.

multiple interpretations apply. We share a world of concrete lived human experience. Moreover, I assume that some moral arguments are better than others, even though I am not sure that any human being has access to the single best argument when it comes to complicated moral issues. And I assume that moral arguments are objective, by which I mean that they can be compelling for others. Nonetheless, I realize that different arguments can be compelling for different people. Our endeavor as philosophers is to examine all arguments in order to find the ones that are most compelling.

My approach is pluralistic, by which I mean that it is possible for different arguments about the same thing to be compelling in different ways. My goal, as a pluralist, is to find many different arguments in support of the same claim. The best claim will be the one that is supported by the most arguments. This is, in fact, the way that thinking works in most parts of our lives. For example, I might want to know whether to take a new job in a different city. To decide, I weigh up all the arguments on both sides and look for the preponderance of evidence. In such a decision, I will need to consider arguments about my own integrity, about my own need for money as well as my family's needs. I will also need to consider my long-term career prospects, nebulous topics about the quality of life, and issues related to my present commitments in my current community. Some of the things I will think about will be "deontological" principles: my new job should not ask me to do something evil. Some of the things I will think about will be about consequences: quality of life, money, etc. My decision will be rational if most of the arguments point in the same direction. This is a pluralistic approach because the fundamental values of some of these arguments may in fact clash. The premises of the argument that focuses on money may in fact clash with the premise about integrity (for example, if I were considering a high-paying job in a factory producing weapons of mass destruction). Such clashes indicate dilemmas that do not have obvious solutions. Nonetheless, one hopes in moral argumentation to find arguments and make decisions in which divergent principles lead to the same conclusion. The ideal decision would be agreed to by many different meta-ethical approaches.

It is a remarkable feature of much philosophical argumentation that this basic point about the practical uses of argument is forgotten. Philosophers are trained to sniff out contradictions and inconsistencies. Thus, moral philosophers like to dwell on problems such as the fact that there are cases in which deontological thinking and consequentialist thinking reach radically different conclusions. This comes up most obviously in the problem of "clean hands" that is often thrown up as an objection against pacifism.[43] Pacifists, the objection goes, are willing to sacrifice the good consequences that might be produced by the use of violence for the deontological purity that comes from refusing to commit violence. The point of emphasizing contradictions is to force a choice. In the case of the clean-hands objection to pacifism, the idea is that a deontological commitment to nonviolence cannot be right because it has the potential to result in bad consequences. This sort of contradiction becomes apparent when we abstract from the real world and dwell on meta-ethical questions about the nature of moral reasoning. However, in practice, the best decision will be one that is supported by both deontological and consequentialist reasoning. The type of pacifism I aim to describe is supported by both deontological and consequential reasons: nonviolence is good both because there is something intrinsically wrong about violence and because violence tends to produce bad consequences. Of course, we cannot ignore the tragic fact that occasionally we fallible humans are confronted by radical dilemmas. I can imagine scenarios in which violence would be the best option. However, my practical commitment to pacifism stems from the idea that such cases are much more rare than most of us suppose.

The best arguments will be those that can be supported from multiple perspectives. Although conflicts will undoubtedly remain within such a synthetic consensus, these conflicts should not discourage us from elaborating the core set of values that are found in the pluralistic middle. I do believe that it is possible for deontological and consequentialist approaches to agree in many cases. Of course, there are cases where there is a very real conflict between different principles. In such cases, it seems that the best we can do is to weigh the evidence and weigh our principles. We occasionally may have to sacrifice one principle for another. If the dilemma were genuine, this would be a genuine sacrifice: we would be giving up something that is good in exchange for something else that is good. Such a sacrifice is a genuine tragedy. The essence of the tragic is a conflict between goods in which we are forced to make a choice in which one good is lost so that another might be gained. As will become clear in what follows, I view the use of violence as tragic. It might occasionally be "justifiable"; but the justification of violence should always be viewed as tragic, since nonviolence is the preferred default position. My argument against some proponents of violence is that they do not see the tragedy that underlies the use

---

43. I discuss this in more detail in Chapter 10.

of violence. Although the just war theory is useful for helping us understand cases in which violence might be justifiable, too often militarists and warriors conclude that violence is a "good" thing. From my perspective, this conclusion should be that violence is morally "acceptable" but nonetheless regrettable.

An important component of my argument has to do with the idea of our prima facie duty to avoid violence. The idea of prima facie duty is most famously developed by W.D. Ross in *The Right and the Good*. I interpret Ross to be arguing for a form of fallibilism with regard to moral systems, found in the fact that moral duties can conflict. Moreover, Ross makes it clear that the question of uncertainty returns in trying to apply ethical principles to concrete cases. "Our judgments about our actual duty in concrete situations have none of the certainty that attaches to our recognition of the general principles of duty."[44] The difficulty is that moral judgments require the application of principles that themselves may conflict. This situation is exacerbated by the fact that we often do not fully comprehend the circumstances in which we must apply moral judgment. The point of emphasizing the "prima facie" nature of our duties is to admit that sometimes duties might conflict. Unfortunately, in such conflicts, there are often no clear answers to what we ought to do. The best we can do in such situations is to weigh our various principles while evaluating the levels of certainty that would be required to draw good conclusions.

In my argument for practical pacifism, I add the notion of the burden of proof, which ordinarily states that the obligation for proof rests on the proponent of risky and uncertain propositions. Different duties bring with them different levels of proof for arguments that would ask us to ignore these duties. Some of the differences among principles are fairly obvious: we have a greater duty not to kill than not to lie. The duty to avoid violence — what Ross calls the duty of "non-maleficence" — is a very important primary duty.[45] Thus the burden of proof for those who would argue that we should use violence is quite high. There are problems with Ross's account, including the fact that accounts of prima facie duties do not seem able provide a coherent system of ethics because the very notion of prima facie duty implies that there will be conflicts within the system.[46] However, if the notion of prima facie duty is simply meant

44. W.D. Ross, *The Right and the Good* (Oxford: Clarendon Press, 1967), 30.

45. Ross, *The Right and the Good*, 21.

46. For sympathetic criticism and discussion of Ross, see Frank Snare, "The Definition of Prima Facie Duties," *The Philosophical Quarterly*, 24: 96 (July 1974), 235-244 or David McNaughton, "An Unconnected Heap of Duties?" *The Philosophical Quarterly*, 46: 185 (October 1996), 433-447.

to imply that we have a duty that could be overridden for good reasons, then it will suffice for my purposes.

Finally, my approach is humanistic. I attempt to understand pacifism without appeal to claims that point beyond the needs and interests of finite human individuals. My emphasis on a humanistic approach is linked to the idea of fallibilism. I am agnostic about claims that are supposed to derive from the mind of God or from direct insight into human nature. I prefer arguments that seek their ground in common human experience without appeal to some external authority. I feel the need to emphasize this because much of the discourse of pacifism comes from a religious perspective. I will argue against these traditions from a humanistic perspective. My basic point is one that was articulated by Plato in his *Euthyphro* and has been reiterated by humanists ever since. Ethics is primary. Something is good because it is good, not because the gods have willed it. Indeed, if the gods are good, they must will the good. Gods who do not do good are not worthy of our worship. While I appreciate the spiritual depth and the cultural importance of the religious approach to pacifism, my effort is to establish the limits of the religious approach in order to clarify a humanistic approach. Ultimately, the question of metaphysical basis — religious or humanistic — is secondary to my real concern: discovering what we citizens of 21st-century democracies should think about military violence that is used in our names.

CHAPTER 2. OF APES AND MILITARISTS: THE *HUMAN* ROOTS OF POLITICAL VIOLENCE

> Blood is the rule when its drops have spilled
> On the ground; a fresh request for blood.
> Slaughter screams for the spirit of vengeance
> To fetch from the first the death it will lay
> On the death it has brought to another.
> — Aeschylus, The Libation Bearers[47]

Western culture, since the Greeks, is permeated with images of rage, vengeance, and impassioned violence. Greek tragedy can be read as an analysis of violence. From the stories of Agamemnon, Orestes, Oedipus, Medea, and others, we learn that violence is almost inevitable for human beings. And we learn that violence is accompanied by a sort of madness. Such stories serve, perhaps, to reconcile us with those violent tendencies that are linked to our lower, unruly, animal parts. However, one must note that the violence of modern militarism does not result from the blind fury of impassioned rage. Indeed, most of the violence of the Greek tragedies was family violence: violence aimed directly at a target who was closely related to the perpetrator. Such violence, while inexcusable, is at least comprehensible in human terms: the violence of Greek tragedy is motivated by emotions we all share and it occurs in the context of concrete, familiar relationships. But modern militaristic violence is both less comprehensible and morally even less acceptable. Large-scale coordinated

---

47. Aeschylus, *The Libation Bearers* in *The Orestes Plays of Aeschylus*, trans. Paul Roche (New York: Meridian, 1996), 122.

violence results from a deliberate choice by groups of individuals to use destructive force against groups of other individuals in pursuit of political aims. For this reason, we should call acts of war and large-scale political terrorism "political violence" and distinguish these actions from more ordinary types of "individual violence."[48] Although these categories may overlap, political violence occurs when a group of individuals deliberately uses destructive force against another group as a means to further a social or political end. Individual violence is destructive force in which individuals act to attain individual ends. Individual violence is usually stimulated by emotions such as anger, rage, jealousy, and hatred. It can be caused by wounded pride or by the spirit of vengeance. But political violence — although it can be quite emotional — is more deliberate and organized. Its disinterested perspective is often linked to claims about justice, duty, and moral obligation, although such claims are often ideological deceptions that disguise the motives of political power. The strange thing about political violence is that its emotional component is often not an immediate reaction. Rather, political violence is facilitated by a deliberate choice to stimulate the emotions of individuals by way of patriotic and militaristic propaganda.

One might claim that the capacity for political violence is uniquely human.[49] Only human beings have the capacity to choose their actions deliberately, to cultivate negative emotions, to carefully plan destruction, to magnify destructive power by the use of technology, and to enact violence by organizing and mobilizing other humans around a political idea. Since political violence is uniquely human, it must be understood in terms of specific human capacities. It cannot, then, be fully understood by reducing it to biological urges. Rather, political violence is the result of what sociobiologist Robin Fox has called, in an attempt to avoid biological reductionism, "the violent imagination."[50] Although it might be the case that human beings have an instinct toward aggressiveness, political violence is the result of our higher,

---

48. Implicit here is a normative definition of violence. I will discuss this further in Chapter 5. For now, let me borrow a definition from John Harris: "An act of violence occurs when injury or suffering is inflicted upon a person or persons by an agent who knows (or ought reasonably to have known) that his actions would result in the harm in question," [John Harris, *Violence and Responsibility* (London: Routledge and Kegan Paul, 1980), 19].

49. For further discussion, see J. Glenn Gray *On Understanding Violence Philosophically and Other Essays* (New York: Harper and Row, 1970).

50. Robin Fox, "The Violent Imagination," in Peter Marsh and Anne Campbell, eds., *Aggression and Violence* (New York: St. Martin's, 1982).

uniquely human, faculties. Aggression is not a "problem" for animals; but it is for us because we are able to question it and imagine alternatives. Although we experience aggressive impulses and negative emotions, we use our imaginations to envision the outcome of aggression and we use our other cognitive faculties to decide whether it is appropriate to express these impulses. In order to judge whether violence is acceptable, we must *see* or imagine violence as good, exciting, necessary, heroic, and perhaps inevitable. We must also be made in a certain sense *not to see* the suffering that is caused by violence. At the very least, we must imagine that the suffering that will be caused by violence is somehow appropriate.

The problem of seeing or imagining is an important political problem. Political ideologies are ways of seeing, or ways of imagining, that color our judgments. Since Plato, political theorists have been aware of the fact that most of us see things through ideological filters. Propaganda and ideology are essential for mobilizing political violence because these create a way of seeing that can legitimate, normalize, and even glorify violence. This is why critical education is necessary as the solution to the problem of political violence. If the imagination can be stimulated to glorify violence, it can also be educated to resist it.

Political violence can reinforce group identity. Patriotism flourishes when our group is attacked or when we are attacking some other. Political ideology and propaganda encourage us to see our group as morally or even metaphysically superior to the other, while it encourages us to see the other as the enemy, worthy of being killed. This shared imagined perspective brings us together in a narcissistic celebration of our shared point of view.[51] Since we like being together in community with others, we find ways to display to ourselves our shared imagination. Political violence is thus a means by which the political community expresses its power over and allure to individuals. This is why it is so difficult to overcome. Political violence, when used against the other, furthermore serves to demonstrate, to those who belong, the power that the political community has over individuals. Thus individuals who might be hesitant about political violence see the risks of resisting and, lacking courage, conform. On the other side of this, political violence promises to empower us, if only we join in the community's way of seeing and participate in its violent

---

51. On politics and the "narcissism of minor differences," see Freud, *Civilization and its Discontents* (New York: Norton, 1961). On the idea of the nation as an imagined community, see Benedict Anderson, *Imagined Communities* (New York: Verso, 1991). I also have in mind here what Durkheim calls "solidarity by similarity" in *The Division of Labor in Society* (New York: Free Press, 1981).

result. Although each individual has the capacity to imagine things differently and thus to resist, resistance is difficult, painful, and can seem futile. And so, we allow ourselves to be beguiled by political violence, which in turn makes the community and its violent imagination even more powerful.

Free will, imagination, and individuality must not be forgotten then when we consider political violence and ways to resist it. Although we often fall back into the language of nations and groups when considering the problem of war, choices must be made by the individual members of these groups at each stage in the planning and execution of any form of political violence. We must not forget that free will and imagination are capacities of individuals. It is true that individuality is colored by group membership. It is also true that many individuals find it difficult to resist the power of the group. But all human beings have the capacity to transcend group membership through the activity of imagination. Art, religion, and philosophy show us this ability in action. To read, think, write, or pray is to expand the imagination beyond the limits of the present, the self, and the group. The cultivation of individuality and imagination is thus essential to the effort to resist and end political violence. Although individuals inherit a tendency toward aggression from our ape ancestors, as well as a tendency to conform to the norms of our group, each individual possesses the ability to resist aggressive instincts and rise above the power of the political imagination. We can resist our violent tendencies by freely choosing to develop cultural and emotional resistance to violence. This is why, as I shall argue in the final chapter, philosophical education is essential to peace: philosophy (like art and religion) creates a space of imagination, what I will call in the final chapter a "zone of peace," that allows for resistance both by calling into question the political imagination and by developing and disciplining the emotions. In general, individuals must be encouraged to raise the question of whether or not destructive force can be justified. This is not to say that we are radically free abstract individuals floating free of our group or our instincts; nor is it to say that a liberal education is a simple panacea. Human freedom and imagination is always grounded in a context and the work of peace is gradual and continual. Nonetheless, to be human is to become conscious of our social and political context so that we can make rational decisions about it. When we become conscious in this way, we open our imaginations and consider other ways of seeing.

One of the most important ways that human beings become conscious of and resist the political imagination is found in the antagonistic relationship between political power and individuality. Political power colors our imaginations and clouds our judgment. This is not to say that political power and the political imagination is all bad. Hannah Arendt, for example, understands political power as the potential for shared human ideas and endeavors. Political power is that which creates community and preserves a public space of shared imagination. Political participation is attractive to individuals because it empowers them. However, there is a dialectical relation between the individual and the community. Arendt points out that "nothing in our history has been so short-lived as trust in power, nothing more lasting than the Platonic and Christian distrust of the splendor attending its space of appearance, nothing — finally in the modern age — more common than the conviction that 'power corrupts.'"[52] It is this distrust of power that promises the end of political violence, for it is a distrust that allows the individual to cultivate a more universal and less violent imagination. Of course, one might be nostalgic for a more organic form of community in which the distrust of power was not so prevalent: the ideal of the organic community is one that promises a release from the responsibility of being an individual. However, the distrust of power is a natural process of human development, seen in the very process by which the son breaks away from the father. Philosophical education develops and refines this process by raising doubts about the shared space of imagination created by political ideology. The philosophical commitment is that individuals should question the homogeneous imagined space of the political community. The hope is that individuals would then be able to judge for themselves whether to adopt the point of view of the polis. This assumes that individuals are able to question, imagine alternatives, and judge them. These abilities are the greatest resources for resisting political violence. We must cultivate individuality, critical questioning, dissent, and resistance, in order to overcome the human tendency to give up individuality in the service of the polis and its violent means.

BIOLOGY AND AGGRESSION

Human violence is not the result of biology. Although sociobiological attempts to understand human violence in terms of animal aggression are interesting, they cannot give us the whole of the story. Most careful

---

52. Hannah Arendt, *The Human Condition* (Chicago: University of Chicago Press, 1958), 204-205.

sociobiologists recognize that we cannot reduce human violence to instinct. E.O. Wilson has concluded, for example, "It is comforting to say that war, being cultural in origin, can be avoided. Unfortunately, that bit of conventional wisdom is only a half truth. It is more nearly correct — and far more prudent — to say that war arises from both genes and culture and can best be avoided by a thorough understanding of the manner in which these two modes of heredity interact within different historical contexts."[53] If we resist simple reductionism, the findings of sociobiology are invaluable for helping us understand our natural tendency toward aggression, our natural investment in defending territory, our instinctive drive to compete for status recognition, and indeed our capacity for altruism and compassion. But sociobiology only shows us our *potential* for both violence and care; we must evaluate these potentials ethically and decide which ones we want to actualize. The ethical question of *justification* is at the heart of the problem of human violence; but animals do not subject their aggressive instincts to the question of justification, so sociobiology cannot tell us how we should ethically evaluate human violence.

Sociobiology has attempted to explain complex social behavior in genetic and evolutionary terms by looking at selective pressures that create the conditions for certain behaviors. Although advances in biological science have given us new data with which to explore violence, the basic assumption of sociobiology is that a look at the state of nature can explain the current state of culture. State of nature arguments are often used in philosophy and political theory. Bernard Gert is tempted, for example, to classify Hobbes as a sociobiologist.[54] Such arguments are notoriously slippery, however, because theories about the state of nature often reflect the cultural biases of the theorizer. For example, an essentially competitive and aggressive idea of human being has been influential in Western thinking. Much of Western moral and political thought thus begins from the assumption that human beings are essentially aggressive, competitive, and egoistic.[55] The risk is that this view of the human essence might merely be the result of the assumptions of Western culture. Recent work in the study of apes and other primates has pointed toward a natural origin of human aggression; but the risk remains that this may be

---

53. E.O. Wilson, *Consilience: The Unity of Knowledge* (New York: Alfred A. Knopf, 1998), 171.

54. Bernard Gert, "Rationality and Sociobiology," *The Monist*, April 1984, 67: 2, p. 216.

55. See Alfie Kohn, *The Brighter Side of Human Nature: Altruism and Empathy in Everyday Life* (New York: Basic Books, 1990), especially Chapter 2, "On the Nature of 'Human Nature'." Also see Gary Greif, *The Tragedy of the Self* (University Press of America, 2000).

merely a projection of our own culture that can be used to criticize certain forms of pacifism as unnatural or hopelessly utopian. Of course, such a use of sociobiology can go both ways. We might choose to emphasize certain forms of altruistic behavior in apes and other animals in order to argue that war and other forms of violence are aberrations that might be eliminated.

This ambiguity can be found in sociobiology itself. One of the interesting theses of sociobiology is that aggression in animals is tied to altruism. Sociobiologists have uncovered the roots of altruism in kin or group selection: those with a predisposition toward altruistic behavior toward their kin or group will flourish because in certain environmental niches a group of altruists will be more likely to survive and thus pass on their genetic predisposition toward altruism. Similarly, aggression aimed at preserving the group is also rewarded by natural selection: animals that defend their groups aggressively will be more likely to survive. Likewise, males that are aggressive both in acquiring mates and in fending off rivals will be more successful in passing on their genes and hence aggression will be inherited — at least by males. Here the so-called "selfish gene" uses group altruism and aggression to preserve itself: animals are benevolent toward members of their group, aggressive toward non-members, and aggressive in the acquisition and defense of mates because these tendencies pay off in the struggle for survival.[56] Of course, this standard approach has not been without its critics even among sociobiologists. Frans de Waal has criticized this as "Calvinist Sociobiology," which imports a cynical idea of animal selfishness into its analyses of biological organisms.[57]

Research on the sociobiological roots of human violence has focused on those species that are most closely related to humans: other apes such as chimpanzees and bonobos. In a fascinating work in this genre, Richard Wrangham and Dale Peterson have argued that humans share with chimpanzees a genetic tendency to produce what they call "demonic males."[58] Several important features of chimpanzee society serve to show us possible natural origins of human violence and indeed of war and terrorism. Among chimps there

56. Richard Dawkins, *The Selfish Gene* (Oxford: Oxford University Press, 1989), Chapters 5 and 12.

57. Frans de Waal, *Good Natured: The Origins of Right and wrong in Humans and Other Animals* (Cambridge: Harvard University Press, 1996), Chapter 1. For a further critical discussion, see Morton Hunt, *The Compassionate Beast: What Science is Discovering about the Human Side of Humankind* (New York: William Morrow, 1990), especially Chapter 2, "In Accordance with Nature."

58. Richard Wrangham and Dale Peterson, *Demonic Males: Apes and the Origins of Human Violence* (New York: Houghton Mifflin, 1996).

is a constant struggle for superiority, especially among males. Superiority provides access to mates. Males tend to form alliances with one another as part of this struggle. Male chimps are aggressive toward females and occasionally "rape" them.[59] Chimps establish and defend territory. Male chimps attack and kill other chimps both in the struggle for superiority and in the struggle to defend and maintain territory. One might argue that chimps are not only aggressive but also that they use terrorism. Indeed, Wrangham describes examples of raids in which members of one troop ambush isolated members of another troop. In such raids, chimps seem to use unprovoked violent attacks to send political messages. Often these attacks result in the death of the victim.

Wrangham and Peterson argue that we can see the roots of human violence in chimpanzee aggression. Homo sapiens show similar tendencies. Humans are status conscious, competitive, and engaged in the struggle for recognition. Moreover, there is a male-dominant tinge to human violence and competition. The status of men serves to provide access to mates and thus natural selection would have strengthened the tendency toward violence among males. Like chimps, men identify with groups as part of the struggle for status. Similarly, men historically have been aggressive toward women and have used violence against them in the form of rape. Men establish and defend territory. Men use violence in the struggle for superiority and to defend territory. And so on. The reductive conclusion is that all of these tendencies can be understood as the result of natural selection.[60]

We should, of course, be cautious with this analogy. Human beings are not chimpanzees. Moreover, other species of ape have different social organizations that provide for different ways of dealing with aggression, mating rights, territory, and group dynamics. Bonobos, for example, are much less prone to violence. Bonobo society is structured around female coalitions which curb male aggression. Bonobo females are more available for sex; thus there is less competition among male bonobos for sex. Indeed, bonobos appear to use sexual

---

59. Wrangham and Peterson, *Demonic Males*, 138. Of course the problem of definition recurs here: if we resist using the notion of violence and the question of justification, as I want to do, to describe animal behavior, then it will be problematic to use the idea of rape to describe aggressive behaviors in chimpanzee sex.

60. It should be noted that Wrangham and Peterson are not so reductive. For further discussion and debate about sociobiological reductivism with regard to human aggression and violence, see UNESCO's "Seville Statement on Violence" and Robin Fox's discussion of this in Robin Fox, "The Seville Statement: Anthropology's Auto-da-fe," *Academic Questions*, Fall 1988. Wrangham and Peterson discuss this in *Demonic Males*, 176. Also Frans de Waal, *Good Natured*, Chapter 5.

pleasure as a way to curb aggression and resolve disputes. The difficulty might be deciding whether humans are more like chimps or bonobos. More profoundly, the difficulty is recognizing that human violence is of a different kind, since human beings have the capacity to choose violence or not and humans raise the question of justification. Moreover, although the analogy with bonobos is tempting, we must keep in mind that no species of ape other than ours has produced altruistic, even self-sacrificing, religious and cultural ideals that seek to overcome aggression. This is a crucial difference: human beings have evolved, for whatever reason, a complex set of social patterns that serve to resist aggression. One possible evolutionary reason for this might be that human beings have evolved the capacity, by way of tool use, to vastly improve the lethal power of aggression. Cultural proscriptions against violence would have been necessary in order to resist the deadly violence of an aggressive ape whose developed brain facilitates and enhances destructive power. Another possibility is to ignore natural selection and state simply that human cultures have found violence to be intrinsically bad precisely because it is natural: we have evolved to resist our natural tendencies and to identify this resistance with humanity and virtue. Or, more humanely, perhaps the logic of culture actually is concerned with moral questions, which transcend mere instinct. The human tendency to name violence, to resist it, to postulate the ideal of a world of peace, and to backslide nonetheless into a world of continued violence puts human violence far beyond the aggressive tendencies of chimps or the pacific tendencies of bonobos. The other apes do not, as far as anyone knows, feel the complex range of human emotions that accompany violence such as deliberate evil, guilt over past violence, despair over the ubiquity of violence, or hope for a world beyond violence. Other apes do not have the rational capacity to raise questions about the justification of violence. And apes do not organize political violence around a shared imagination.

There are sociobiological theories that discount the conclusion about "demonic males" in the ape family. Frans de Waal argues that animal aggression has been overblown and that the real asset of ape society is the capacity for altruism and for reconciliation after aggressive displays. De Waal argues that *both* aggression and reconciliation are essential for society. The first helps to establish the social hierarchy, while the second serves to smooth the disruptions caused by the first. "Aggression turns out to be an integral part of social relationships: it arises within them, it upsets their dynamics, and its harmful effects can be 'undone' through soothing contacts... As with expressions of sympathy, conflict resolution by peaceful means would never have come into existence were it not for strong attachments based on mutual dependency and cooperation."[61] Just as reconciliation serves a social purpose, so too does aggression. De Waal's conclusion is that human societies should not try to find ways to completely eliminate aggression but rather should understand its social role. Some aggression is useful: it promotes group solidarity, it promotes self-assertion, it stimulates competition, and it is necessary for the defense of important assets and values. The key, from de Waal's perspective would be to find ways to prevent aggression from becoming unjustified violence. This moves us beyond sociobiology toward philosophical questions about culture and the way in which culture is used to curb aggression by defining limits for justified uses of destructive force.

The big worry about sociobiology is that it reduces human violence to genetic tendencies and so serves to justify violence in a version of the naturalistic fallacy: since it is in our genes, there is nothing we can do — or should do — to resist it. One can look to sociobiology without being reductivist about human culture, however. Our genetic tendencies are one thing; what we do about them culturally is another question. It seems hard to deny that human beings have a predisposition to violence. This predisposition is not merely the inheritance of defective culture, as some social constructionists might argue. Rather, violence seems ubiquitous to human cultures and is genetically linked to our ape-like ancestors. Nonetheless, human beings do possess (also genetically) reason, culture, and free will. We can choose whether or not to express our aggressive tendencies in violent actions. And indeed, we have erected cultural barriers to violence including religion, politics, and philosophical ethics.

The real question for human beings is: how is it that despite barriers to violence, violence still occurs? Two remarkable facts about human beings must be accounted for. First, almost all human cultures have resources that aim beyond violence (although they allow for religious sacrifice, warfare, self-defense, punishment, and the competition of games and sports, which are all thought to be *justifiable* forms of violence). Second, violence persists sometimes in spite of cultural proscriptions and sometimes with the tacit support of them. This leads us to think either that human beings in general (and men in particular) are so aggressive that violence cannot be stifled by culture, or that culture is simply not doing its job. Sociobiology leads us to believe that we are

---

61. Frans de Waal, *Good-Natured*, 165.

naturally aggressive, so it may well be that no amount of cultural tinkering can totally prevent violence. However, I want to suggest that we simply have not yet stumbled upon effective cultural remedies for violence. The hope to end violence, if there is hope, must come from political and cultural forces that will find a way to redirect human aggression away from violence.

WAR AND CULTURE

As stated at the outset, war is political violence. One of the reasons that political violence is so difficult to overcome is that contemporary culture is based on a belief in its value. This belief can either be militarism, a belief in the pragmatic necessity of military power, or it can be outright bellism, the belief in the value or glory of war. It is important to recognize the pervasive nature of militarism and bellism in order to understand what practical pacifism is up against. It may seem natural for the practical pacifist to resist war because, from this perspective, it is obvious that violence is prima facie an evil to be avoided. However, this pacifistic assumption is not shared by all. Militarists imagine war and preparation for war as a necessary part of political life. Moreover, bellists imagine war as an activity productive of values that cannot be discovered in peace.

It is not an exaggeration to say that human culture has always celebrated martial values. Gilgamesh, the most ancient hero of literature, was a warrior king whose initial impetus was to pursue strife and the glories of battle. The ancient heroes of Western culture were all warriors. Among the Greeks and Romans we have Achilles, Odysseus, Hercules, Oedipus, Pericles, Alexander, Aeneas, Caesar, etc. Among the Hebrews we have Samson, Joshua, David, etc. Greeks and Romans deified war as Ares or Mars; but most of the gods of the Greek pantheon were themselves warrior gods who took part in human battles and who battled amongst themselves. The two great epics of ancient Greece, the *Iliad* and the *Odyssey*, are war narratives, with the first focusing on the event of war and the second focusing on the warrior's attempt to return from war. This celebration of war and of the warrior's virtue is not unique to the Greeks and their mythology. The God of the Hebrew Bible and Christian Old Testament is a warrior God, Yahweh Shabaoth, the Lord of Hosts, or literally, the God of Armies. The first great moment in Hebrew history is a metaphorical military victory in which the Hebrews win their freedom from the Egyptians by luring the Egyptian army into a battle at the Red Sea. Throughout the Pentateuch and the books of the prophets, the Hebrew God is also concerned to demonstrate His might both by using miraculous powers and by using the force of arms of His people, the Hebrews.

The phenomenon of war was even turned into a metaphysical power by Greek philosophers. Heraclitus, at the dawn of Western philosophy, famously said, "War is the father of all." Empedocles identified the dialectical process of becoming as the result of the conflict between Love and Strife. This view is reflected in the Hebrew tradition, where the preacher of Ecclesiastes tells us that war and peace, love and hate are engaged in a vain struggle: "A time to kill, and a time to heal; a time to break down, and a time to build up;... a time to love, and a time to hate; a time for war, and a time for peace." Indeed, in the Hebrew tradition, the first truly human generation is tinged with violence. Cain kills Abel in the first episode of post-Edenic human life.[62] It is important to note the details of this story of the advent of violence, because it gives us insight into the nature of violence as a basic human problem. Cain's violence is religiously and economically motivated. Cain is a "tiller of the ground," while Abel is a sheepherder. Cain is jealous of Abel because Abel's sacrifices were pleasing to God. Violence erupts as the result of competition between brothers. Thus within the Hebrew tradition, violence is discovered at the origin of human culture and violence is understood as related to religion, to economic competition, and ultimately to the struggle between men for dominance. Finally, this story is important because it shows us God's ambiguous judgment about violence. Cain's sin cannot be atoned — his violence results in his expulsion from the human community and from nature. The Lord says to him that the ground will no longer yield its strength to him. However, seeds of peace can be found in this passage as well: God prohibits any human from taking revenge upon Cain. Rather, the punishment of the first purveyor of violence is that he must wander the earth as an exile. Violence, culture, and the experience of human exile go together. We develop culture to prevent violence; but violence results from human culture — from religious and economic advancements; and all of this — violence and culture — result in our estrangement from an Edenic home in which humans and animals are at peace.

---

62. For a discussion, see Rene Girard, *Violence and the Sacred* (Baltimore: Johns Hopkins University Press, 1977).

In the Western tradition bellism — the worship of war — develops within the context of exile and alienation. At one extreme of the bellistic culture, war is seen as a moral necessity for separating good and evil. At the very least, if war is a necessary part of human life, we must become inured to its pernicious effects and learn to celebrate its purgative power. At another extreme, war is celebrated for its ability to produce value by stimulating warriors to exhibit courage, loyalty, and a spirit of sacrifice. The Western tradition holds peace out as the ideal toward which we are directed as a point of origin and return. Christians hope for peace at the end of days and Odysseus longed to return home after his battles. Unfortunately, the Western tradition focuses on the necessity of going through purgative battle in order to arrive at peace. In the Christian tradition, the City of God will only be obtained after the final climactic battle of Armageddon; in the Greek tradition, Odysseus can return to Penelope only after he has slaughtered the suitors who threaten his home.

We inhabit the middle region of history and culture — between Eden and the end of time. In this middle region, it often seems that militarism is necessary for self-preservation. Although we believe in peace and hope for its rebirth in a new age, we find that we must use violence to deal with the facts of life as they are in the "real" world. But many in the West have also celebrated war as an end in itself. Many of us continue today to be seduced by the adrenaline thrills of war and the virtues and valor of bellistic culture.

The dialectic between real and ideal haunts the discussion of pacifism and militarism in the West. Although there have always been voices against war, it is not until the advent of Christianity that the voice of peace was truly heard in the West. The Christian message is one that transforms the relation between real and ideal. The kingdom of God is not an earthly kingdom: the real world in which we live and die is no longer thought to be real. Rather, the ideal world — the kingdom of heaven — becomes the ultimate reality. The hope for peace is "otherworldly" insofar as true peace will only prevail in the City of God, which is the paradigm for those of us who are merely passing through the degenerate world of appearances. This idea in its theological development borrows from Platonic philosophy the idea of a perfect world of ideas in reference to which the appearances of this world make sense.

Most of the Western tradition looks for absolute answers to the problem of war, as written in God's law or articulated by His inspired interpreters. A more pragmatic approach considers each situation and asks whether the use of violence can be justified in light of the best moral principles that we fallible humans can derive from experience. The difference is crucial: absolute pacifism can only develop in a context in which violence is condemned from a transcendental perspective. For the rest of us — those who are agnostic about our access to such a transcendental level of justification — only a practical form of pacifism can be justified: pacifism derived from a philosophical commitment to values such as modesty, tolerance, and reflective self-consciousness. Nonetheless, whether one's pacifism is pragmatic or absolute, pacifism is antagonistic to the militaristic status quo. Many of the great pacifists — Socrates, Jesus, Thoreau, Gandhi, Martin Luther King, Jr. — were imprisoned and/or killed. Pacifists are always ridiculed because their alternative way of imagining the world opens the possibility that those who are committed to militaristic and/or bellistic values are both deluded and immoral. The risks of pacifism continue to be great because warrior values continue to thrive. This may be why a more absolute approach to pacifism — one that offers an otherworldly reward for nonviolence — is appealing.

MILITARISM AND THE STATE

Warrior values continue to thrive because military societies inculcate their citizens with the belief that military service is valiant and that a strong military is necessary. This process occurs, most obviously, when the military indoctrinates new recruits who then defend the military system. This process was criticized almost 100 years ago by Karl Liebknecht in his controversial book, *Militarism and Anti-Militarism.*[63] Although he was not the first to use the term (as mentioned in Chapter 1, Jane Addams had discussed militarism before the turn of the century), his discussion of militarism shows us the way in which militarism impacts both foreign affairs and domestic policy. Arguing from certain basic Marxist presuppositions, he claims that militarism is the way in which a dominant elite keeps the rest of society in line. "Its [militarism's] task is to uphold the prevailing order of society, to prop up capitalism and all reaction against the struggle of the working class for freedom."[64] Although Liebknecht points to the direct use of military force to suppress domestic opposition, his

---

63. As if to prove his point that the militaristic state was poised against those who question its basic presuppositions, he was charged with treason by the German government and his book was banned.

64. Karl Liebknecht, *Militarism and Anti-Militarism* (New York: Garland, 1973), 20.

analysis is interesting for showing us the more subtle forms of pressure — by way of patriotic propaganda and other forms of indoctrination — that the military state uses to create a domestic consensus which supports its continued existence.

Most importantly, Liebknecht indicates the ideological process by which the military state produces soldiers, what he calls "shooting automatons."[65] The state needs "intelligent" soldiers; but these soldiers' intelligence must not be applied to a critique of the military system itself. The military therefore relies heavily upon young men who are thrown together under the control of the military ideology, who are isolated from outside influences, and who are then beguiled by the trappings of military life. All of this is necessary because militaristic societies have to transform human beings into killing machines who are asked to perform duties that are ordinarily condemned by other parts of culture. As Jonathan Glover has interpreted this, military training purposefully aims to inhibit or neutralize the "moral resources" that the non-military part of culture emphasizes. "Armies need to produce something close to a 'robot psychology', in which what would otherwise seem horrifying acts can be carried out coldly, without being inhibited by normal responses."[66] Glover details the ways in which modern warfare further distances soldiers from these normal responses by distancing them — by way of technology — from the killing that they do. In other words, military training creates a new form of imagination in which individual virtues such as courage and loyalty are connected with political violence.

If Glover and Liebknecht are even partially correct, this idea should be disturbing. Clearly, the idea of conformity that is found in the "robot psychology" of the military is antithetical to the ideals of a liberal state. While the modern American (post-Vietnam) military does attempt to educate its members about the ideas of the just war tradition, and while military personnel and veterans by and large do possess moral sensibility of the sort that Liebknecht and Glover suggest they lack, it remains true that conformity is required if a fighting force is to function effectively, and soldiers must be taught to stifle doubts and ignore certain of their more altruistic and less aggressive impulses.

---

65. Liebknecht, *Militarism and Anti-Militarism*, 24.
66. Glover, *Humanity*, 48.

The larger problem, however, is that the values of militarism — its conformism and aggressiveness — are encouraged and supported by society. The irony of American military power is that, in the name of liberal values, we ask individuals to sacrifice their individuality in military service. The whole of American society values military service and its violent presuppositions. This is explicit in patriotic displays that ask us to "support the troops." It is a constant theme in the dominant American narrative, which emphasizes our military successes such as the Revolutionary War, the Civil War, and the First and Second World Wars. It is an ongoing presence in war movies, in war monuments, and in advertisements for the military. And it is accentuated by the way in which military heroes are honored and given power (from George Washington and Dwight Eisenhower to local parades and the honor rolls listed in small-town newspapers). This leads to a self-sustaining cycle: military leaders and a militaristic culture support militarism. This self-catalyzing process can take over the whole of culture, becoming what Eisenhower himself recognized as the military-industrial complex.

The problem of the military-industrial complex and the permanent militarization of the United States is real; it has not gone away with the end of the Cold War. Fifty years ago, C. Wright Mills described this problem in terms of the "military ascendancy." Mills noticed that there was a feedback loop that connected military power to capitalism. This linkage between military power and business is found in the way in which top government officials, top corporate officials, and top military officials are interconnected. It is also found in government spending on military contracts. All of this combines to create what Mills described as "the great structural shift of modern American capitalism toward a permanent war economy."[67] The same facts hold true today: many large corporations rely upon defense spending. Although the idea that there is a separate, free-standing economic monolith called the "military-industrial complex" has been discredited, it is undeniable that there is mutual support between and among business, military, and political leadership.[68] There is a closed community of "defense intellectuals" who move among lobbying groups, think-tanks, government positions, and private corporate jobs. When

---

67. C. Wright Mills, *The Power Elite* (Oxford: Oxford University Press, 1956), 215.

68. For an analysis that rejects the idea of the "military-industrial complex" but still holds onto the idea of a power elite, see G. William Domhoff, *Who Rules America?* (Mountain View, CA: Mayfield Press, 1998), 52-53.

one further considers how the media too is entangled with the defense octopus, the militaristic problem can appear to be insoluble.

Militarism is not just an ungrounded ideology; there is an argument to support it. Militarism begins from the basic idea that international relationships are best described as a Darwinian struggle among nations. In this context, each society must struggle to preserve itself against others who would challenge its very existence. Such an understanding of international relations follows from some of the basic assumptions of modern political philosophy following Hobbes: that in the state of nature there is a war of all against all. In contemporary political theory, this is the realist presupposition that international affairs are anarchic.[69] In such a condition, national survival and self-interest are promoted through militarism, with peace being understood in terms of the balance of power. Peace under this assumption is only possible as a *modus vivendi*. There can be no ultimate agreement on principles of international cooperation, only an armistice based upon an unwillingness to further pursue the battle. Under such conditions, a continued commitment to militarism is essential on all sides because the *modus vivendi* can be disrupted when the balance of power is upset. There can be no unilateral disarmament or commitment to the end of militarism under this conception of international affairs because to disarm would be to invite invasion and a return to the state of war.

Militarism thus describes a pragmatic recognition of the necessity of military force in an anarchic world. However, this is a crass form of pragmatism in which the ends justify the means. As we shall see subsequently, a more philosophical form of pragmatism, while it may allow for the use of military force, will see the problem that militarism poses for democracy. In Liebknecht's usage it is also connected with the drive to dominate and this drive to dominate proves to be a disaster for democracy. This is why democratically minded pragmatists such as Addams, James, and Dewey were critical of militarism. When the drive to dominate comes to be seen as an end to be celebrated, as in Nietzsche's idea of the will-to-power, we move beyond militarism toward bellism. But bellism or "war-ism" goes further than a pragmatic justification of war and celebrates war in itself. Democratic critiques of militarism emphasize that the idea of democracy aims to move beyond the use of force. Although force might be necessary to defend democracy against internal and external enemies, a

---

69. See Michael Doyle's description of realism in *Ways of War and Peace* (New York: Norton, 1997), Part I.

democratic society is not grounded in force. Thus, true democracies cannot be militaristic; and they are miles away from the bellistic celebration of war as an end in itself.

Of course there is no standard agreement about how to use terms such as these. The word "militarism" has been used by Robert Holmes, for example, to describe the idea that "military preparedness and the fighting of wars, when necessary, is the best way to achieve peace."[70] Here, militarism is not necessarily linked to the will to dominate. Rather, militarism can be restrained, as Holmes suggests, by the idea of a justice in war. The danger is, of course, that pragmatic militarism used as a means to the end of justice can easily become a sort of social end in itself, as society dedicates its resources to producing military power, which stimulates arms races and helps to create international instability by continuing to manifest the threat of war. Moreover, militarism can slip toward outright bellism, as a militaristic society must convince its members of the glory and necessity of war. History shows that militaristic cultures are not just interested in using military force as a last resort. Rather, they are often interested in the values promoted by war: loyalty, courage, sacrifice, discipline, order, hierarchy, domination, and power.

The theory of international relations that seems to be favored currently by the US foreign policy establishment is one that views the world as an unstable vacuum waiting for the expansion of US power. American militarism easily becomes expansionist and imperialistic, thus leading to a cycle whereby the threat of US power stimulates resistance, which in turn leads the US to work harder to expand its power. The problems of terrorism and the "war on terrorism" are best understood along these lines. It is important to note that, to create support for US militarism and expansionism at home, the media has to promote bellistic values that make war out to be a glorious thing. We are ironically taught to see war-making as a means to supposedly "liberal" ends. We celebrate our commitment to "democracy" by glorifying the Second World War and down-playing both expansionist US policy even during that war and the unjust means (e.g. the atomic bomb) that we employed to achieve our war objectives. We are taught that patriotism means to support the troops no matter what and we are conditioned to fear that this war — the war on terrorism — is a war in which homeland security is at stake.

---

70. Robert Holmes, *On War and Morality* (Princeton: Princeton University Press, 1989), 114.

This promotion of militarism occurs despite the fact that the just war tradition tries to meliorate these bellistic values by focusing on the idea that war is a tragic expedient. Thus, the war in Iraq was initially justified as an unfortunate last resort in pursuit of a just cause and is more recently justified in terms of humanitarian intervention and democratization. This shifting discourse of justification in the war in Iraq indicates the difficulty of distinguishing in practice between just war necessities, militaristic pragmatics, a bellistic celebration of war for its own sake, and the interests of empire.

Militarism can be understood in terms of the claim that for a culture to survive it must be able to defend itself. Bellism can be understood in terms of the fact that human beings — especially men — are biologically and culturally predisposed to violence: at a certain level, we like violence. Pacific cultures, if there were any, would not have had the evolutionary advantage necessary in the struggle for survival. Of course, broad claims such as these must be viewed with skepticism. History, culture, and biology are too broad and various to permit such facile generalizations. Although it certainly seems to be the case that militarism is ubiquitous, one counter-example will serve to undermine the generalization. Although it is generally true that men are more violent than women, this is not absolutely true. Nonetheless, contemporary global culture is based upon militaristic assumptions. The division of the world into nation-states is both the cause and result of militarism. International institutions of governance — as weak as these are — rely upon the pragmatic assumptions of militarism. A nation-state can be defined as a geographical region of concentrated military power. The government of a nation-state controls the legitimate uses of violent power — in the form of both police and army. The governmental power possesses a monopoly of legitimate violence in a region. The idea of legitimate violence is key, here: the violence of police and army is thought to be legitimate if it has been justified by political procedures which are accepted by those who are subject to this violence. This idea assumes that subjects would agree that the use of violence is necessary and this militaristic assumption is built right into the idea of the social contract. It is quite difficult to imagine today a nation-state that is not committed at some level to military force. And at the international level, order is maintained by military alliances such as NATO and by treaties enforced with the threat of military force. The United Nations itself is organized as a military hierarchy. The Security Council is the most powerful arm of the United Nations and the permanent members of the Security

Council are global military powers. Today, states must build military power, if they are to survive.

MILITARISM AND PRAGMATISM

The problem for those who would work for peace, then, is that the contemporary political landscape is not constructed for peace. A brief look at military budgets and weapons stockpiles shows us that the world is organized for war, not for peace. In 2001, global military expenditures were estimated at $839 billion by the Stockholm International Peace Research Institute.[71] According to the Bulletin of Atomic Scientists, "more than 31,000 nuclear weapons are still maintained by the eight known nuclear powers, a decrease of only 3,000 since 1998."[72] Pacifism is confronted by militarism at every turn. If a nation became pacifistic and renounced its territorial monopoly on violence, it would rapidly be overrun by enemies both internal and external. Thus we must admit that militarism is a pragmatic response to the facts of the status quo. I want to emphasize the pragmatic nature of militarism for three reasons.

First, if militarism is merely pragmatic, it might be the case that if the status quo were altered the pragmatic justification of militarism could be undermined. Let's admit that militarism is at best a pragmatic approach to survival in a militarized world. But let's dismiss, then, those bellistic arguments that glorify war as such. We need to emphasize the fact that war is not good in itself but that it is only a useful expedient. If this shift to a pragmatic view of war could be accomplished (and I'm not sure that it has been), the next step in working toward peace would be to realize that if the world were different we might be able to move away from militarism. This utopian aspiration for a world beyond militarism is my deepest hope. I realize, of course, that this hope is unrealistic at present. However, we can work to create the conditions under which the need for militarism might gradually disappear, if we work to imagine alternatives and call our leaders' militaristic presuppositions into question.

---

71. See *SIPRI Yearbook 2002*. A summary is available online: *http://editors.sipri.se/pubs/yb02/highlights.html*.

72. *Bulletin of Atomic Scientists*, February 2002 (http://www.thebulletin.org). This number does not include decommissioned nuclear weapons that sit in stockpiled reserves. The SIPRI Yearbook of 2002 estimates the number of nuclear weapons at 36,800 warheads.

Second, the idea of military pragmatism is explicitly related to what is called "realism" about international relations and war. The realist holds that we must recognize that the world of international affairs is a world of power and might. Thus the realist is not constrained by discussions of morality, except insofar as morality itself is of pragmatic value in pursuing power or national interest. It is my contention that all forms of militarism from outright military realism to the just war tradition are pragmatic. This claim is meant both to undermine the sanctity of the idea of the just war and to open up the possibility for a pragmatic approach to peace. If it is the case that all considerations made in international affairs are ultimately pragmatic, then perhaps there is room for a move toward what I call practical pacifism. The development of practical pacifism will occur if we realize that the ends of peace and justice can only be attained by peaceful and democratic means.

The final reason for focusing on the pragmatic nature of militarism is to point out that support for war happens at a variety of levels, none of which is absolute. The only approach to war that is absolute is the bellistic approach, which celebrates war in itself. Recognition of different levels of support for war leaves us with the opening in which practical pacifism occurs. Practical pacifism is essentially a movement for peace on the part of citizens. Such a peace movement is pragmatic and strategic. While not giving up on the security and goods created by the militaristic culture of 21st-century civilization, practical pacifism argues against and resists militaristic culture. To a pure pacifist such as Gandhi, this may seem like hypocrisy, although even Gandhi made compromises that involved, for example, serving in the ambulance corps during the First World War. In the global civilization of the 21st century, any movement for peace must come from within militaristic culture. The pragmatic interpretation of militaristic culture focuses on the fact that pragmatic militarism views war as a means and not as an end in itself (i.e., militarism is not bellism). The pragmatic pacifist reminds the militarist of the dangers of war and of the pragmatic and strategic mistake of preparing for war in order to work for peace. Nonetheless, the pragmatic pacifist does not call for the immediate overthrow of military culture. Such an approach would be a strategic mistake for at least two reasons: it would not be politically successful and a complete renunciation of military power in the present world would simply give power to terrorists, tyrants, and zealots. If we distinguish militarists who pursue the balance of power to ensure stability from bellists who celebrate war for its own sake, we can conclude that the shared goal of militarists and pacifists is peace, not war, anarchy, or disorder.

At issue is the question of the proper means toward this end. Practical pacifists must argue that in the current world situation, militarism is no longer the best means to the ends of peace and justice. There is — despite the problem of terrorism and forms of Western imperialism — stability and consensus in the global society. This newfound international unity must now be leveraged so that we can begin to move beyond the pragmatic need for militarism. The basic idea of pragmatism is that the means will change when the conditions change. I argue that our shared human goal should be to move beyond the idea that military means can produce either peace or justice. And, now is the time to recognize that the present conditions are auspicious for moving beyond militarism.

The practical conclusion is that we must actively condemn the glorification of war that tends toward bellism. We must remind our militaristic leaders of their responsibility to promote peace by peaceful means, while arguing against their militaristic assumption that peace and justice can be created by violent means. Of course, one might object that the leading military powers in the world today — the United States, to cite the main example — are not really interested in peace. It might be the case that the United States is actually bellistic: while the US claims that it is interested in justice and peace, such claims may be ideological propaganda used to disguise the imperial will-to-power. To argue against this we must mobilize internal critique against these bellistic and hegemonic tendencies. Obviously, many of our leaders are self-professed religious believers who at least pay lip service to Christian and other religious ideals. Moreover, they routinely invoke ideas such as human rights, democracy, and justice. We must force them to acknowledge that imperialism and bellism are antithetical to these beliefs. It is rare to hear a leading military or civilian leader argue that war or US imperial domination is good in itself. Thus, we can turn the pragmatism of militarism against the militarist by arguing that now there are other more practical means to the ends of peace and justice. The key to discovering these means is to liberate our imaginations from the presupposition of war. We are not fully determined either by nature or by culture. We must use our freedom to imagine alternatives to human aggression and political violence.

CHAPTER 3. ABSOLUTE PACIFISM AND JUST WAR THEORY

> Blessed are the peacemakers,
> For they shall be called sons of God.
> — Jesus[73]

Pacifism is the belief that peace is good, that we must work for peace, and that war should be avoided, if not abolished. There are many varieties and degrees of pacifism, from the absolute commitment to nonviolence in all parts of life to a pacific version of the just war theory. There are also many reasons to believe that some version of pacifism is good. In the present chapter I will look critically at a traditional approach to pacifism that stems from a commitment to a religious point of view. It would be false to say that all religions are pacifistic. It would also be false to say that all pacifists are religious. However, there is a strong affinity between pacifism and certain forms of religious belief. Indeed, the most thoroughgoing form of pacifism is grounded in a larger metaphysical view that is committed to ideas such as the beloved community, the brotherhood of men, the interdependence of beings, and the spiritual power of love and truth. These profoundly moving ideas support what I call absolute pacifism. This approach and its metaphysical/religious foundation set the stage for my subsequent argument for a humanistic form of pacifism. My own version of practical pacifism is focused primarily on the political question of war and is not necessarily connected to a claim about nonviolence in all parts of life. My position builds upon some of the basic assumptions of the just war theory, which is one step removed from the pacifist position. The just war theory holds

---

73. Matthew 5: 9 (Biblical passages are quoted from the Revised Standard Edition).

that some wars may be justifiable, while nonetheless adhering to a strong presumption against the use of force. Practical pacifism holds that although it might be the case that some wars may be justifiable in theory, in practice it is difficult, if not impossible, for most of us to say that any given war is in fact justifiable. This approach leads to a prima facie commitment to pacifism. It is not absolute, however, since it might be possible for a given war to be justified in practice. Practical pacifism is a rough-and-ready political position that is open to the possibility of refutation. It is thus to be distinguished from those more absolute forms of pacifism that usually stem from religious belief.

My conclusion is that war should be avoided and that militarism should be abolished. However, this conclusion does not require appeal to a religious justification. Rather, it follows from an analysis of the facts about war and peace, about politics and power, as they present themselves to finite beings in the real world. A common assumption, which I reject, of both most forms of absolute pacifism and certain versions of the just war theory is an appeal to knowledge claims that, for the most part, are unsupportable based on fallibilistic assumptions of a pragmatic form of humanism.

ABSOLUTE PACIFISM

By absolute pacifism I mean that form of pacifism that is committed to nonviolence and peace as inviolable first principles of ethics. This idea goes beyond the claim that war can rarely be justified in practice to a much broader claim that violent action of any sort can never be justified. In the Christian tradition this is the idea expressed by Jesus in the twin ethical commandments of love and obedience: "You shall love the Lord your God with all your heart, and with all your soul, and with all your mind, and with all your strength," and "You shall love your neighbor as yourself."[74] Loving the neighbor as the self leads to the famous ethical pronouncements of the Sermon on the Mount. "You have heard that it was said, 'An eye for an eye and a tooth for a tooth.' But I say to you, Do not resist one who is evil. But if any one strikes you on the right cheek, turn to him the other also... You have heard that it was said, 'You shall love your neighbor and hate your enemy.' But I say to you, Love your enemies and pray for those who persecute you."[75] With love as the foundation of ethics, pacifism

74. Mark 12: 30-31.
75. Matthew 5: 38-48.

60

follows. Of course, it must be noted that a long tradition of thinking about justice in war derives the idea of a just war from Christian principles such as love. I shall describe the Christian just war tradition later on. Here, I want to describe the form of absolute pacifism that can be derived from Christian principles.

Jesus' pacifist ethic is ultimately connected to the larger question of God's will, our obedience to God, and the nature of love. This ethic makes sense in a dualistic universe where the world of the flesh, the world of appearance, is not the real world. The Christian ethic is admittedly an ethic that reverses the normal values of commonsense. One need not be a Nietzschean to recognize this. Paul says as much in his first letter to the Corinthians, when he says, in the context of a discussion of love, that the Christian approach requires us to transcend ordinary categories. "For now we see in a mirror dimly, but then face to face. Now I know in part; then I shall understand fully, even as I have been fully understood. So faith, hope, love abide, these three; but the greatest of these is love."[76] Love may not seem to be the solution to problems of this world; but the problems of this world find their significance and solution in the spiritual world. The Christian message aims to overcome the traditional values of a warrior culture. Jesus himself says that he came to abolish and fulfill the ancient laws. And he claims that traditional values shall be reversed by instituting spiritual values that are opposed to the warrior spirit of traditional morality. For Jesus, it is the meek, the merciful, and the peacemakers who are to be rewarded, not the violent, the strong, and the war-like. The Christian message of loving enemies, turning the other cheek, conquering with love rather than with a sword, all of this runs counter to the "reality" of political power and violence in this world. Pacifism of this sort must be otherworldly because it asks us, in some sense, to "sacrifice" ourselves or our interest in worldly power, in the name of peace and spiritual power. The Christian model of political action is ultimately Jesus himself, who willingly sacrifices himself to the political authorities. In early Christianity, then, we find a form of absolute pacifism that is tied to the idea of martyrdom and saintly sacrifice.

For pacifism of this sort, which is tied to a doctrine of loving others and defending the innocent, one cannot win a battle in this world without employing means that are unsuitable. Thus even to defend the meek, protect the innocent, and help the suffering, war cannot be justified. Rather, the proper way

---

76. First Corinthians 13: 12-13.

of service is a way of sacrifice: we substitute ourselves for victims of violence out of the realization that this sort of sacrificial pacifism follows exactly on the model of Christ's own sacrifice.

As Paul interpreted the gospel, love was to be the foundation of an ethics of peace and harmony in a world that the believer had already in part transcended through the death and resurrection of Christ. Moreover, Paul's pacifistic pronouncements make sense in light of his eschatological vision: for Paul, the kingdom of God was close at hand and our task was to prepare for the final judgment and resurrection. Such spiritual enthusiasm is found in Paul's overwhelming emphasis on love.

> Let love be genuine; hate what is evil, hold fast to what is good; love one another with brotherly affection; outdo one another in showing honor... Live in harmony with one another; do not be haughty, but associate with the lowly; never be conceited. Repay no one evil for evil, but take thought for what is noble in the sight of all. If possible, so far as it depends upon you, live peaceably with all. Beloved, never avenge yourselves, but leave it to the wrath of God; for it is written, "Vengeance is mine, I will repay, says the Lord." No, "if your enemy is hungry, feed him; if he is thirsty, give him drink; for by so doing you will heap burning coals upon his head." Do not be overcome by evil, but overcome evil with good.[77]

All of this makes perfect sense if one believes in the Kingdom of God, which is to be won by such pacifism, if one believes that evil will in fact be punished by God, and if one believes that the end of time is nigh.

Lest we think that the religious concern for peace is a Western phenomenon, recall that Indian traditions celebrate the virtue of *ahimsa*, or nonviolence. Like the Christian tradition, Indian religions recognize that violence is an inescapable feature of the human universe. While Christianity aimed to overcome the idea that God's kingdom is a political kingdom to be won by the sword, the Hindu tradition contains a recognition of the futility of war and our all-too-human tendency to be stuck in a cycle of violence. It is of no small significance that *The Bhagavad-Gita* is a conversation between Krishna and Arjuna that takes place during the prelude of the Battle of Kurukshetra. Although Krishna ultimately urges Arjuna to fight, the larger moral of the story is a sort of resignation that ensues from recognizing the futility of war.[78] Pacifism in Indian traditions such as Jaina, Hinduism, and Buddhism follows

---

77. Romans 12: 9-21.

from this basic insight. But it is also connected to a more profound metaphysical view. In the Jain and Hindu traditions, everything is interconnected by way of karma and other cosmic forces. Because *atman* is ultimately Brahman, violence to others is, in effect, violence to self. Likewise, Buddhism holds a similar theory of interconnection and dependent co-arising. However, even though Buddhism ultimately claims that even the self is an illusion, the interdependent nature of no-self leads to ahimsa. In all of these traditions, everything is mutually dependent and everything is sacred. The idea is that once this is recognized, ahimsa should follow.

The most famous pacifist in the Indian tradition is probably Gandhi. Gandhi's ahimsa is closely connected with his faith in the unity of humanity and in God's grace. Moreover ahimsa, for Gandhi, is closely connected with other spiritual practices categorized under *brahmacharya*.[79] Brahmacharya is a way of renunciation, which includes sexual abstinence, dietary restrictions, and fasting. Such self-abnegation and its connection with pacifism only make sense in a spiritual tradition in which there are higher spiritual goods and in which the pain and even death of the body have no ultimate significance. Gandhi links his own approach to that of Christianity and the Christian teachings about love. "Ahimsa means 'love' in the Pauline sense, and yet something more than the 'love' defined by St. Paul... Ahimsa includes the whole creation, and not only humans... It is the only true force in life."[80]

Gandhi elucidated his commitment to nonviolence in various places. One concise summary of the philosophy of nonviolence can be found in the following.[81]

1. Nonviolence is the law of the human race and is infinitely greater than and superior to brute force.
2. In the last resort, it does not avail to those who do not possess a living faith in the God of Love.

---

78. For discussion, see Christopher Key Chapple, *Nonviolence to Animals, Earth, and Self in Asian Traditions* (Albany, NY: State University of New York Press, 1993), Chapter 4, "Otherness and Nonviolence in the Mahabharata." This is also Gandhi's interpretation of the *Bhagavad-Gita*, see "God of Love, Not War," in Mohandas K. Gandhi, *Non-Violence in Peace and War, 1942-1949* (New York: Garland Press, 1972), 117-119.

79. See discussions throughout Gandhi, *Autobiography: The Story of My Experiments with Truth* (Boston: Beacon Press, 1993).

80. Gandhi, "A Talk on Non-Violence," in Gandhi, *Nonviolence in Peace and War*, 113-114.

81. Mohandas K. Gandhi, "God of Love, Not War," in *Non-Violence in Peace and War*, 119.

3. Nonviolence affords the fullest protection to one's self-respect and sense of honor, but not always to possession of land or movable property, though its habitual practice does prove a better bulwark than the possession of armed men to defend them. Nonviolence, in the very nature of things, is of no assistance in the defense of ill-gotten gains and immoral acts.

4. Individuals or nations who would practice nonviolence must be prepared to sacrifice (nations, to the last man) their all except honor. It is therefore inconsistent with the possession of other people's countries, i.e., modern imperialism, which is frankly based on force for its defense.

5. Nonviolence is a power which can be wielded equally by all — children, young men and women or grown-up people, provided they have a living faith in the God of Love and have therefore equal love for all mankind. When nonviolence is accepted as the law of life it must pervade the whole being and not be applied to isolated acts.

6. It is a profound error to suppose that whilst the law is good enough for individuals, it is not for masses of mankind.

The metaphysical and religious roots of Gandhian nonviolence are obvious. The law of nonviolence is infinitely higher than the laws of brute nature. Faith in God is required for a full commitment to nonviolence. There is a revaluation of the values of this world such that those things that can be won through force in this world are not of value. Faith in nonviolence is a life-transforming faith that changes all of our actions. And so on. Some of this is reminiscent of the Christian approach, which emphasizes love and faith. But Gandhi's approach is developed from within the Hindu tradition.

When Gandhi speaks of ahimsa, or nonviolence, it is important to remember that this is the negation of violence (*himsa* means violence and *a-himsa* means nonviolence). Violence is seen as a disorder, an unproductive or unnatural action. The goal is to resist the temptation toward violence by cultivating ahimsa, or nonviolence. According to Gandhi, we need to wake up from our immersion in violence in order to discover the compassion that flows from recognizing our interdependency.

> We are helpless mortals caught in the conflagration of himsa. The saying that life lives on life has a deep meaning in it. Man cannot for a moment live without consciously or unconsciously committing outward himsa... A

64

votary of ahimsa therefore remains true to his faith if the spring of all his actions is compassion, if he shuns to the best of his ability the destruction of the tiniest creature, tries to save it, and thus incessantly strives to be free from the deadly coil of himsa. He will be constantly growing in self-restraint and compassion, but he can never become entirely free from outward himsa.[82]

Gandhi is realistic about the fact that in this world, violence will continue to occur. The task before us is, then, to resist our tendency toward violence by cultivating virtues such as self-restraint and compassion. The same message can be found in the Christian approach. Paul says the following, in his letter to the Galatians.

> Now the works of the flesh are plain: fornication, impurity, licentiousness, idolatry, sorcery, enmity, strife, jealousy, anger, selfishness, dissension, party spirit, envy, drunkenness, carousing, and the like. I warn you, as I warned you before, that those who do such things shall not inherit the kingdom of God. But the fruit of the Spirit is love, joy, peace, patience, kindness, goodness, faithfulness, gentleness, self-control; against such there is no law. And those who belong to Christ Jesus have crucified the flesh with its passions and desires.[83]

The Christian message, like the Hindu, is that love, peace, gentleness and self-control are the result of a spiritual gift that ultimately comes from the grace of God. No doubt it is up to us to be open to this gift and to work actively to cultivate it, but the foundation for it is the religious absolute. And these virtues are themselves justifiable within a larger metaphysical view.

This approach was developed into a nonviolent philosophy and practice that has had a direct impact on the society and politics of the United States. Martin Luther King Jr. unified the Pauline Christian idea of love with Gandhi's doctrine of ahimsa and his strategic political nonviolence. King's approach is summed up in his discussion of Paul's idea of *agape*, or ethical love. "Agape means a recognition of the fact that all life is interrelated. All humanity is involved in a single process, and all men are brothers... Because men are brothers, if you harm me, you harm yourself."[84] King and Gandhi also point out that this absolute form

---

82. Gandhi, *Autobiography*, 439.

83. Galatians, 5:19-24

84. Martin Luther King, Jr., "An Experiment in Love," in *A Testament of Hope: The Essential Writings of Martin Luther King, Jr.* ed. by James Melvin Washington (San Francisco: Harper and Row, 1986), 20.

of pacifism leads to a sort of internal nonviolence. From King's perspective, not only must we refrain from violence, we must also learn to turn hatred into love. It is important to keep the example of King in mind because, like Gandhi, he showed in practice that nonviolence can have a practical effect in the world. Although there are open questions about the reason for its success, from within the Gandhi-King philosophy the reasons have to do with the justice of God. For King, "the believer in nonviolence has deep faith in the future... For he knows that in his struggle for justice he has cosmic companionship. It is true that there are devout believers in nonviolence who find it difficult to believe in a personal God. But even these persons believe in the existence of some creative force that works for universal wholeness."[85]

It is "easiest" to articulate a pacifist philosophy from within a larger metaphysical scheme or religious tradition that supports the sacrifice and suffering that may be required of the devotee of nonviolence. By this, I do not mean that the faith of religious pacifists is easy to come by or that the work of nonviolence is easy. Rather, I mean that the unified metaphysical system which underlies a religious commitment to nonviolence makes it easy for pacifists to make judgments in the real world and provides the tranquility and certainty that can come with faith. Again, I do not want to minimize the struggles, sacrifice, and suffering of faith. A passing familiarity with the lives and works of Jesus, Paul, Gandhi, or King shows that their lives were characterized by profound suffering. My point is only that the consistency and metaphysical comfort provided by absolute pacifism provide a set of resources that include courage and hope that are not available to a humanist.

We should note that the sacrifices and suffering demanded by nonviolence are not that different from the sacrifices and suffering demanded by a commitment to violence and war. Those who go to war risk being killed, in the same way that those who choose to practice nonviolence risk being killed. Thus, it is not surprising that religion is also invoked to justify the sacrifices made by warriors. The difference is that while warriors are willing to die for their cause and use religion to celebrate and justify their sacrifice, they are also willing to kill for it, and likewise use religion to justify their killing. Pacifists are willing to die, if necessary, but are unwilling to kill.[86] It is significant that both warriors and pacifists can invoke the same deities to support their efforts — and this indicates

---

85. King, "An Experiment in Love," 20.
86. This difference is brought out by Duane Cady in *From Warism to Pacifism* (Philadelphia: Temple University Press, 1989), 105.

one of the problems with the religious approach. The Christian religion, for example, seems to support both a pacifistic and a just war approach.

It should be noted that pacifists, like warriors, are willing to act and to act with vigor, for their cause. Pacifists are not "passive-ists." That is, they do not roll over and give up. Rather, like Gandhi and King they are committed to active nonviolence. However, pacifists impose certain limits on the means that can be used in their active pursuit of justice. One of the reasons for this has to do with some idea of the unity of means and ends. For the pacifist, the end cannot justify the means.[87] Moreover, the absolute pacifist who approaches nonviolence from a spiritual tradition is ultimately concerned not with the transitory ends of this life but with the eternal values of the spirit. Religious nonviolence emphasizes the fact that the spirit ought to resist hatred, prejudice, enmity, and strife. In other words, the nonviolent spirit is to be a spirit of love. Although love can actively work for justice, the pacifist finds it hard to imagine that love can use violence as a means.

Of course, not all pacifists are religious and not all religions are pacifistic. Indeed, the just war tradition, which despite its affinities to pacifism is not pacifistic, developed out of the Christian religion and has adherents who are religiously committed. Moreover, one might be an absolute pacifist for ethical reasons that are not connected to a religious doctrine. Deontologists and consequentialists can both be pacifists in an absolute sense. This form of ethical absolutism can be pacifistic if the foundational ethical principles are thought to result in a thorough commitment to nonviolence. The deontologist might claim that the principle "do no harm" should never be violated, while the consequentialist might claim that war always creates more negative effects than positive ones. While consequential and deontological approaches are philosophically significant, most humans do not clarify their values by way of meta-ethical argumentation. Rather, most humans use religion along with their own critical intelligence to help them figure out where to stand on important ethical issues. The nonviolent activism of Gandhi and King is much more influential and widely known than the pacifism of ethicists and philosophers. The message of religious pacifism, because it appeals to widely held religious beliefs, is able to reach a wide audience. This is why it is important to understand the religious approach. The religious approach has the added element of offering a larger metaphysical picture in which we can be consoled in

---

87. See King, "Love, Law, and Civil Disobedience," in *A Testament of Hope*, 45.

light of the risks and dangers of pacifism. Such a larger metaphysical view is not available to a humanistic approach such as the one I defend.

The religious approach to pacifism is absolutist in the same way that religion is absolutist. By this I mean that religions make claims about the absolute truth with regard to metaphysics and ethics. Thomas Merton clarifies this in what follows.

> The nonviolent resister is not fighting simply for "his" truth or for "his "pure conscience, or for the right that is on "his side." On the contrary, both his strength and his weakness come from the fact that he is fighting for the truth, common to him and to the adversary, the right which is objective and universal. He is fighting for everybody. For this very reason, as Gandhi saw, the fully consistent practice of nonviolence demands a solid metaphysical basis both in being and in God.[88]

As is quite well known, Gandhi's idea of *satyagraha* can be translated as "truth-force" or, as King translates it, "love-force."[89] The commitment to nonviolence is a commitment that is based on an absolute claim about the truth of the interconnectedness of beings, about God's will, and about the common goal for all persons, which is peace and the unity of love. Although religious approaches certainly need to be interpreted by human beings, they find their ultimate ground in claims about the ultimate nature of human and non-human reality that must be taken on faith. Such faith is absolutist when it is not revisable in light of further experience.

A HUMANISTIC APPROACH

My own approach is humanistic and pragmatic. By this I mean that I make no claims about the absolute truth of metaphysical reality, nor do I claim to have an infallible source for my ideas about ethics.[90] Although I am sympathetic to the idea of interconnectedness and brotherhood, I am not sure that this is the best description of the human experience. Moreover, I am unsure of the theological underpinnings of this claim. For a humanist, the answers to

88. Thomas Merton, "Blessed are the Meek: The Christian Roots of Nonviolence," in *Thomas Merton on Peace* (New York: McCall Publishing, 1971), 209.

89. King, "Pilgrimage to Nonviolence," in *A Testament of Hope*, 38.

90. A useful introduction to humanism is found in Paul Kurtz, *Embracing the Power of Humanism* (Lanham, MD: Rowman and Littlefield, 2000).

metaphysical and ethical questions are in an important sense underdetermined — experience does not lead us to final or absolute answers about metaphysical and ethical questions. For example, the facts do not lead me to conclude either that there is a God or that there is no God. Nor do the facts lead me to conclude either that the soul is immortal or not. Nor do the facts lead me to believe that humans are all brothers or that we are not. The religious view stakes a claim with regard to such questions that ignores the tragic fact that human experience is limited and our conclusions are uncertain. From a humanistic perspective, in our condition of uncertainty, the best method for proceeding is a pragmatic one that focuses on the concrete empirically verifiable results of beliefs, while side-stepping large metaphysical questions with a respectful agnosticism. This approach runs counter to the mainstream of religious thinking, which emphasizes a realm of verification that is non-empirical, which is encountered either through direct intuition or through some system of authority.

While absolute pacifism may not be "easy" to enact, given problems such as weakness of will or human "sinfulness," it is not beset by the skeptical problems that are found in a more humanistic approach. Christians, Jains, Hindus, Buddhists, and other religious pacifists have the "luxury" of arguing that peace is mandated by God or by the nature of the karmic universe. I say that this is a luxury because the humanistic approach is open to the doubt. The humanist must constantly wonder if it is really true that peace is a good for human beings. Moreover, the humanist who is informed by the brutal facts of history must continually wonder whether peaceful means can be effective "in the real world." Absolute religious pacifism circumvents this particular skeptical problem by postulating another world in which suffering can be redeemed and by retreating to a metaphysically-inspired hope that in the long run God's will will be done. Even innocent suffering, which might be prevented through use of force, can be allowed when it is located within a larger structure in which evil deeds are punished and innocent suffering is redeemed. King, for example, was quite clear about the fact that his approach is based on the assumption that "unearned suffering is redemptive" and that God provides us with the foundation in hope that is necessary for the struggle.[91] This foundation in hope seems to be essential for the total devotion required of a commitment to nonviolence; and it is a form of hope that is best supported by theological commitment. As Merton says, "Christian nonviolence derives its hope from the promise of Christ: 'Fear not,

---

91. King, "An Experiment in Love," 18.

little flock, for the Father has prepared for you a Kingdom' (Luke 12:32). The hope of the Christian must be, like the hope of a child, pure and full of trust."[92] It is precisely this type of childlike hope that realists about violence find to be absurd.

I reiterate that I am not saying that religious pacifism is easy to enact or that the theological hope it requires is easy to cultivate. Indeed, religious belief is a constant struggle, in part because it asks us to go beyond our ordinary world of experience and demands the great leap of faith. But the difficulties of pacifism are not unique to the religious variety. Violence is one of the possibilities for human action, a possibility that has been celebrated and encouraged in most cultures. Religious pacifism asks us to turn away from our potential to use violence. This process of turning is a difficult one. However, the religious pacifist may be strengthened in this process by faith in a larger system of rewards and punishments. My own approach parsimoniously refrains from appealing to another world of justification and redemption. Pacifism becomes much more difficult to defend when the resources for such a defense are limited to the natural universe of human interaction. And it becomes more difficult to enact, when there are no metaphysical resources to support it other than a commitment to the idea that war and violence are prima facie wrong. Indeed, there are those who argue, on ethical grounds, that pacifism is self-contradictory, as indeed an absolute form of pacifism would be if it did not appeal to religious justification.[93] If we reject — or are doubtful about — the religious ground of pacifism, then a more pragmatic approach is necessary, i.e., one that looks at the relationship between ends and means in the real world.[94]

The conclusion of the version of practical pacifism that I am defending in this book is that violence in general and war in particular are, as a rule of thumb, to be avoided, because, in practice, violence and war create more suffering than they prevent. This is a general rule: there might be exceptions. Moreover, the reasons for avoiding war are practical, by which I mean that they are discovered in the present world by way of empirical considerations. War is to be resisted not because of any absolute reason discovered by way of metaphysical or religious speculation but, rather, because human reason tells us that war is bad.

---

92. Merton, "Blessed are the Meek: The Christian Roots of Nonviolence," 216.

93. Jan Narveson, "Pacifism: A Philosophical Analysis" in *Ethics*, 75: 4 (1965), 259-271. The limitation of Narveson's approach is that it does not account for the religious ground of pacifism.

94. For an example of this approach, see Martin Benjamin, "Pacifism for Pragmatists," in *Ethics*, 83: 3 (1973), 196-213.

This conclusion is reached not through religious epiphany or indoctrination but through the tough work of continued self-critical analysis that is demanded by philosophy. This is not to say that certain religious pacifists cannot agree with the stance of practical pacifism. Indeed, many religious pacifists give reasons for pacifism that are decidedly practical. The Dalai Lama has recently written:

> I am a fervent believer in non-violence. Violence begets violence. And violence means only one thing: suffering. Theoretically it is possible to conceive of a situation where the only way to prevent large-scale conflict is through armed intervention at an early state. But the problem with this argument is that it is very difficult, if not impossible, to predict the outcome of violence. Nor can we be sure of its justness at the outset. This only becomes clear when we have the benefit of hindsight. The only certainty is that where there is violence, there is always and inevitably suffering.[95]

The practical point is that, in reality, violence does not produce the result we want, which is peace. Although the Dalai Lama's faith in nonviolence is ultimately tied to his larger faith in the precepts of Tibetan Buddhism, this statement makes it clear that one can be committed to pacifism without bringing in religious justifications.

The difference in tone is important. Practical pacifists begin from the facts of this world and recognize the horrors of war. Absolute pacifists begin from transcendental claims about the soul and derive rules for the redemption of the soul, including a variety of ideas about sacrifice, self-abnegation, and submission to enemies (This is true despite the vigorous activism of both the nonviolent action of pacifists such as Gandhi and King). The religiously motivated nonviolent activist ultimately will find his own suffering and even his own death redeemable in another realm. "One of the first principles of nonviolence is the willingness to be the recipient of violence while never inflicting violence upon another."[96] Moreover, in the depths of a metaphysical scheme such as is found in Hindu or Buddhist approaches to pacifism, the connection between the nonviolent agent and the violent one is quite complex. Interconnectedness means that violence done to another is violence done, in some sense, to oneself. Likewise, within such a scheme violence is bad; it creates bad karma, or it is a sin. Given the interconnectedness thesis, we all suffer when our brothers sin; so the question arises whether it would be better to prevent the violent offender

---

95. Dalai Lama, *Ethics for the New Millennium* (New York: Riverhead Books, 1999), 201.
96. King, "Interview with Kenneth B. Clark," in *A Testament of Hope*, 336-337.

from committing violence in the first place, perhaps through the use of force, so that he does not hurt himself and upset the community. A further difficulty is found in the fact that nonviolent protest can in fact elicit violence from authorities and others. This is tantamount to tempting the other to sin, by tempting the other to commit violence. Again, the theological and metaphysical speculations needed to solve this problem are many. Gandhi's hope was that his own suffering could redeem his fellows from the sinfulness of their own violence. Thus his fasts were not only undertaken to provoke pity and reflection. They were also undertaken to atone for the sins of those who had committed violence, as if through his own suffering the bad karma created by others could be reduced. It is interesting that Gandhi was very careful to have the right intention in his fasting. The fast cannot be undertaken as an attempt at coercion — it cannot be done "against" someone. Rather the fast was a way of atoning and a way of participating in the suffering of others.[97]

These religious approaches are inspiring in their comprehensiveness and in the devotion that they can inspire, despite their metaphysical complexities. The difficulty confronted by the practical pacifist approach comes from two directions. First, the practical pacifist is a humanist who is not certain about the metaphysical claims — such as the principle of interconnectedness — that are made by the religious approaches. Moreover, the practical humanist approach uses the criteria of rational ethics to evaluate even religious claims. The struggle between divine command and humanistic ethics has been going on since Plato wrote his *Euthyphro*. The humanist maintains that moral claims are good not because God commands them, but because reason justifies them — even God should be constrained to command only those things that are in fact morally justifiable. Of course, this merely moves the conversation about pacifism from religion to ethics. But this move is important for the humanistic approach, because ethical principles can be debated rationally without appeal to religious epiphany, authority, and faith. Second, the practical pacifist is worried about the zealotry and extremism that can be tied to religion in general. While we do admire the courage of pacifists such as Gandhi and King, this courage always runs the risk of becoming unthinking enthusiasm. I will not develop this criticism of religious enthusiasm further, here — but will return to it in Chapter 8. The practical approach thus seeks to hold onto the courage of the absolute religious approach, while avoiding the excesses of zealotry that religion can give

---

97. Gandhi, *Autobiography*, 430-32 or 342-44.

rise to. Again, the solution is a commitment to ethics and a realization, based on philosophical analysis, that war should be avoided.

JUST WAR

Eventually the pacific message of Christianity was tied to militarism. The doctrine of the just war in Christianity, which most scholars trace to Augustine, can be understood as an idea which made it acceptable for the pacific Christian culture to become militaristic. One could argue that Christian militarism resulted when Christianity finally obtained political power in the 4th century. Indeed, the idea of a just war — a war that could be sanctified by God — represents a turn away from the otherworldly focus of early Christianity. Jesus, the Apostle Paul, and the early Christians lived under the expectation that the Kingdom of God would triumph in their lifetimes. They did not make provisions in their thinking for the problem of how to obtain and maintain political power. Nor did they worry much about saving others from suffering, since all suffering was to be redeemed with the second coming of Christ. Thus, several centuries later, with Augustine we arrive at a Christian theory that justifies war in the name of a set of other-worldly values. Although this theory is surely an advance over the ancient deification of warrior gods and praise for warrior virtues, Christian civilization was still founded upon the idea that war is necessary and that it can be justified.

Of course, the just war idea is not an easy one to reconcile with the pacifistic ideal found in the scriptures. Even Augustine, to whom the more vigorous approach of the just war tradition can be traced, worried about whether killing another in self-defense was justifiable.[98] Augustine's emphasis is on killing in order to save someone other than yourself — an idea that gives support to the idea of humanitarian intervention. Within the dualistic scheme of Christianity, it may not be justifiable to defend your own miserable body at the expense of your soul. Rather, killing can be justified only when it is undertaken as an act of charity or sacrifice. Indeed, if killing is a sin, then when one kills to defend some innocent other, one is committing a serious sacrifice — risking the good of one's own soul in order to save another. Of course Augustine's position becomes quite complicated: is it permissible to kill to save your own skin so that

---

98. This discussion follows Richard B. Miller, *Interpretation of Conflict* (Chicago: University of Chicago Press, 1991), Chapter 1.

you might be able to work to defend others? Complicated questions such as these require detailed theological speculation. Such questions were developed further by Thomas Aquinas and eventually came to be known as just war theory. However, the heart of the just war tradition is a presumption against violence.[99] Violence must be avoided and used only as a last resort. Moreover, violent intentions are not to be encouraged. Violence must be carefully restrained to appropriate levels, even within war. Despite its complexities, it is hard to avoid the conclusion that the just war tradition is a pragmatic accommodation in which otherworldly Christian love is linked to the practical demands of political power.

Similar pragmatic approaches can be found in other traditions. The Chinese produced that important theory of war, known as "the Sun-Tzu." It is important to remember that even Sun-Tzu denies that war is good in itself. Sun-Tzu seems to emphasize that one should avoid war if possible and wage it decisively when it is inevitable: "There has never been a state that has benefited from an extended war. Hence, if one is not fully cognizant of the evils of waging war, he cannot be fully cognizant either of how to turn it to his best account."[100] Even a pacifistic Chinese religious-philosophy such as Taoism recognizes the necessity of war. The Taoist sage Lao-Tzu recognized that the resort to war was regrettable and to be avoided because war was not a natural action. Taoism is known for focusing on "non-action" or "effortless action" (*wu-wei*). This idea is perhaps best understood as simplicity and grace that is attained by avoiding unnatural action. Like other philosophies that advocate pacifism, the focus is on negating violence. The *Tao te Ching* focuses on the regrettable necessity of war as follows:

> Even the finest arms are an instrument of evil, a spread of plague, and the way for a vital man to go is not the way of the soldier. But in time of war men civilized in peace turn from their higher to their lower nature. Arms are an instrument of evil, no measure for thoughtful men until there fail all other choice but sad acceptance of it. Triumph is not beautiful... The death of a multitude is cause for mourning: conduct your triumph as a funeral."[101]

---

99. For a different interpretation, see George Weigel, "The Just War Tradition and the World after September 11," *Logos*, 5:3 (Summer 2003).

100. *Sun-Tzu: The Art of Warfare* (trans. Roger T. Ames, New York: Ballantine Books, 1993), Chapter 2, p. 107-108. Roger Ames complicates the question of whether militarism is ubiquitous to human culture quite a bit. He argues that ancient Chinese philosophy was intimately concerned with warfare and that warfare was considered to be applied philosophy. The point here is that Chinese philosophy utilized metaphors that were derived from warfare (Roger T. Ames, translators introduction to *Sun-Tzu: The Art of Warfare*).

This recognition of the tragic necessity of war has much in common with Christian just war thinking. However, these Chinese approaches are not based on ultimate claims about the blessed soul or about redemption from suffering. Rather, these are pragmatic analyses of the fact that war is hell and that it should be avoided. Such a conclusion can be linked to the presumption of nonviolence that should underlie just war theory

Much has been written about just war theory in recent years. Two of the more important humanistic approaches can be found in Michael Walzer's *Just and Unjust Wars* and more recently in John Rawls' *The Law of Peoples*. These texts will be discussed in more detail in Chapter 6. The basics of this approach to the idea of a just war set the stage for my own approach, which is itself a version of this just war approach. My conclusion is that the just war theory is not careful enough about its militaristic or bellistic assumptions.[102] The problem of the just war approach can be discovered when we try to locate it on a continuum between pacifism and realism.[103] I prefer to think of the just war approach as closely linked to pacifism. There are historical reasons for this — the just war theory in the West developed in a Christian context. But without the religious connection, the just war approach is committed to a certain reluctance about war that shows close affinities with pacifism. Just war theory follows from the basic idea that occasionally it might be justifiable to use violence. Just war theory attempts to set up the conditions under which violence might be justifiable. This approach is not pacifistic in that it allows for the use of violence. However, it shares with pacifism the basic idea that we should avoid violence if possible. The just war theory adds that we may use violence when it is absolutely necessary. I extend just war thinking toward practical pacifism by claiming that it is extremely difficult to know when the use of violence is in fact necessary and justifiable.

Of course, it is possible that just war theory is more closely related to realism. The point of the just war theory may not be to avoid violence and war. Rather, the just war approach might simply be an attempt to regulate war. The assumption of the just war theory, when seen in this light, is that the world itself

---

101. Lao Tzu, *The Way of Life* or Tao-te-Ching (trans. Witter Byner, New York: Perigree Printing, 1980), Verse 31, p. 44.

102. Duane Cady points out that our culture rejects pacifism as absurd because the culture presumes that war is normal and unavoidable (Cady, *From Warism to Pacifism*).

103. See Miller, *Interpretation of Conflict*.

is best understood in terms of something like an ongoing war of all against all, such as Hobbes described. Hobbes' solution was to call for the creation of a strong state that could ensure peace. The problem for the military realist is that in the international arena, there is no party to ensure the peace. This is a condition of what some have called "international anarchy": the war of all states against all states.[104] Since there is no hope that an international sovereign will ensure peace, each nation must arm itself in order to provide for its own self-defense. Moreover, in this armed international anarchy, no state can trust any other. Indeed, if the Hobbesian psychology can be applied to states, each state is interested ultimately in power and glory. Thus each state has a reason to fear every other. Nonetheless, realists can be concerned with peace. And the realist might support certain ideas about restraint in war that lead, if not to an idea of a just war, then to the idea of a limited war.[105] In this case, the just war would be defined in terms that examined consequences of war for international stability and the prospects for peace. Hobbes tells us that the social contract will result from the exhaustion of continual war and from the common human interest in peace. The rules generated in Hobbes' social contract constitute a "peace treaty" and they establish certain principles of justice. In the domestic arena, a sovereign is elected to enforce the peace treaty. This sovereign is empowered by giving him a monopoly of force. However, in the international arena, there is no cosmopolitan sovereign. In light of international anarchy, the best sort of peace that can be obtained from this perspective is a "balance of power" peace that results when self-interested nations realize that the costs of war will exceed the benefits. Such a peace was characteristic of the deterrent policies of the Cold War. The costs of military action were so high for the superpowers that they refrained from moving beyond the MAD stalemate of Cold War.

While military realism tends toward the Machiavellian conclusion that "The end justifies the means" or that "All's fair in love and war," realism can reach principles which regulate warfare. Certain principles, which would be agreed to by all parties, must be respected in order to ensure the stability of the balance of power. Nonetheless, because international anarchy is total and because there is no trust that the other states will restrain themselves in war, the realist recognizes the necessity of preparing for total war. If the enemy will stop at nothing to win, then we must be prepared also to stop at nothing. In other

---

104. See Michael Doyle, *Ways of War and Peace*.

105. For the distinction between just war and limited war, see James Turner Johnson, *Just War Tradition and the Restraint of War* (Princeton: Princeton University Press, 1981), Chapter 7.

words, for the realist, nothing is in principle out of bounds in terms of methods or strategies, including terror bombing, sieges, and other means that are prohibited by a more robust form of just war theory. Just war principles might be useful for preventing escalation and ensuring the possibility of peace. But a realist leaves open the possibility of a "supreme emergency exemption" in which the principles of the just war theory can be overridden.[106] Limited (but not necessarily just) war principles are established for the realist by arguing that it is in our self-interest to avoid certain methods and strategies because they may make it impossible for us to achieve our goals in the long run. Aggression, invasion, expansive imperialism, genocide, the use of rape, poison, and weapons of mass destruction might be condemned from a realist perspective not because they are wrong but because they are not useful either for helping us to assert our power or for creating a stable balance of power.

In opposition to this realist approach to limited war, which argues for limitation of force from consequentialist ideas about the future balance of power, the just war theory is much more concerned about intentions and the inherent rightness or wrongness of differing violent means to good ends. The realist idea of limited war does not reject any means on principle. The just war theory does. This makes the just war theory something of a deontological theory. The best we can do is to approach such principles as prima facie duties, rather than as absolute deontological principles.[107] The preponderance of evidence shows us that means and ends are interdependent and cannot be considered in isolation. This interdependence shows us that, usually and for the most part, violent means cannot be used for peaceful ends. Thus there is a prima facie duty not to use violent means and the burden of proof rests on the one who would argue otherwise. Moreover, since peace and justice are such important ends (and means), the burden for overriding the prima facie duty not to use violence and unjust means is quite high.

The just war theory can be closely linked to pacifism. The basic idea is that war and violence are wrong and that they should be avoided. Like pacifism, the just war approach, as I interpret it, is reluctant to utilize war and would like to avoid conflict if possible. However, unlike the absolute pacifists described above, just war theorists acknowledge that in this world violence is a means that occasionally must be employed. One obvious reason that violence might be

---

106. This realist component is found in both Walzer and Rawls. For further discussion, see Chapter 6.

107. Cf. W.D. Ross.

necessary can be seen in discussions of self-defense. Most of us would agree that we have a right to life. If we have such a right, most of us would also agree that we have a right to use violence to protect it.[108] In international affairs this would amount to the right of a sovereign nation to defend itself. This might be extended also to include a recognition that violence might be necessary to protect some other whose right to life is threatened. This basic insight would ground a discussion of humanitarian intervention.

The implementation of the idea of self-defense is not as obvious as it might seem. In the Christian tradition, Aquinas complicates it a bit by claiming that our intention must be pure when we utilize violence in self-defense. We cannot intend to kill our assailant. Rather, we can only intend to defend ourselves, with the death of the assailant being an unintended side-effect. This is the basis for the controversial doctrine of double effect that is appealed to in the just war tradition to defend the killing of innocents that happens in war. Christian just war theorists, such as Augustine and more recently Paul Ramsey, focus on love as a motivation for war. From this perspective, we go to war to save innocent people who might be harmed were we not to fight. In these cases, the intention matters. Violence is supposed to be a reluctant last resort and it is to be undertaken with regret and repentance.

Violence cannot be blood-thirsty or malicious and still fall within the Christian justification. The difference from a realist perspective is telling. Realist limitations on war do not worry about intention, so long as the balance of power and conditions for peace are maintained. This is a difference in ultimate ethical justification. The approach which emphasizes intention is, at least in part, deontological, while the realist approach is consequentialist. The import of this distinction can be understood as follows. For the deontological approach, there are certain principles that should be respected without exception. Respect for principles has as much to do with intentions as with consequences. Thus intentions matter, with the primary intention being some variant of "Do no harm." The problem that gives rise to the just war approach is that occasionally it is necessary to do harm in order to protect others from harm. The reason the intention matters is that violence and war — to be morally acceptable — will have to intend to create justice and other conditions for peace. We are supposed to intend to fight only to prevent harm. For the consequentialist approach, what

---

108. This is Jan Narveson's point in "Pacifism: A Philosophical Analysis," in *Ethics*, 75: 4 (July 1965).

matters is results. If the end to be pursued is peace or justice, then it does not matter how these ends are obtained, so long as they are obtained. Of course, this is a bit of a caricature: it might be the case that the consequentialist would like us all to adopt peaceful intentions — i.e., the intention to do no harm because if such intentions were ubiquitous, peace and justice would be more likely to result. However, for the consequentialist, this intention is not good in itself. It would be good only if it actually led to the goal in mind, that is, if it actually led to the promotion of peace.

The pragmatic approach to this debate proposed in these pages focuses on both intentions and consequences. There is something to be said for good intentions but these alone are insufficient to generate justice. Likewise, consequences do matter — but so does character. By cobbling together as many approaches as possible, deontological, consequentialist, even virtue ethics, we may discover broad support for the prima facie argument for the just war theory. There may be conflicts among these approaches. However, it is possible that each of these various meta-ethical approaches can give us a good reason to be concerned about questions of justice in war.

The most recent influential discussion of just war principles can be found in John Rawls' *Law of Peoples*, which draws heavily on Walzer's *Just and Unjust Wars*. For Rawls, just war principles are necessary for ensuring a stable international society of peoples. Rawls' approach is linked to his approach to liberal values. He argues for the just war theory by way of a hypothetical contract situation, in which representatives of peoples would agree to the principles of the just war theory (he calls this, alluding to his previous work on social contract theory, "the second original position"). The point of this method is that Rawls thinks that it would be rational for nations to agree to the principles of the just war theory based upon the attempt of the parties involved in the international contract situation to maximize self-interest under conditions of ignorance. The imposition of a hypothetical ignorance condition is a heuristic designed to ensure that each party would be as impartial as possible. Rawls' approach is pluralistic and so I am quite sympathetic to it. Rawls implies that different peoples could support the just war theory for different reasons, coming from different metaphysical, religious, and ethical worldviews.

Regardless of the way in which the just war theory is grounded, it has developed into a set of criteria both for going to war and for conduct in war. They can be summarized in the following lists.[109]

Jus ad bellum (Justice in Going to War)
1. Just cause
2. Right intention
3. Proper authority
4. Last Resort
5. Probability of Success
6. Proportionality

Jus in bello (Justice in war)
1. Discrimination
2. Proportionality
3. No intrinsically bad means

The first list, the *jus ad bellum* principles, have to do with judgments made about going to war. We must have a just cause, a right intention, and the proper authority. Moreover, war must be a last resort, must have a likelihood of success, and must be proportional to the end aimed at. The second list sets out the *jus in bello* principles, which are about evaluating actions within a war. A just war should discriminate between combatants and noncombatants, should use strategic means that are proportional to strategic ends, and should avoid intrinsically bad means such as rape and slavery.

The just war theory can be criticized on two grounds. First, one wonders whether the idea of a just war even applies anymore in the era of total war that includes aerial bombing and other means of mechanized killing that cannot discriminate between combatants and noncombatants. Second, who is to apply the theory? The first worry has been discussed extensively in recent literature, especially in light of the MAD-ness of nuclear deterrence strategy. In his book, *On War and Morality*, Robert Holmes quite appropriately argues that the question of *jus ad bellum* collapses into the question of *jus in bello* because ultimately the question of the justification of war is not a question of causes for going to war but a question of whether we can justify the means used to prosecute a war, even one in pursuit of a just cause. "Unless one can justify the actions necessary to waging war, he cannot justify the conduct of war and the pursuit of its objectives; and if he cannot do this, he cannot justify going to war."[110] Holmes

___

109. Sets of just war criteria can vary somewhat and some might list a third set of criteria having to due with a just peace after hostilities have ceased. My point in listing these criteria is to give some content to the just war theory.

connects this with an account of the means of modern war that makes it clear that modern war uses means that are morally offensive. Since modern war results in widespread indiscriminate destruction, it cannot be justified. "Given the presumption that killing innocent persons is wrong, the fact that war inevitably kills such persons means, in light of our argument that war can be neither just nor justified if the means necessary to waging it are not justified, that modern war is presumptively wrong."[111] Holmes goes on to examine the principle of double effect to see if it can be used to justify the unintentional killing of innocents in war.[112] His conclusion is that it is a vacuous moral principle, since it can be used to justify almost any action by tinkering with the scope of the intention. Finally, Holmes responds to the objection which says that the pacifist will "let innocent people die" if he is unwilling to use force to protect them. His response is that we have "a greater obligation to refrain from killing innocent persons than we do to save them," because "no one has a right to be saved by others... But everyone has a right not be harmed or killed by others."[113] If war is an activity that includes the killing of innocent people, then from Holmes' perspective, it cannot be justifiable, even if the prohibition of war means that we will have to let some innocent people die.

I agree with Holmes' approach for the most part, although I can imagine cases of limited modern warfare in which it might be possible to claim that the just war principles were upheld. Holmes' conclusion about letting innocents die represents a form of deontological reasoning that is not interested in consequences. His commitment to purity of motives is admirable, but perhaps, at least sometimes, the consequences do matter. Counter-examples are numerous: what if we only had to kill one person to save thousands? A more pragmatic approach would take into account both consequentialist and deontological principles. Absolute pacifists and just war theorists differ about this problem. As Duane Cady has written: "Perhaps one possible difference between the pacifist and warist at this point is the difference between believing that something is worth dying for (pacifists and warists may often agree on this) and believing that something is worth killing for (pacifists and warists may

---

110. Holmes, *On War and Morality*, 181.

111. Holmes, *On War and Morality*, 189.

112. For further critical discussion of the principle of double effect, see G.E.M. Anscombe, "War and Murder," in James Rachels, ed., *Moral Problems* (New York: Harper and Row, 1971) and Alison MacIntyre, "Doing Away with Double Effect," *Ethics*, 111 (January 2001), 219-255.

113. Holmes, *On War and Morality*, 210.

often disagree on this)."[114] An absolute pacifist, whether religious or deontological, will be reluctant to kill, while a just war theorist may acknowledge that occasionally killing — even killing of the innocent — can be justified. Practical pacifism assumes that the deontological position is correct as a starting point and it establishes a very high burden of proof for those who would claim that the principle of "do no harm" is to be set aside. Nonetheless, practical pacifism is open to the consequentialist counter-example. It would in fact be the worst form of callousness and hubris to allow large numbers of people to die when we could act to prevent their deaths by killing some innocents, if there truly were no other resort in this case.

There are other limits besides the deontological ones — i.e., prudential and empirical conditions — that strengthen the practical pacifist's presumption against killing and against war. For example, war is always risky and uncertain and history shows us that violence is rarely a suitable means toward the creation of a just and lasting peace. Moreover, practical pacifism recognizes the deceptively easy option presented by the culture of militarism and its assumption that force is usually necessary, as well as the allure of bellism and its glorification of violence.[115] Thus, again, a plurality of arguments lead to the conclusion that the burden of proof that would justify war must be set quite high and that we must err on the side of peace.

A second worry about the just war theory is that it is unclear who is to apply these criteria in practice. According to our founding documents, in the US ordinary citizens should be the ones who ultimately apply these criteria. If a war is being fought in our name, with the support of our tax money, and with the sacrifices that we ourselves as well as our relatives, friends, and neighbors are asked to make as they serve in the military, we ought to make certain that the war is a just one. The problem is that, as ordinary citizens, we do not have the capacity to judge whether these criteria apply, at least in part because we do not possess the information needed to make the judgment. Thus, perhaps the just war criteria are, in practice, only to be applied by our military and civilian leaders. Indeed, we must hope that our generals and civilian military strategists are worried about just war concerns. However, we cannot be certain of this, given the mediated world in which we live. Thus, in practice, for an average citizen, the just war criteria are merely theoretical principles which we cannot

114. Duane L. Cady, *From Warism to Pacifism*, 105.
115. Cf. Holmes, *On War and Morality*, Chapter 8: "Alternatives to War."

apply in practice. It is our task to hold our leaders responsible for applying these principles in practice. We do this by questioning and resisting them when they insist that we must go to war. Finally, when war has already broken out, it is the citizen's duty to vigorously remind military and civilian leaders that they have a responsibility to prosecute the war justly and that what we want is not victory and glory, but justice and peace.

CHAPTER 4. CITIZENSHIP, EPISTEMOLOGY, AND THE JUST WAR THEORY

> The less government we have, the better, — the fewer laws, and the less confided power. The antidote to this abuse of formal Government, is, the influence of private character, the growth of the Individual...
> — Emerson[116]

Ordinary citizens of advanced democracies should be strongly committed to pacifism in practice. This conclusion follows from a commitment to the basic principles of the just war tradition, from an analysis of the division of labor in society, and from a certain set of assumptions about the relationship between citizens and government. This social and political analysis shares much in common with the libertarian strain of modern liberal theory and with the individualism of the American philosophical tradition. However, one need not be an anarchist to agree that citizens must be empowered to question and resist political power. Anarchism is a utopian political philosophy, which could never be implemented in reality. The state is an unavoidable expedient for dealing with social reality. The danger is that the state and its military power can come to overshadow the lives and the commonsense of its citizens. It is the duty of citizens to cultivate their own virtues, to develop practical wisdom, and to question and resist those powers that seek to dominate individuality.

---

116. Ralph Waldo Emerson, "Politics," in *Essays: Second Series* in *Ralph Waldo Emerson, Essays and Lectures* (Library of America), 567.

Although the ideas of practical pacifism are linked to the larger questions of political theory, the concerns of the present chapter are limited to the question of what citizens who accept something like the just war theory ought to do in light of the facts of modern military and political power. The basic idea that a theory about justice in war could lead to a version of pacifism is known as "just war pacifism," as described toward the end of the previous chapter.[117] This position became popular in light of the destructive power of 20th century weaponry and the era of total war. According to the just war pacifist, aerial bombardment, total mobilization, and the possible use of weapons of mass destruction makes war impossible to justify according to the terms of the just war theory, which prohibits indiscriminate killing of noncombatants. The just war tradition is committed to the idea of producing justice through a moral use of appropriately limited violent means. No doubt occasionally some violence is necessary in the real world. The problem is whether ordinary citizens are able to judge whether military force is justifiable. The thesis of practical pacifism is that most of us cannot know that any given war is in fact justified. Since war is horrible and prima facie immoral, ordinary citizens should resist war until a strong case has been made that any proposed war would be justifiable.

Most people who think about the just war theory reject its pacifist interpretation. For example, Keith Pavlischek — a colonel in the Marine Reserves — concludes that the just war tradition focuses on providing a normative ground for statecraft, on providing guidance for military leaders, and on offering guidance for individuals as they decide whether to support the use of force. He concludes that judgment about the justice of war "rests with those

---

117. The discussion in Chapter 3 focused on Robert Holmes, *On War and Morality*. But also see Richard B. Miller, *Interpretations of Conflict* (Chicago: University of Chicago Press, 1991); Duane L. Cady, *From Warism to Pacifism* (Philadelphia: Temple University Press, 1989); and Stanley Hauerwas, *Should War be Eliminated?* (Milwaukee, WI: Marquette University Press, 1984). In the background of this discussion is the US Catholic Bishops' pastoral letter of 1983, "The Challenge of Peace: God's Promise and Our Response." Also see Richard Wasserstrom, "On the Morality of War," *Stanford Law Review*, 21: 1627-1656, reprinted in James Rachels, ed., *Moral Problems* (New York: Harper and Row, 1971) and Martin Benjamin, "Pacifism for Pragmatists," *Ethics*, 83: 3 (1973), 196-213. George Weigel and James Turner Johnson reject just war pacifism as discussed in Weigel, "The Just War Tradition and the World after September 11." For a recent discussion by Turner, see "Just War Tradition and the New War on Terrorism," a Pew Forum on Religion and Public Life Discussion (with Jean Bethke Elshtain and Stanley Hauerwas) (www.pewforum.org). The present chapter also relies upon the following sources for discussions of just war and of pacifism: Michael Walzer, *Just and Unjust Wars* (New York: Basic Books, 1977), John Rawls, *The Law of Peoples* (Cambridge, MA: Harvard University Press, 1999), Paul Ramsey, *The Just War* (New York: Charles Scribner's Sons, 1968), Jenny Teichman, *Pacifism and the Just War* (Oxford: Basil Blackwell, 1986), Jonathan Glover, *Causing Death and Saving Lives* (New York: Penguin, 1977), Chapter 19.

who have the competence to render such judgments. Put bluntly, it resides with those who know what they are talking about. In almost every instance, that does not include bishops, theologians, and professors."[118] Pavlischek is undoubtedly right; it is ultimately up to our military and civilian leaders to decide whether a given war is just, as they have access to the necessary information and expertise to make the judgment. However, this still leaves the rest of us with the problem of deciding whether to support the judgments made by our leaders. Pavlischek recognizes this: "For most Americans... the just war tradition illuminates the responsibilities of citizens in a self-governing democracy under God."[119] However, he does not recognize the complexity of this claim. The division of labor in society includes a division of responsibility for judgment. Democratic institutions allow, indeed demand, debate and disagreement among and between the parts of society. The responsibility of a citizen in a self-governing democracy is not simply to acquiesce in light of the expertise of our leaders. Rather, our duty is to question and demand proof, especially in light of actions that have momentous moral implications, such as the question of whether to support a war.

The pacifistic interpretation of just war theory referred to derives from the question of whether the means of modern warfare are immoral because these means inevitably involve indiscriminate killing of innocents. This thesis developed in the last few decades amid concern for nuclear war, the means of which included deliberate targeting of population centers. An understanding of the means of modern war gives us a strong reason to reject war, in addition to the difficulty, for ordinary citizens, of judging whether there are good reasons to go to war. Thus practical pacifism is about both the causes of war and the means employed. In both cases, ordinary citizens should adopt a policy of erring on the side of peace until a compelling argument is made that shows that any given war is justified. Put more strongly, citizens ought to presume that war is usually not justifiable. The burden of proof rests upon those who propose to resort to war: they must show that there is a just cause for war and that the means of war will not be immoral. This is not a final argument against war, however, unless we adopt a form of absolute pacifism that completely rejects the use of violence. The just war tradition attempts to clarify limits on causes for and means of war, while accepting that violence can sometimes be justifiable. Those who are

---

118. Keith Pavlischek, "Just and Unjust War in the Terrorist Age," *The Intercollegiate Review*, Spring 2002, p. 31.

119. Pavlischek, "Just and Unjust War in the Terrorist Age," 31.

sympathetic to the idea of a just war admit that it is possible to imagine some tragic scenarios in which war and its inevitable risks and horrors would be justifiable.

What is the rational response for citizens who want to know how to evaluate any given war? The prima facie argument against war is based upon the problem of the indiscriminate destructive means of modern warfare. George Weigel has argued against this view by noting that its prima facie presumption against violence is too strong because it focuses too much on the contingencies of *in bello* concerns, while ignoring the "moral clarity" that is possible with regard to the *ad bellum* question of just cause.[120] Weigel's insistence that the just war theory is more interested in the question of ends (identifying the just cause) than in the question of means is worrying. Unless we recognize the interdependence of means and ends, we can easily end up slipping toward the immoral doctrine that the end justifies the means. In good pragmatic fashion, it won't do to ignore the means and focus only on the ends — as Weigel seems to indicate. The ideal is one where peaceful democratic means are employed to obtain peaceful democratic ends. Until this ideal is possible, it may be necessary to resort to war. However, we must resist the idea that war is the solution to political problems. Very often there are other solutions that are overlooked by those who advocate military power.

Practical pacifism follows from a recognition of human fallibility and of alienation within political institutions. As Paul Griffiths writes of the source of information upon which ordinary citizens would base their judgment, "Our principal sources are three: the US government itself, in the person of those appointed to speak for it; the US media; and foreign governments and media. But we have no good reason to think that any of these sources is sufficiently reliable to provide what we need, and we therefore also have no good reason to think that we have access to the evidence and argument we would need if we were to judge the burden of proof to be met."[121] This assumption follows from a basic skepticism not only about the justification of killing in light of modern means of war, but also about the transparency of modern political life.[122] In general, even in a liberal democracy such as ours, most citizens are precluded from knowing

---

120. George Weigel, "The Just War Tradition and the World after September 11," *Logos* 5:2 (Summer 2002), 13-44. For his emphasis on ad bellum questions and moral clarity, see p. 24.

121. Griffiths, "Just War: An Exchange," 32.

122. Cheyney C. Ryan has argued that pacifism is essentially a "skeptical" position in "Self-Defense, Pacifism, and the Possibility of Killing," in *Ethics*, 93: 3 (1983), 508-524.

whether many actions of state are justified. This is especially true with regard to war because information about war is kept secret or is obscured by propaganda. Even if we accept the idea that violence can sometimes be justified in theory, a practical version of pacifism will result if we admit that we simply do not have enough information to judge whether any given war is justified.

PRESUMPTIONS FOR OR AGAINST VIOLENCE

Two rival assumptions color thinking about war and violence. Either human beings are essentially aggressive and violent, or we are not. If we assume that people are basically violent, we will be quicker to argue for the necessity of violent means to our ends. If we assume people are basically nonviolent, we will avoid violent means and be willing to allow nonviolent means to work. There is a bit of circularity in the arguments made for either assumption. If one holds the first assumption — that human beings are naturally violent — then one will interpret cultural and sociobiological evidence accordingly. Such an assumption makes it easy to see the roots of human violence in the "violence" of chimpanzees and thus lends credence to the assumption that human beings are essentially violent. This in turn leads to militarism, to Hobbesian arguments for a powerful security state, or at least to the claim that some form of "justified" warfare is necessary in order to ensure stability, justice, and peace. The "fact" of militarism and the security state thus supports the violent assumption and vice versa. And just war theory is then understood as an attempt to limit the use of violent means, which themselves are supposed to be inevitable. One has only to appeal to our chimpanzee relatives and to the long human history of warfare, terrorism, and violence to show that the military state and war itself are necessary. Likewise, the existence of the military state "proves" the fact that we are violent. If one holds the opposite assumption — that human beings are not naturally violent — then chimpanzee aggression will not count for much (while bonobo pacifism will count for more), warfare and terrorism will seem like aberrations from the norm, and militarism will be seen as a retrograde ideology which serves the interests of the ruling elite. Likewise, the idea of a just war will be seen as a tragic oxymoron that we must strive to overcome. Such rival assumptions about our nature can be found in religious discussions. Some religions hold that human beings are originally violent and so must be saved from ourselves by some superior external force. Others hold that human beings are originally nonviolent

89

and must shake off the illusions of violent culture to return to our originally pure state.

The presumption of violence is often held by conservatives who follow Hobbes in arguing that strong governments and rigid moral codes are needed to prevent evil.[123] The presumption of nonviolence is often held by liberals, pacifists, and anarchists who follow Rousseau in arguing that if human beings were not corrupted by violent social forces, we would all be able to get along better. Both of these presumptions are precisely that, presumptions. Depending upon which one chooses, one will view the empirical evidence differently, identifying human beings either with chimpanzees and devils or with bonobos and angels.

The truth is probably some synthesis of the two: we possess the capacity to be both devil and angel; we are genetically related to both chimp and bonobo. It is crucial to note that each rival assumption brings with it a closed system of interpretation. Since the synthesis of these two views is not immediately forthcoming, a pragmatic response is appropriate. Indeed, when confronted with the hermeneutical circles described here, a good pragmatic response is to ask the question of which circle works better to promote the ends we have in mind. Those who value peace, who dread the horrors of violence, and who value democracy, will adopt the anti-militarist presumption of nonviolence. But the nature of this pragmatic resolution to the problem is one that is open to revision. We must continually reconsider whether the presumption of peace is actually working to fulfill our ends.

Many theorists in the Western tradition — Machiavelli, Hobbes, Nietzsche, and Freud to name a few — adopt the presumption of violence: they agree that human beings are fundamentally — naturally — aggressive and prone to violence.[124] Freud, for example, writes in *Civilization and its Discontents*: "Men are not gentle creatures who want to be loved, and who at the most can defend themselves if they are attacked; they are, on the contrary, creatures among whose instinctual endowments is to be reckoned a powerful share of aggressiveness. As a result, their neighbor is for them not only a potential helper or sexual object, but also someone who tempts them to satisfy their aggressiveness on him, to exploit his capacity for work without compensation, to use him sexually

---

123. Cf. John Kekes, *The Case for Conservativism* (Ithaca, NY: Cornell University Press, 1998).

124. For a critical account of the competitive assumption shared by Hobbes, Nietzsche, and Freud, and a consideration of the alternative moral psychology of Heinz Kohut, see Gary Grief, *The Tragedy of the Self* (University Press of America, 2000).

without his consent, to seize his possessions, to humiliate him; to cause him pain, to torture and to kill him. *Homo homini lupus.*"[125] This idea that "man is a wolf to man" leads to the conclusion that violence is not surprising and that political and cultural arrangements must be set up that work to counter violence with control. If, as Hobbes claims, the state of nature is a state of war, then the only hope for peace is a strong set of cultural prohibitions against violence. But, as Freud has indicated, these strong cultural prohibitions bring with them their own price in terms of repression, guilt, and other forms of internalized aggression. As Herbert Marcuse — a critical theorist beloved by the counter-culture — understands Freud, "the notion that a non-repressive civilization is impossible is a cornerstone of Freudian theory."[126] The irony of this approach is that its conclusion is that violence — albeit subtle forms of internalized violence — must be used to combat violence. And so the circle of violence is grounded on the presupposition of violence. Despite the seeming inevitability of violence which follows from the presumption of violence, Marcuse hopes, following some of Freud's more hopeful ideas, that the solution to violence and militarism can be found in education about the violent presuppositions of militaristic culture. For Marcuse, opposition to militarism requires "the spread of uncensored and unmanipulated knowledge, consciousness, and above all, the organized refusal to continue to work on the material and intellectual instruments which are now being used against men."[127] But the very idea that knowledge can be used to combat violence is one that points beyond the closed circle of the conservative view, toward liberal faith in the nonviolence of reason.

Opposed to the conservative view is a more optimistic or melioristic approach which works from the presumption of nonviolence. This view is found in liberals who dream of progress toward a world of reasonable consensus in pursuit of justice and in hopeful religious thinkers and others committed to forms of absolute pacifism. Rousseau is perhaps the most famous of those who have argued that it is the development of society, industry, and technology that have led to an increase in violence, inequality, and injustice. Unlike Hobbes, Rousseau argues that self-love is limited in primitive man by pity, "an innate abhorrence to see beings suffer that resemble him."[128] Of course, as Martha Nussbaum has argued, pity, empathy, and compassion are insufficient to ground

---

125. Sigmund Freud, *Civilization and its Discontents* (New York: W.W. Norton and Co., 1961), 68-69.

126. Herbert Marcuse, *Eros and Civilization* (Boston: Beacon Press, 1966), 17.

127. Marcuse, *Eros and Civilization*, "Political Preface 1966," xxiv.

a public policy based on justice.[129] A more developed notion of compassion must go beyond immediate identification with the sufferer and include the idea that the suffering is not deserved — an idea that leads to the question of justice. The idea that some forms of suffering can be deserved can lead to the justification of violence and war. The just war theory can be interpreted as stating the principles that would control and justify the creation of suffering through violence. Often, the idea of justifiable use of violence is linked to the idea that violence can be used as a means to the goal of ending violence. However, most liberals hold some version of the idea, developed by Kant, that since individuals are ends in themselves worthy of moral respect, war can only be justified when free citizens give their consent to "the waging of war in general, but also to any particular declaration of war."[130] Kant's basic presumption is that violence is a bad thing that can only be justified by allowing people to consent to it.

Absolute pacifists go further and postulate nonviolence as our true destiny or ideal, despite the fact that we must struggle with and against violence to achieve this ideal. This requires quite a bit of hope grounded in religious eschatology and soteriology. Thomas Merton has described a Christian approach to nonviolence that assumes both the ultimate union of all of us within God and the fact that the truth itself is only accessible and defensible by nonviolence. "The quality of nonviolence is decided largely by the purity of the Christian hope behind it."[131] This hope comes from the assumption that the world is directed toward good and that human beings can be redeemed from original sin and violence. The presumption of nonviolence is that nonviolence is humanly attainable, not that violence is inevitable. The presumption of nonviolence leads us to expect more out of ourselves than simply to restrain our inevitable violent tendencies. It asks us to work for a world in which violence is truly the exception and is not a constant expectation. As Merton says of his approach to nonviolent conflict resolution: "It appeals above all to the highest ethical motivations..."[132] These motivations are toward the good, the true, and

128. Jean-Jacques Rousseau, *Discourse on the Origin of Inequality* in Rousseau, *The Social Contract and Discourse on the Origin of Inequality* (New York: Washington Square Press, 1967), p. 201.

129. Martha Nussbaum, *Upheavals of Thought* (Cambridge: Cambridge University Press, 2001), Part III.

130. Immanuel Kant, *Metaphysical Elements of Justice* (New York: MacMillan, 1965), 118.

131. Thomas Merton, "Blessed are the Meek: The Christian Roots of Nonviolence," in *Thomas Merton on Peace* (New York: McCall Publishing, 1971), 215. In addition to Christianity, Merton also draws his ideas from Gandhi.

132. Thomas Merton, "Note on Civil Disobedience and Nonviolent Revolution," in *Thomas Merton on Peace*, 227.

the just. Merton and Gandhi go further and claim that it is untrue of human beings that we are essentially violent. There are many important metaphysical and theological questions here. However, such an approach is not only about metaphysics but also about the political and ethical implications of one's descriptions of human being. To emphasize nonviolence is to hopefully work for peace; to emphasize violence is to cynically prepare for war.

Those who assume that the human essence is nonviolent are not passive pacifists who refuse to do anything to actualize this human essence. Both Gandhi and Merton realize that concrete human action is necessary to defend the just, the good, and the true: the ideal of nonviolence can only be actualized through human effort. However, they do not hold onto the pessimistic assumption of conservatives who argue that human beings cannot be perfected and that violence will thus always be necessary. Rather, they argue that the resources of culture must be used to help us both to remember our essential goal — nonviolence — and to remind us of the only acceptable means toward this goal, which are peaceful.

The presumption of either violence or nonviolence connects to the issue of burden of proof. If we agree that violence is bad and if we presume that the human goal is to work toward nonviolence, then the burden of proof that would justify violence will be quite high. If we argue that violence is useful or at least inevitable, then the burden of proof will be shifted and proponents of nonviolence will be asked to prove that their means can be effective. There is no definitive argument that can justify either the presumption for or against violence. Nor, then, is there a final answer to the question of the burden of proof. However, the nonviolent presumption is better for pragmatic moral reasons, because peace is a good that we all pursue and because violence is prima facie bad. This is not to say that absolute pacifism is right. Rather, I am merely postulating a basis for the burden of proof. The proponent of violence must prove his case because the presumption of nonviolence is morally preferable to the presumption of violence. This is so because of a basic commitment to the interdependence of means and ends: the basic presumption of a pacifist approach is that violence begets violence and that peace can best be promoted through peaceful means.

PACIFISM AND JUST WAR THEORY

I assume that some version of just war theory is morally defensible. That is, I allow that it may sometimes be justifiable to use violence to resist injustice. However, as stated above, we should adopt the presumption of nonviolence and put the burden of proof on the proponent of violence. The questions of justification and proof thus open all sorts of other questions that demand practical analysis in any given circumstance. This is true for both *ad bellum* and *in bello* principles. I will focus on one criterion from each set, show their interrelation, and pose a skeptical problem.

The primary *ad bellum* criterion is the question of just cause. The most obvious example of a just cause is the idea of self-defense. When one nation is attacked by another, the victim has the right to defend himself against the aggressor. Indeed, it is the duty of the government to defend the people against aggression. If our leaders did not act to defend the nation, they would not be doing their duty. Another example of a just cause is connected to the question of humanitarian intervention. Humanitarian intervention is justified when, Michael Walzer's words, it is a response to acts that "shock the moral conscience of mankind."[133] To know that the cause is just in the case of proposed humanitarian intervention, one would have to know that there were egregious violations of human rights, genocide, or other acts that shock the collective human conscience. With modern media and an open society, it should be fairly easy for any concerned citizen to know when there is a just cause for war in either of these two cases. The September 11 attacks were clear examples of aggression and the ethnic cleansing in Yugoslavia obviously demanded humanitarian intervention. The evidence that would help us decide whether there is a just cause in either case is fairly obvious and can be provided by the mainstream media.

However, things become more complicated as we decide what a proper response to those cases in which there is a just cause. Just cause alone is not enough to precipitate a war. Prudential concerns matter with regard to the question of how best to respond to an act of aggression or the need for humanitarian intervention. We need to know whether the proposed military

---

133. Michael Walzer, *Just and Unjust Wars*, 107. For an update, see Walzer, "The Argument about Humanitarian Intervention," *Dissent* Winter 2002. For further discussion, see the debate between Duane Cady and Robert Phillips in their *Humanitarian Intervention* (Lanham, Maryland: Rowman and Littlefield, 1996).

action will be successful, whether it will cause more suffering than it seeks to prevent, whether there is the prospect of a stable peace, etc. And we might be concerned with the question of who has the proper authority to authorize military action or we might be concerned about the purity of the motives of those who propose to intervene. The practical question is whether a concerned citizen could know the answer to these sorts of queries, to the prudential question of success and the question of proportionality; and we cannot ever know about the purity of our leaders' motives. However, these issues do not focus exclusively on the question of whether the cause is just. Indeed, they are taken up by other *ad bellum* criteria and point beyond the *ad bellum* criteria toward *in bello* principles.

With regard to the issue of the purity of motives and intentions, the connection between means and ends comes to the fore. Michael Walzer argues, on consequentialist grounds, that mixed motives do not matter so long as the result is that evil is eradicated. Indeed, he argues that political motivations are always mixed.[134] This analysis runs counter to the issue of "right intention" that is part of the *ad bellum* criteria, showing us that it is difficult to live up to the standards of the just war theory in practice. But, the issue of intention gives us a reason to question those who would drive us toward war. Walzer seems to imply that we should support those with less than pure intentions simply because we value the ends that they seek to pursue. This can push us toward a slippery slope of accommodation with advocates of war who happen to share our ends. This has been a problem for intelligence gathering and law enforcement agents who must cooperate with and even reward criminals in order to attain their ends. Can we ever be sure of the purity of the motives and intentions of those who would lead us to war? Obviously, we have no way of knowing the true intentions of our military and civilian leaders. For this reason, we should actively engage them by asking them to justify themselves and state their intentions.

Let us turn then to the question of means as discussed under the *in bello* criterion of discrimination. The principle of discrimination has been held to be perhaps the most important principle for *in bello* consideration because it is thought to be something like an absolute duty not to deliberately kill innocents. As Ramsey describes this, it is a question of the relation between means and ends. "Acts of war which directly intend and directly effect the death of non-

---

134. Walzer, "The Argument about Humanitarian Intervention."

combatants are to be classed morally with murder, and are never excusable. If the excuse is that victory requires this, then we would be saying that the end justifies an intrinsically wrong means or that men may be murdered in order to do good."[135] In a just war, a good faith effort must be made to avoid employing unjust means which include deliberate killing of innocent noncombatants. Unintentional killing of noncombatants is covered by the doctrine of double effect.[136]

To justify a war in light of this principle, one would need some idea of the intended strategies of a given war and of the circumstances under which these strategies will be implemented. Some have argued that the practical strategies of modern warfare — which include aerial bombardment and other forms of mechanized killing — lead to an almost sure violation of the principle of discrimination. But in addition to that, ordinary citizens lack the ability to evaluate claims made about the intention of the military to constrain its operations in light of the principle of discrimination. Ordinary citizens are excluded (for good strategic reasons) from having access both to battle plans and to a concrete analysis of the "facts on the ground" that could inform a decision about whether this principle were respected. Furthermore, we can imagine the difficulties for anyone — even someone who has access to more information — who must make judgments about discrimination and the other aspects of the just war theory. As Johnson describes this, "Even with the best attempts to measure an enemy threat and one's own ability to avert or withstand it, and even with the most conscientious use of such attempts in judgments about the good and evils associated with a particular war, these judgments ultimate hinge upon perceptions about the enemy and one's own nation. Such judgments are inevitably of the character of art: in this case, the art of statecraft."[137] Although Johnson intends to support the idea that political judgment is required of military and civilian leaders, he opens the question of whether one can trust the moral judgment of one's leaders; and he points out

---

135. Paul Ramsey, *The Just War* (New York: Charles Scribner's and Sons, 1968), 154. For discussion, see James Turner Johnson, *Just War Tradition and the Restraint of War* (Princeton: Princeton University Press, 1981), 196-228.

136. See, for example, G.E.M. Anscombe, "War and Murder" in James Rachels, *Moral Problems*, op. cit. For a recent discussion see Alison McIntyre, "Doing Away with Double Effect," *Ethics* 111 (2001), 219-255. Johnson distinguishes between double effect in terms of discrimination and in terms of proportionality (Turner, *Just War Tradition and the Restraint of War*, 221-22). I have focused here only on the issue of discrimination.

137. Johnson, *Just War Tradition and the Restraint of War*, 206.

that the type of judgments that must be made in war are complex and demanding. While we do not have a prima facie reason to distrust the judgment of leaders, in evaluating them we must acknowledge the complexity of the judgments required, the pressure to ensure victory, and the temptations of power. None of this alone gives us reason to question their integrity. However, we should not blindly trust them until they have demonstrated their good intentions and ability to make these moral judgments.

In general, while it is possible for ordinary citizens to judge that there are good causes for war, we do not have access to the kind of information we would need in order to know whether the means of war — even a war proposed for good cause — were justifiable. This problem of knowledge holds, even if we are willing to temporarily suspend the principles of justice in war under something like the supreme emergency exemption discussed by Walzer and Rawls. Most ordinary citizens do not have the kind of geopolitical and strategic knowledge that would be needed to know whether a supreme emergency loomed. Finally, with regard to preemptive or preventative wars that seek to defeat potential threats that are identified by military intelligence, the epistemological problem is perhaps even worse.[138] Even if we admit that preemption or prevention could be justified on consequentialist grounds, the epistemological problem remains. Ordinary citizens do not have access to the kind of military intelligence that would be needed to judge that a preemptive or preventative war would be justified.

KNOWLEDGE AND THE BURDEN OF PROOF

It should be clear that I am demanding a fair amount of certainty with regard to the question of the justification of war. There are important uncertainties when we consider utilizing violence, and in light of these we must resist the move toward war. Violence and killing are such evils that we should establish a high burden of proof in an effort to justify them. This is especially so for citizens in a democracy, whose passive acquiescence implies tacit consent.

---

138. For a discussion of preemptive war, see Walzer, *Just and Unjust Wars*, Chapter 5. Walzer says that preemption is justified at the point of "sufficient threat." But he admits that this phrase is "necessarily vague" (Walzer, p. 81). This vagueness points us to the epistemological problem. Preemption occurs when there is a threat of an imminent attack from one's enemy. Preventative wars occur when the threat is not yet imminent. The current war in Iraq was, in part, a case of preventative war (although it has also been interpreted as a case of humanitarian intervention).

Especially in a democracy, wars are fought "in the name" of all citizens. If war is prima facie wrong, then citizens have a duty to demand justification. Until such justification is forthcoming, we should resist the drive to war. In a liberal democracy, it is not a citizen's immediate duty to support a war. Rather, it is the government's duty to convince the citizen that he should support the war by offering proof about the justice of the cause and about the intention to utilize just means.

The idea of a burden of proof perhaps requires some explanation. In most ordinary cases, the *less plausible and more risky* proposition must be proved. I assume that the use of violence is an implausible means toward humane ends. And I assume that the use of violence is risky. Violence is implausible as a means because there is something right about the pacifist assumption that "violence begets violence." Moreover, violence is risky both for those who propose to use it and for those innocents who will inevitably be its victims. This does not suggest that violence can never be a means; it only suggests that the burden of proof rests on the one who proposes violence. Of course, one might argue that the goal of the just war theory is not peace or some other "humane" end. Rather, the point of the just war tradition is to ensure justice. Such an objector might argue that in the real world, violence is often a means to justice, as can be seen in the use of police force and criminal punishment. But in pursuit of domestic justice, we have established a fairly high burden of proof precisely in order to prevent harm from being done to the innocent. The same high burden of proof should hold for war.

Some of the questions we might have about any given war are prudential: can we be sure that our effort will be successful? This is not directly a moral concern. It can become one, however, if we link it to questions such as the following: can we be sure that the war will be successful, given the limitation on means that is imposed by the just war theory, that it will not escalate beyond these limits, and so on? Skeptical responses to this question seem appropriate, especially in light of the brutal history of the 20th century and in light of our more efficient means of mass killing.[139] Wars have a tendency toward escalation beyond the limits imposed by the just war theory.

George Weigel has dismissed the focus on the *in bello* question of means as an overemphasis on "contingent" issues. "There is nothing wrong, per se, with contingent judgments; but they are contingent. In the nature of the case, we can

---

139. See, for example, Jonathan Glover, *Humanity: A Moral History of the 20ᵗʰ Century* (New Haven: Yale University Press, 2000).

have less surety about *in bello* proportion and discrimination than we can about what have previously been assumed to the be the prior *ad bellum* questions."[140] While Weigel seems to suggest that, because these questions are contingent, they matter less for moral analysis, his idea of a "contingencies" with regard to the issue of discrimination is in fact a euphemism concealing the fact that it is real innocent human beings who will be killed. The practical pacifist wants, most basically, to know whether a war even in pursuit of a just cause will kill innocent people and create suffering. The question of means is an essential part of the moral evaluation of whether we ought to pursue justice or whether we ought, rather, to employ nonviolent means or possibly even learn to forgive our enemies. The question of justice comes in when we use war as a means to preventing greater suffering. But pacifists have been at pains to point out that there are other means that can work to prevent suffering. Moreover, sometimes the prevention of suffering itself can be evil if it employs means that are evil. Weigel's point may be that military planners cannot account for all contingencies and absolutely ensure justice *in bello*. There are risks in war. Nonetheless, these risks — however contingent they may be — should be taken seriously, not ignored for the "easier" question of whether we are pursuing a just cause.

But ultimately I am concerned with the problem for citizens who are at a remove from the calculations of the military strategist. Most of our pundits and fellow citizens claim to know more than they do when they offer us definitive answers about proposed wars. We must continually criticize this bit of hubris: very few of us are in a position to be able to definitively answer the skeptical challenge.

This is not to say that there is no truth to the matter. It is either true or false that any given war would be a just one. The problem is that ordinary citizens cannot know the truth. This is especially true in light of the unpredictability of war and the so-called "fog of war." We in the midst of history simply do not have access to all of the facts. If this is true, then we should be skeptical of those who propose any given war. A practical form of pacifism results from this point of view. We should raise skeptical objections to those who would justify war, and demand that a clear and compelling case be made both with regard to just cause and with regard to assurances that just means will be used. Until such a case has been made, we should err on the side of peace.

---

140. Weigel, "The Just War Tradition and the World after September 11."

Patriotism, Protest, and Civil Disobedience

One might object that the standard of proof demanded here is too high and that in practice, this would lead to the inability of a government ever to justify war to its people. I accept this objection and readily admit that my position leads to a form of pacifism. However, I leave open the possibility that citizens could be persuaded that any given war is justified. Moreover, I claim that it is the duty of a democratic government so to persuade its citizens by providing as much evidence and argument as is possible while still maintaining levels of secrecy that are necessary for security. The problem is that, since some secrecy is necessary, citizens can never be absolutely sure that the government's claims are justified.

One might further object that patriotism requires obedience to and support of the government. "Whether a war is just or not is not for the private man to judge: he must obey his government."[141] This may work for hierarchical governments that demand blind obedience. But liberal government requires trust based on reasons, consent, and open information.[142] One might object that the position I advocate breaks down the trust that is necessary for the adequate functioning of government. My position does hinge upon a certain amount of distrust of those in power. This distrust is rational, in light of a long history that shows a tendency toward manipulation and abuse of power by those in power. In liberal states — which since Locke have been understood as fiduciary institutions — citizens have a right and possibly even a duty to raise skeptical objections to ensure that their trust is not broken. This is especially true with regard to actions as momentous as war. The "patriot" objection might hold if war were merely an action of an entity called the nation or state, which was not reducible to the will of its citizens. However, wars are fought by citizen-soldiers and they are supported by tax dollars generated by the labor of citizens. Moreover, and this is the decisive point, citizens do not abdicate the moral demand that they evaluate and judge actions done "in their names."

---

141. This objection is stated by G.E.M. Anscombe, "War and Murder," 282. Anscombe agrees with this to an extent, although she is worried about those who would hide immorality behind reasons of state. For a concrete analysis, see also John Somerville, "Patriotism and War" in *Ethics*, 91: 4 (1981), 568-578.

142. For a recent discussion of the importance of social trust and its relation to democracy and social equality see Eric Uslaner, *The Moral Foundations of Trust* (Cambridge University Press, 2002).

It is a citizen's moral duty to question and judge actions of state. It is also a moral duty to resist those actions of state that are judged to be immoral, through civil disobedience and other forms of nonviolent resistance. In light of a skeptical analysis, the question of civil disobedience becomes quite vexing. There is an open question here. I have not claimed that all wars are in fact immoral. I have merely claimed that we do not know whether or not they are justified. Civil disobedience is certainly called for in wars that are clearly immoral. In a situation of agnosticism, however, perhaps the best we can do is question and protest, while supporting our leaders, who we hope are also concerned with the morality of their actions. Civil disobedience and active nonviolent resistance should be employed only when we have good reason to believe that an unjust war is being fought. Here we might reverse the question of the burden of proof. In this case, since civil disobedience is risky, we might impose a high burden of proof on those who would claim that we should actively resist the war effort.

There is an important ambiguity in political analysis that must be admitted by practical pacifism. There are many levels within the division of labor in society. Two should be emphasized: the level of military and civilian leadership and the level of the ordinary citizen. The question of justification, in light of the just war criteria, is ultimately a question that must be directly answered by our military and civilian leaders. They must consult their own moral consciences to answer the question of whether any given war is justified. For ordinary citizens, however, the question is whether they trust their leaders to make sound moral judgments. One of the practical results of this thesis is that citizens must actively engage their leaders in order to demand information and justification. This is necessary so that citizens can reach conclusions, however tentative and incomplete, about wars that are fought in their names. A further reason to actively question political and military leadership is to remind our leaders of their political and moral obligations: in actively questioning them, we force them to provide justifications and thus to confront their own moral consciences.

CONCLUSION

Most practical pacifists will initially resist the drive to war. As such they are closely allied with absolute pacifists, at least at first. However, the practical pacifist is open to argument and evidence, while the absolute pacifist will never accept that any given war is justified. One of the points of the practical pacifist approach is to recognize that our militaristic culture tends to promote war at the expense of peace, even in the name of the just war theory. The culture is primed to use violence to combat violence. Thus the just war theory is often interpreted not as a regrettable and tragic oxymoron but as a defense of continued militarism. A pessimist may not be surprised that a bellistic and militaristic culture such as ours would assume that the obvious answer to the problem of violence is more violence. But, this *should* be surprising — especially if we are genuinely committed to the prima facie immorality of violence. It should be surprising that anyone would adopt violence without a profound internal struggle, serious self-analysis, and intense doubt. Of course, we know that this is not the case. Rather, our present militaristic and bellistic culture makes it appear surprising that anyone would adopt the nonviolent presumption. And this is the problem: the presumption of violence is too easy, too deeply ingrained in the heart of the contemporary world.

A cynical interpretation of the peace movement might see it as a sublimated form of aggression, rather than a genuine human impulse. Such an approach is colored by the conservative and pessimistic assumptions of a Hobbesian political philosophy, which turns social norms into self-interested contracts, and which use the power of the state to limit the supposedly innate destructive tendency of private self-interest. The pessimistic presumption of violence leads us, then, to underestimate our own commitment to peace. This conclusion is worrisome because it makes it seem as if a commitment to peace involves either naivety or self-deception. But notice that the tables could be turned and the presumption of violence could be viewed as itself a piece of self-deception in which the pessimist refuses to admit that it is humanly possible to want and to achieve peace.

The evidence of sociobiology leads to the conclusion that aggression is present in us as a genetic inheritance. Thus we must seriously consider ways to redirect aggression. In order for such redirection to occur, we must seriously reassess our cultural norms. By "our culture," here, I mean human culture in general, although my remarks apply most directly to American culture — we must begin with self-criticism. Our culture celebrates aggression and violence in films, television shows, literature, sports, and even music and visual art. Our economy celebrates competition and aggression that easily becomes violent. Our politicians celebrate violence in their inflammatory war rhetoric. Many of our religions, despite rhetoric to the contrary, have been used as cover for violence. And yet, a rival strain in our tradition recognizes that violence is bad and that there are nonviolent moral resources to resist violence. Freud himself recognizes that Eros is also a primary drive. Christianity conceives of love as the pacific and universal agape. And Rousseau and others link love to pity and compassion.

During the "war on terrorism," when we have all been deeply impacted by violence, when we see violence continue around the world, when the US is plotting to continue to expand its use of violence, we must self-critically consider whether it is not time to redirect our culture — the human culture — away from violence by making it clear that violent individuals are not heroes, that murderers and suicide bombers are not rewarded by any God worthy of worship, and that the means of war must be carefully guarded and used only in self-defense, as a last resort, and with deep regret. We need to reassert the hope for a world beyond violence that underlies the presumption of nonviolence.

It is utopian to imagine a world beyond violence; but utopian visions motivate our highest human possibilities. As Camus says, "If he who bases his hopes on human nature is a fool, he who gives up in the face of circumstances is a coward."[143] Utopias embody our aspirations, direct our activities, and stimulate our best capacities. Utopian thinking is as useful and as natural for us as is pessimistic thinking that is only concerned with mitigating damage and avoiding the dystopian worst-case scenario. Our thinking since September 11 has been too caught up with dystopian nightmares that make us willing to advocate violence as the only way to prevent terror. As a remedy we need to reinvigorate utopian hopes for a world beyond violence. One might joke that such a world could only occur if females wrest control from "demonic" males, as has apparently happened in bonobo society. But the means for change is nonetheless just as radical. We need a complete reexamination of our presumptions about violence and the way our culture embodies these presumptions (and neglects our nonviolent aspirations). If we agree that violence is bad, then we must do our best to resist the forces of violence in our own culture: the media glorification of violence, the religious support of violence, and the political and philosophical rhetoric that seeks to justify and normalize violence.

We cannot end violence completely. Our utopian hope must be guided by pragmatic acknowledgement of the fact of violence — perhaps because aggression and violence are hardwired into our genetic make up. And occasionally, some violence may be justified (albeit with regret) in the name of

---

143. Albert Camus, *Neither Victims nor Executioners* (Philadelphia: New Society Publishers, 1986), 55.

self-defense or just war. Nonetheless, if we agree that violence is bad, then we must constantly struggle to resist it by postulating as our uniquely human task the construction of a world beyond violence. This means that we must self-critically examine our rhetoric about violence. To transform our culture and move it away from its ubiquitous presumption of violence we must constantly remind ourselves that the forces of natural and cultural inertia, which continue to lead us toward violence, are not inevitable. We can begin to resist violence if we only self-critically remind ourselves that we can.

Resistance to violence must become practical. The relation between the practical pacifist and the state is like Socrates' relation to Athens: a relation of questioning aimed at justice. Like Socrates, practical pacifists admit that their knowledge is far from perfect. But they believe that their duty is to serve their society by questioning and clarifying evidence and arguments. Of course, unless we are to actively embrace a certain form of anarchy, we must have some trust in our leaders and must hope that they are concerned with the morality of the actions to which they are committing us. And yet the tension of the division of labor persists. Our leaders cannot provide us full access to all of the evidence that would support their claims about the prudence of their proposed response to a purported just cause. Nor can they provide us with access to battle plans that would help to support the claim that the war would be conducted in a just manner. But this tension is crucial in a democracy. The people must demand evidence and justification from their leaders, while leaders must act based upon knowledge that they cannot share with the people. Such a complex system requires us both to trust our leaders' moral judgment and to constantly demand proof of their good judgment. It is the obligation of a practical pacifist who is a citizen of a democracy to continue to resist, question, and demand proof. Such questioning should be understood as a sign of respect for those of our compatriots who will make the ultimate sacrifice in service to their country, as a concerned reminder to those who would lead us into war, and as a symbol of solidarity and compassion for the innocents at home and abroad whose lives will be disrupted by war.

CHAPTER 5. VIOLENCE, TERRORISM, AND WAR

> All war propaganda consists in the last resort, in substituting diabolical abstractions for human beings. Similarly, those who defend war have invented a pleasant-sounding vocabulary of abstractions in which to describe the process of mass murder.
> — Aldous Huxley[144]

Most of us would intuitively agree that violence is bad, that terrorist assaults on innocent civilians are wicked, and that war is an absurdity that must be abolished; but some philosophers have defended violence in war by appealing to ideas about justice in war and others have gone so far as to argue that terrorism might be justifiable.[145] The thesis of this book is that violence is such an evil and our ability to control it and justify it is so limited that we must err on the side of peace. Practical pacifism results from modesty about our ability to justify violence. If we fully comprehend the evil of violence and the horror of war, we will establish a strong presumption toward peace that could only be overcome with great reluctance in dire emergencies. The purpose of the present chapter is to understand why violence is bad, to clarify the rhetoric and propaganda that accompany war, and to analyze the ideological understanding of terrorism and war.

---

144. Aldous Huxley, "Pacifism and Philosophy," in *The New Pacifism*, ed. by Gerald K. Hibert (New York: Garland Publishing, 1972), 35.

145. See Kai Nielsen, "Against Moral Conservatism," *Ethics* 82 (1972) and Virginia Held, "Violence Terrorism, and Moral Inquiry," *The Monist*, 67: 4 (Oct. 1984).

VIOLENCE AND CONSENT

Most of us assume that violence is a normative term: violence is, by definition, bad. But why? Let's begin by stipulating a neutral definition of violence: *violence is the deliberate use of destructive force.*[146] A key issue in this definition is the notion of deliberation. Although we can use the term "violent" metaphorically to describe storms and such, in the present context we are ultimately interested in destructive force for which human agents are responsible, where their responsibility is connected to their ability to deliberate and choose to use destructive force.[147] The problem of assuming a normative value for violence arises when we consider cases of "justified violence" in which violence — a bad thing — can be used for good ends. To keep things precise we might call such occurrences "justified force," where force is the power to move another. However, we must be aware that by avoiding the word violence and substituting the word force in such cases, we retreat to euphemism. In war, the use of "force" can involve widespread destruction, killing, and suffering. And indeed warriors are trained in the frenzied ways of destruction, encouraged to develop the will to destroy. We would be lying if we said that the destructive force of war is not violence. Indeed, the paradox of "justified violence" points us toward the tragedy of being human. Sometimes we must use violence, even though violence is prima facie a bad thing. The idea of justified violence should be tragic and disquieting. The use of justified violence is not to be celebrated. Rather, it is to be approached with fear and trembling and to be considered with caution and regret.

---

146. For definitions of violence and related terms such as *force* and *power*, as well as general discussions of violence, see the following: Paul R. Robinson, *Anger, Aggression, and Violence* (Jefferson, NC: McFarland and Co., 2000); Virginia Held, "Violence Terrorism, and Moral Inquiry," op. cit.; Graeme Newman, *Understanding Violence* (New York: J.B. Lippincott Co., 1979); John Harris, *Violence and Responsibility* (London: Routledge, 1980); J. Glenn Gray, *On Understanding Violence Philosophically* (New York: Harper and Row, 1970); Hannah Arendt, *On Violence* (New York: Harcourt Brace and Co., 1970); Robert Paul Wolff, "On Violence," *The Journal of Philosophy*, 66: 19, 601-616; Bernard Gert, "Justifying Violence," *The Journal of Philosophy*, 66: 19, 616-628; John Dewey, " Force, Violence, and Law," *John Dewey, Middle Works* (Carbondale: Southern Illinois University Press) 10: 211-215 and "Force and Coercion" *John Dewey, Middle Works*, 10: 244-251.

147. John Harris clarifies the distinction between "violent" as an adjective, which can be used to describe storms, etc. and "violence" as an activity, as I have described it above (John Harris, *Violence and Responsibility*, Chapter 2). As an adjective, "violent" implies vigorous physical activity. In this sense, Harris notes, we can stir tea "violently," which serves to make violence a bit muddy and ambiguous. I prefer to reserve "violence" to describe deliberate unjustified acts of destructive force. The extension of violence beyond this is, to my mind, only metaphorical and poetic: storms, quite simply, are not "violent" although they might be destructive and vigorous.

106

A less neutral consideration of violence can be found in the following: *violence is destructive force that harms people.* This definition makes is clear that violence is bad insofar as harming people is bad. There is a subjective component to the idea of harm and violence. Harm is defined in part by the perception of the victim: destructive force is force that is viewed as harmful by those parties that might suffer from the harm. Violence is, in part, in the eye of the beholder. It is up to the victim to determine, within limits, whether he or she has been harmed. Likewise, the degree of harm or the seriousness of the violence is determined by the victim and the context. To some, words can be harmful and thus violent. Others might not view even a minor physical interaction — perhaps a scuffle on the playground — as harmful or violent. Although there is room for interpretation, it is obvious that for a harm to occur there must, on the one hand, be some form of interaction, while on the other hand, actions resulting in extreme physical suffering and death are in all likelihood harmful. A further subjective aspect of violence has to do with the intentions of the agent who is utilizing force. Violence is usually thought to be deliberate. Someone might harm another accidentally by running into him with his car. However, unless the driver consciously aimed the car at the victim with the intention of hurting him, we would not say that this action was violent. At issue in clarifying the intentional aspect of violence is the question of culpability. Violent acts are perpetrated by responsible agents. Violent individuals are thus responsible for their violent actions; they should be punished and should feel guilty, if their violence is unjustified.[148]

How would we justify violence and what sorts of violence are unjustified? One easy answer to the question would focus only on ends. Justified violence would then serve some justifiable human end, while unjustified violence would not. The danger of such a view is that it can be Machiavellian, with the end justifying any means whatsoever. The question of just means must be considered also. Dewey and other pragmatic liberals focus on the *interdependence* of means and ends. We must recognize that there can be just and unjust means and there can be just and unjust ends. The crucial question is a complex one: which means are justified in light of which ends? A liberal approach to this question focuses on the issue of autonomy. Just means are those that respect the right that each

---

148. One might object that punishment is an act of violence. However, the notion of justification is important here. Punishment, like self-defense, is a justified application of destructive force. Of course, the notion of justification is still left unclear. Suffice it to say that punishment and self-defense utilize destructive force in pursuit of higher ends.

individual has to decide for himself which ends he will pursue. This is why genuine education is not violent. Education is a means for allowing individuals to choose their own ends. Although some form of coercive force might be necessary in education (rewards and punishments to stimulate pedagogy), the goal of education is to produce autonomy, which would, in theory, be a goal that the autonomous individual would choose for himself in retrospect.

The paradigm case of justified violence is self-defense. Although absolute pacifists condemn violence that is used for any end, the idea of self-defense suggests that violent means can be employed if they are unavoidable and necessary to defend oneself and, by extension, others who need defense. Some forms of violence can thus be justifiable, although the very idea that violence is necessary and unavoidable suggests that there has been a previous failure to fend off the attacker by nonviolent means. Although our culture glorifies the violent hero, we must not lose sight of the fact that often nonviolent means can be more successful in the long run. But the use of nonviolent means requires creative intelligence; and unlike the use of violent means, this is not often viewed as heroic or courageous.

An important component in a definition of violence is that violence is a violation of autonomy. Thus one criterion for the justification of violence is the issue of consent. Violence can be justified, if it is possible to imagine that the victim of an act of violence would *consent in principle* to the harm that will result from it. Self-defense is justifiable because almost everyone, including potential attackers who might be killed by their potential victims in self-defense, would agree that it is acceptable for people to defend themselves. The basic idea of the social contract is that we consent, in advance, as it were, to those uses of destructive force that the police monopolize. Likewise, the use of military force for humanitarian intervention could be justified if we were sure that the people suffering under a brutally oppressive regime would consent in principle to the destruction that would be caused by military intervention.

I do not mean to minimize the problem of justification. While it might be possible to imagine the type of consent I have in mind, the idea of consent is supposed to make it quite difficult to justify violence in practice: it is a difficult task to ensure that those who would suffer under violence would consent in principle. Likewise, the idea of consent is supposed to limit the power of the state. If we seriously consider what people would consent to, we would arrive at a less powerful and less militaristic state. It is difficult to imagine that anyone would actually consent to being a citizen of a militaristic state such as ours, if we were actually allowed to deliberate and vote on the question. Militaristic states almost by definition have to be paternalistic, since individuals cannot be "trusted" to support a state that taxes them to fund the defense industry while also putting them at risk by escalating military power and stockpiling weapons — including weapons of mass destruction — that beg to be used. Have many of us explicitly consented to US military power? At best, we do so indirectly by way of our elected representatives. But often these representatives defend military power from the vantage point of the elite vanguard, who — if they care about the interests of the people — claim that the people cannot know what is in their own interest when it comes to national defense.

This idea of "consent in principle" is found in social contract theories, from Hobbes to Rawls. I have in mind something like what Rawls describes under the rubric of "the original position."[149] We are to imagine what reasonable individuals would consent to, if they were able to discuss the social contract under conditions of equality and fairness. A recurrent criticism of the Rawlsian approach is that this abstract form of consideration cannot account for the actual diversity of human life. Indeed, some have argued that abstraction itself is linked to violence: the abstraction of the contracting situation violates those who refuse to deal in abstractions. This concern is linked to a profound anarchist and deconstructive critique of law and political violence.[150] The large and important worry is that political systems are founded on violence and that they hide this violence behind the authority of the law by claiming, in the abstract, that everyone would support the system. I must admit that I am quite sympathetic to this problem. However, unless we are to retreat to anarchism, we must have some standard by which to judge when political authority and even violence can be justified. Rawls' approach to the original position and the development of the conception of right aims both to justify authority and to go beyond violence. He says explicitly, "It is to avoid the appeal to force and cunning that the principles of right and justice are accepted. Thus I assume that to each according to his threat advantage is not a conception of justice."[151] In other words, the idea of justice is one that aims to reach reasonable agreements

---

149. This discussion relies upon John Rawls, *A Theory of Justice* (Cambridge: Harvard, 1971), and *Political Liberalism* (New York: Columbia University Press, 1995).

150. See for example, Walter Benjamin, "Critique of Violence," in *Reflections* (New York: Schocken Books, 1978); Jacques Derrida, "Force of Law: The Mystical Foundation of Authority," in Drucilla Cornell, ed.., *Deconstruction and the Possibility of Justice* (New York: Routledge, 1992); or Robert Paul Wolff, "On Violence," *The Journal of Philosophy*, op. cit.

151. John Rawls, *A Theory of Justice*, 134.

that are beyond violence. The deconstructive and anarchist critique views this claim as utopian and ideological: in the real world, agreements are not made by reasonable beings; rather they are the result of interest and power.

Violence is wrong, then, because it violates autonomy. If someone does something to another to which he did not consent, not only might there be physical pain, but this is also an assault on the person's integrity, autonomy, and dignity.[152] Violence is more than "destructive force." Force moves or somehow affects a thing. Destructive force affects a thing negatively, causing harm. Violence is destructive force used against autonomous human beings. It affects us in a way to which we did not consent. It creates ends that we did not choose to pursue. This is why the destructive force used by dentists and doctors is not thought to be violence: we consent in advance to have our teeth drilled or to have an organ removed. Thus, the negative result of such a procedure — pain, etc. — is not considered by the patient to be a "harm." The issue of consent shows us why killing is thought to be the worst form of violence: we assume that no one would voluntarily consent to be killed. Of course the issues of suicide and euthanasia remain outstanding problems.

The spiritual harm that results from violation of autonomy is ultimately more important than whatever physical harm is caused by violence, which is why consent is crucial for the question of justification. Violence is thus bad, first and foremost, because it violates the autonomy of the victim. From this thesis, two important conclusions follow.

First, this explains why terrorism and acts of war that kill civilians are usually thought to be unjustified, while allowing for the possibility that certain forms of limited war might be justified. Soldiers, in theory at least, consent to be cannon fodder; civilians do not. Thus we might allow destructive force to be used against enemy soldiers, while condemning the killing of innocent civilians.[153]

---

152. This idea derives in part from Jonathan Glover, *Causing Death and Saving Lives*, Chapter 5 and Peter Singer, *Practical Ethics*, 2nd edition (Cambridge: Cambridge University Press, 1993), Chapter 4.

153. Of course, soldiers themselves often have no choice in the matter, when they are conscripted. During the recent US invasion of Iraq, thousands of Iraqi soldiers were slaughtered as they fought against the vastly superior US forces. One wonders if they actually consented to launch themselves in futile human waves against the tanks and machine guns, just as soldiers have done throughout the 20th century. Indeed, there were reports that they and their families were under threat by their officers. The military hierarchy has always had to use coercive force to "convince" scared and confused soldiers to leap out of the trenches toward their deaths. Is it really possible to imagine that a soldier would consent to such activity if he knew that his charge were in fact totally useless?

This becomes complicated when we consider something like humanitarian intervention. One obvious way of deciding whether the use of military violence for humanitarian purposes would be justified is to imagine whether those who are to be affected by the use of violence would, at least hypothetically, consent to it. For example, we might consider whether the Jews and others who were murdered by the Nazis would consent to the use of destructive force that ultimately resulted in their liberation. It is possible to imagine people saying that they would be willing to take the risk of being killed by a war fought by those who were there to liberate them. The idea of imagining such consent is still problematic. Even if a large majority would consent and could make their consent known, consent is not a sure guarantee of respect for human rights. The way around this is to imagine some sort of ideal hypothetical decision procedure such as Rawls has described in order to imagine what a disinterested rational human would consent to.[154] When applied to the question of humanitarian intervention, we ought to ask whether any disinterested rational being would consent to the use of military force being used to rescue them from human rights violations, in light of the inherent risks of military force. The risks of military force should not be minimized, however. There is often no clear answer to the question of whether military intervention by a foreign power would be preferable to domestic oppression.

Second, by focusing on consent, we move beyond a consequentialist justification of terrorism and war. Kai Nielsen, for example, has argued on consequentialist grounds that terrorism might be justifiable: "There are circumstances when such violence must be reluctantly assented to or even taken to be something that one, morally speaking, must do."[155] The example he has in mind is those "terrorists" or "freedom fighters" who fought for Algerian independence in the 1960s using terror tactics. One assumes that Palestinian suicide bombing and perhaps the World Trade Center bombings could be justified on consequentialist grounds as promoting the general welfare of the Palestinian people or as working toward the freedom of Islam from foreign intervention. A consequentialist might argue that if these actions serve some further legitimate purpose for a person or group, then they are justifiable.

---

154. Rawls does this in his *The Law of Peoples* (Cambridge, MA: Harvard University Press, 1999). However, for Rawls, the participants in the "second original position" are not individuals. Rather, they are representatives of "peoples." The approach I defend here focuses on the consent of individuals, not peoples.

155. Kai Nielsen, "Against Moral Conservativism," *Ethics* 82 (1972), 222.

However, if violence is always a violation of autonomy, and if autonomy is something to which we all have a right by virtue of being human, then violence against innocents can only be indirectly justified by something like the principle of double effect. Or we might imagine, as described above, that a disinterested rational being would accept the risk of being killed by the terrorist act as a means to larger political ends.

The problem with this "consent in principle" approach is that it merely provides a heuristic to facilitate the judgment of whether any use of violence is justified. But this heuristic provides us with no certain conclusion and indeed makes the task of justifying violence more difficult. It is hard to imagine that any of the victims in the World Trade Center would consent to the violence used against them. Thus, it is fairly easy to condemn the destruction of the towers as unjustified violence. But is it so clear that victims of Nazi oppression living in Germany would have consented to the bombing campaigns that were used there? Hawkish advocates of humanitarian intervention like to imagine that the answer to this question is fairly obvious. Michael Walzer articulates a defense of humanitarian intervention, stating that it is just when it is a response to acts that "shock the moral conscience of mankind."[156] But the idea of the moral conscience of mankind is so abstract that it cannot sufficiently include inevitable diversity of views — even among those who are oppressed — about the question of whether military intervention would be justified.

If the idea of "consent in principle" is useful, it is useful because it focuses on the choices that individuals would make about their own fates: we aim to respect the autonomy of potential victims of violence by asking ourselves whether they would be willing to take the risk implied by the use of violence. However, individuals — almost by definition — differ with regard to the risks they are willing to take, just as they differ with regard to the amount of certainty they require about potential costs and benefits. Perhaps there would be consensus that cases such as Rwanda do "shock the moral conscience of mankind." However, it is more difficult to imagine consensus, even among the victims themselves, about whether foreign intervention is an acceptable remedy for specific atrocities. This does not mean that international indifference to the suffering in Rwanda is justified, either; rather, it indicates the sorts of questions that must be asked as we think about the justification of violence.

---

156. Michael Walzer, *Just and Unjust Wars*, 107.

RHETORICAL PROBLEMS

In discussions of war and violence, language is always a problem. Those who want to advocate and support certain activities use euphemisms to describe them; those who want to condemn certain activities use dysphemisms to describe them. Anarchists and others who reject the social contract view of the state claim that all of politics is "violence" and that such violence can never, in principle, be justified. Anarchists think that no one should ever consent to transfer their rights to a third party, and so they believe that government is violent. They worry that rhetorical manipulations sell us the ideology of "law" as somehow different from violence. The idea that someone would abstractly consent to the use of violence is thus put into serious doubt. From the anarchist position, it is bizarre to imagine that any individual would agree to allow himself to be put at risk of violence. There is something to be said for the consistency of the anarchist position: according to the anarchist, an autonomous being would never consent to give up his autonomy. However, it is in fact easy to imagine counter-examples, which call this consistency into question. If a man and his family and were at risk of violence from some criminal, we can imagine they would be willing to allow the police to use violent force against the criminal, even if the violence might kill one of them, provided that the violence would result in the rescue of the rest of the family. Some such idea lies behind the idea that the victims of totalitarian regimes would consent in principle to the violence of a war that aimed at their liberation.

We must keep such rhetorical and ideological analyses in mind as we consider questions about violence, terrorism, and war. We condemn "terrorists" and are fighting a "war on terrorism." However, for the supporters of al-Qaeda or for supporters of the Palestinians, "terrorists" can be called "freedom fighters" or "martyrs." Indeed, the US has supported "freedom fighters" in Central America and in Afghanistan, whose destructive power the US claimed was justified by the higher cause they served — although one supposes that from the opposite side, these looked like terrorists.[157] The word "martyr" as used by supporters of recent suicide bombers is telling: it assumes that the suicide bomber is dying for a higher cause, that his use of violence is justified. Moreover, the idea of humanitarian intervention can be used as an ideological obfuscation through

---

157. For a discussion of US "terrorism" throughout the world, see Noam Chomsky, *The Culture of Terrorism* (Boston: South End Press, 1988).

which imperialistic motives can work. In the recent war against Iraq, the claim that the Iraqi people would welcome the liberating forces of the United States was used to garner support for what, from another perspective, looked like a war of imperial expansion.

We must be careful with our language because humans have a tendency — especially in times of distress such as wartime — to choose language that is convenient in order justify whatever suits our immediate interests. Orwell noted that "political language has to consist largely of euphemism, question-begging and sheer cloudy vagueness. Defenseless villages are bombarded from the air, the inhabitants driven out into the countryside, the cattle machine-gunned, the huts set on fire with incendiary bullets: this is called *pacification*."[158] We should be careful with the language of "collateral damage" and "smart bombs" because these serve to sanitize the facts on the ground. War is violent and innocent people are inevitably killed by the actions of war. This tendency toward euphemism and doublespeak can be inflated to the point that we lose track of what we are doing in war. Chris Hedges has argued that a whole culture can be caught up in what he calls the "myth of war" that includes our whole history of valorizing the warrior and ignoring the futility and dehumanizing effects of combat. In the throes of war, we blindly adhere to the myths that portray "our" side as the side of truth and justice. And we easily succumb to a negative, sometimes overtly racist, view of the "other" side.

This linguistic influence becomes quite complicated by the constrained and controlled information that we have about terrorism, war, and military force. Our primary sources of information are the government and the corporate media, and these sources provide us with a one-sided view of things. Howard Zinn has pointed out that "Official terrorism, whether used abroad or at home, by jet bombers or by the police, is always given an opportunity by the press to explain itself, as is never done for ordinary terrorists."[159] What is worse, we do not even call the violence and bloodshed caused by our military forces "terrorism." But clear-eyed analysis shows that it often is, if terrorism means using violence that violates the principles of justice in war. One could cite terror bombing during World War II (Hamburg, Dresden, Tokyo, Hiroshima, and Nagasaki) and in the Vietnam War (the bombing of Cambodia and the use of napalm). And the problem continues.

---

158. George Orwell, "Politics and the English Language," in *George Orwell: Essays* (New York: Knopf, 2002), 963.

159. Howard Zinn, *On War* (Seven Stories Press, 2001), 22.

The new US doctrine of "pre-emptive" or "preventative" war is another example of rhetorical distortion. The US invasion of Iraq violates the international consensus about justice in war, which says that no nation can invade another unless the target is a clear and present danger to the nation in question. We claim that we need to invade rogue states in an effort to secure ourselves against terrorism. We also claim that wars such as the Iraq war are aimed at liberating the local population. But·one wonders whether this policy does not also hide less noble and more imperialistic US ambitions. Let's avoid this contentions claim, however, and recognize that despite new and improved weaponry, no modern war occurs without terrorism in the form of civilian deaths and other forms of fear and dislocation. Just war theorists will try to justify such occurrences as unintended and therefore acceptable consequences. It may be that in rare cases war is justifiable; but modern war is almost always terroristic.

The myth, stereotypes, and euphemisms of war are given to us by the government and reinforced by a supportive and uncritical media. Hedges concludes that this is a disaster for serious moral reasoning. "Destruction of honest inquiry, the notion that one fact is as good as the next is one of the most disturbing consequences of war. The prosecution of war entails lying, often on a massive scale — something most governments engage in but especially when under the duress of war."[160] Chomsky adds, more darkly, that militaristic democracies must use "thought control" to manufacture consent about war that citizens would reject if they really knew how violence was being used in their names.[161] Political narrow-mindedness leads everyone to think that "our" use of "terror" is justified while "theirs" is not.[162] If Chomsky and Hedges are at least partially correct, then our duty is to criticize, question, and resist. We must be careful as we discuss the justification of violence, terrorism, and war, not to be misled by the rhetoric and ideology that makes these seem to be good when they are employed by us. At best violence is a regrettable means that should be avoided. When we must use violence, this is a tragedy, not a triumph. And we

---

160. Chris Hedges, *War is a Force that Gives Us Meaning* (New York: Public Affairs, 2002), 149-150. For further discussion of the way in which propaganda is used in war (with a focus on the Gulf War), see Glover, *Humanity*, Chapter 20.

161. Noam Chomsky, *Deterring Democracy*, Chapter 12.

162. This is Noam Chomsky's point in *Media Control* (New York: Seven Stories Press, 2002) and *Power and Terror* (New York: Seven Stories Press, 2003).

must not let patriotic rhetoric mislead us into thinking that violence and war are to be celebrated.

TERRORISM

Let us turn more explicitly to the question of terrorism. Terrorism, like violence, is a normative concept. It is, by definition, thought to be wrong. Even within war, terror tactics are usually ruled out by the principles of justice in war. This is so because terrorism is destructive force deliberately directed at innocent targets. The just war doctrine says that it might be permissible to harm innocent civilians if this harm is an unintentional side effect of a legitimate military goal. Such unintended killing might be justifiable by way of the doctrine of double effect. However, terrorism is not justified by the doctrine of double effect because it aims directly at killing innocents.[163] Of course, a realist would not accept this principle and would argue that any means are suitable for intended ends, especially if the world is such that we are always already at war with terrorists who themselves have no respect for the "rules of war." Terrorist acts are, according to standard definitions of justice in war, war crimes. "Terrorist tactics, in most cases, violated the rules that governed armed conflict — for example, the deliberate targeting of noncombatants or actions against hostages."[164]

Again, we must be careful about the ideological nature of political language. The distinction between terrorism and justifiable force is a slippery one — even within the just war theory — that depends upon the abstract question of whether civilian casualties are directly intended. During World War II, it seems obvious that terror tactics were intentionally employed by both sides: deliberate bombing of civilian population centers is a form of terrorism. The fire bombings of Tokyo and Dresden were terror attacks. And the two atomic bomb blasts that destroyed Hiroshima and Nagasaki represent perhaps the most destructive terrorist attacks in history.[165] It might be the case that in

---

163. Alison McIntyre has recently clarified that the doctrine of double effect only applies to those rare occasions when the harm caused is indeed unintended, is only a side-effect (and is not a direct means), is unavoidable given the intention, and is proportional to the good intended. She uses the terrorism as an example and contrasts terrorism with strategic bombing campaigns. Alison McIntyre, "Doing Away with Double Effect," *Ethics* 111 (January 2001): 219-255.

164. Ian O. Lesser, et al., *Countering the New Terrorism* (Santa Monica, CA: RAND Corporation, 1999), v.

the era of total war — in which whole populations are mobilized in the war effort — the distinction between combatants and noncombatants has been effaced. In that case, either there is no such thing as terrorism per se or all war is terrorism. Realists might adopt the first part of this disjunction, when they claim that any means are suitable to the end of victory. Pacifists, of course, worry about the other side of the disjunction. This can be seen in the signs saying "War is Terrorism" that appeared at anti-war protests during the lead up to the US invasion of Iraq. The just war theory attempts to find a third option that distinguishes between justifiable and unjustifiable uses of violence. Justifiable use of violence would not be terrorist, while unjustifiable uses would be.

The realist approach that would allow terrorism is not irrational. Most politically motivated terrorists are not merely pathological (as opposed to what we might call "nihilistic terrorists," whose only goal is to disrupt and destroy). Political terrorists are rational agents who utilize what might be called a calculus of terror. The terrorist uses destructive force in order to antagonize a people and destabilize a social structure in order to make a political point aiming at some future political end. In this sense, political agents who use terrorism are, in fact, quite rational: they know how to do cost-benefit analysis in order to maximize the results of their activity. The September 11 terrorists were quite efficient if we consider that this one act, which involved only a handful of operatives, resulted in a radical change in US policy.[166] Likewise, the use of the atomic bomb during World War II was a rational policy decision that helped the United States obtain its ends — including the Machiavellian end of deterring the Soviets — in a cost efficient way, by avoiding a full-scale invasion of Japan.

Some philosophers have argued that terrorists might justify their actions as necessary for the good they intend or they might redescribe their activities in an effort to appeal to something like the doctrine of double effect.[167] Ultimately — if we adopt something like the just war theory — these efforts to justify terrorism must fail because terrorists aim directly at creating civilian casualties as a means. Thus the doctrine of double effect does not apply. It is doubtful that the World Trade Center bombers or those who authorized the use of the atomic

---

165. See Zinn, *On War*, Chapters 18 and 21 or Glover, *Humanity*, Chapter 12.

166. Of course, it is possible that the changes in US policy brought about by the terrorists were counterproductive to their ends. The declaration of a war on terrorism and the destruction of the Taliban regime were undoubtedly unanticipated negative outcomes for the terrorists.

167. Virginia Held has suggested that terrorism may be justifiable in light of the just war tradition (Held, "Violence, Terrorism, and Moral Inquiry," op. cit., 619-620).

bomb in World War II only meant to destroy the buildings and create panic without directly intending to kill innocent human beings, as would have been required if this act could have been justified by the principle of double effect.

The just war tradition's doctrine of double effect is suspicious because it tends to ignore the value of individuals who will suffer from the "unintended" consequences of war. It is also questionable to argue that anyone should be willing to sacrifice himself for a larger political end, although it is conceivable that some victims of some totalitarian regimes would consent to a war in the hope that their children could be liberated. Of course, the difficulty is that we have to make this judgment, as it were, in our imaginations, without access to the thoughts of the intended victims. It is hard to imagine how it might be possible to justify actions which cause harm to innocents without their consent, even if these actions are not intended or if these harms can serve some higher purpose.[168] We are safer adopting something like a presumption of nonviolence and setting a very high burden of proof to justify violence, such that we would have to be certain that innocents would consent to being harmed in the war effort. We must always be skeptical of such a decision procedure, precisely because it is always tinged by subjectivity and self-interest. To imagine what other people want is to imagine them as similar to you. We should be careful to recognize the limits of our moral imaginations.[169]

What is so frightening about violence and terrorism is that rational agents can deliberately choose to harm innocents. There is, at first, something odd for most of us in imagining what it would be like actually to do violence to another human being, especially an innocent being who has not directly provoked us. Imagine yourself, for a moment, into the minds of Eric Harris or Dylan Klebold, the Columbine killers; or into the mind of Timothy McVeigh, the Oklahoma City bomber; or into the mind of Mohammed Atta, named as the leader of the World

---

168. The doctrine of double effect is complex and includes issues such as the problem of defining negative vs. positive actions; the distinction between killing and letting die; the problem of intentionality of harm vs. foreseeing harm; and the question of whether or not the numbers matter (See McIntyre, "Doing Way with Double Effect"). There are no easy answers to these questions, but I assume that there is a prima facie obligation not to harm innocents without their consent. In this regard I am also sympathetic to Wolff, who holds that no violation of autonomy can be justified and who thus roundly condemns violence: "If 'violence' is taken to mean an unjustified use of force, then the answer to the question [of when it is permissible to resort to violence] is obviously never. If the use of force were permissible, it would not, by definition, be violence, and if it were violent, it would not, by definition be permissible" (Wolff, "On Violence," 608).

169. See my essay, "Toleration and the Limits of the Moral Imagination," *Philosophy in the Contemporary World*, 10:2 (Fall-Winter 2003).

Trade Center bombers.[170] We can understand the potential for violence that results from a momentary passion: we get angry in our cars, honk our horns, swear, etc. We can even imagine the violence that would be used for self-defense: self-defense classes, in fact, teach us to be comfortable using violence to resist attack. But it is difficult to imagine what it would be like to deliberately plot and carry out the destruction of innocent people. Dostoevsky's *Crime and Punishment* provides us with one famous attempt to get into the mind of a killer and we find, in the course of the novel, that Raskolnikov's mind is not a normal one.

And yet, such a cold and deliberate approach to violence happens in the normal course of war. An American soldier in Iraq killed a woman who was being used as a "human shield" by an Iraqi militant. The soldier justified his actions by saying, "the chick got in the way." [171] Military training aims to produce this sort of callousness because it is essential for getting the job done. Of course, the rhetorical problem recurs as we justify our killing as somehow superior to theirs and even seek to shift the blame onto the enemy for creating such situations. But we cannot deny that military strategists deliberately plan the killing of innocents in designing bombing campaigns, especially in targeting nuclear missiles. A rhetorical disconnect makes us find terrorism unimaginable, while allowing us proudly to celebrate the accomplishments of our military forces by hiding their destructive force behind the doctrine of double effect. We would be better off admitting that terrorism and war are violent horrors that cause the destruction of innocent lives, regardless of the cause that is being pursued. Likewise, even the use of economic sanctions can be a form of violence that deliberately causes the destruction of innocents, by depriving them of the means of life.[172] It might be that by appealing to the just war theory we might accept certain of these activities as justifiable. But if violence is bad and if unjustified uses of violence are wicked, we must be very careful to be certain that any proposed use of violence is in fact justifiable. Moreover — and here we return to the tragic element in the use of violence — we must recognize that the terrorist has a theory of justification of his own.

---

170. For a discussion of the distorted view of reality of Harris and Klebold as well as other terrorists such as McVeigh and Kaczynski, see Suzanne Laba Cataldi, "Making a Game of Killing," *Philosophy in the Contemporary World*, 9: 1 (Spring 2002), 19-26.

171. This was reported in *The New York Times* on March 29, 2003. For a discussion, see Matthew Rothschilds, "The Chick Was in the Way," *The Progressive*, March 31, 2003.

172. This argument has been forcefully made by Joy Gordon in "Economic Sanctions, Just War Doctrine, and the 'Fearful Spectacle of the Civilian Dead,'" *Cross Currents*, Fall 1999, Vol. 49, Issue 3.

I am not claiming that terrorism, such as occurred in Oklahoma City or on September 11 is justifiable. And I am not claiming that all uses of military force are unjustifiable or terroristic. The just war theory might be interpreted as aiming to prevent justifiable military force from becoming terroristic. But one wonders whether this is ever possible. We hope that we do not become terrorists ourselves. However, this hope should not delude us about the terrorism of war. One way of ensuring this is to be very clear about our language and our methods. We should avoid euphemism and frankly describe the facts of violence. We should also demand transparency and honesty from our political and military leaders, so that we can assess military actions done in our names and on our behalf. Finally, when we are not certain of the justness of military action, we should protest and resist.

WAR

War utilizes violent methods and these methods tend to slip toward terrorism, even when our warriors and leaders do their best to ensure that the highest ideals of the just war theory will be upheld. For this reason alone, we should be skeptical of war and conclude that war is prima facie to be avoided. We must demand that our leaders assure us that when they decide to utilize military force, they will do their best to uphold the principles of the just war theory. But there is more to war that is pernicious than the question of its violent methods. It is not too much to say that war represents the worst aspects of human nature. In this section I will discuss two problems both of which are linked to the question of moral identity. The first problem has to do with the inversion of personal values that occurs in war. In war, ordinary values such as compassion and commitment to higher order human functions are subverted. The second has to do with the political nature of war. War shows us the instability of individuality and the pernicious influence of large scale social and political institutions. In war, individuals sacrifice their individuality for the group in multiple ways. And in war, groups press forward with a destructive hubris that would be morally repugnant in individuals. War also perverts basic intellectual tendencies toward the preservation of truth, self-criticism, and tolerance for the opinions of others. During wartime, cultures clamp down on dissent; they search for scapegoats; and they demonize enemies.

This last sentence contains a phrase that is important for understanding war — the notion of "wartime." In war, the ordinary experience of time and the values of ordinary time are disrupted. Glenn Gray has described the dislocation of war by saying that there is an "abyss between war and peace."[173] Warriors tend to be immersed in the present, forced into a state of concentration by the struggle for survival. For the rest of us, wartime leads us to ignore long-range plans that, given the destructive forces of war, are uncertain. All other pursuits are put on hold until the war is over, as a whole society is mobilized for action. The American experience of September 11, 2001 gives us an indication of this disruption; but it also shows us the American problem. The shock of September 11 was in part the result of our own ignorance about the fact that we send troops to war and fund armies, terrorists, and warriors around the globe. And while our country exercises military power around the world, none of us really felt — until September 11 — that we were at war. September 11 was a trauma for those of us who grew comfortable with our power and our ignorance — but the trauma was soon forgotten as the President urged us to continue shopping and go on about our ordinary activities. And war became abstract and distant again as we watched from the safety of our living rooms the invasions of Afghanistan and Iraq. We must remember that our soldiers and theirs (and the civilian populations of these distant war zones) are experiencing the world in and as war time, as if every day were September 11.

The dislocation of war creates an intensity of experience and the thrill of wartime. This may help to explain the tendency of wartime to push us toward a form of hedonism that sacrifices loftier intellectual and ethical commitments. During wartime, the future is ignored for focus on the present. This form of *carpe diem* is connected to a deeper form of nihilism found in war. Glenn Gray writes that his deepest fear is that "these happenings had no real purpose."[174] Although we like to imagine that wars happen for noble reasons, it might rather be that war is not the result of rational action at all. War might rather be something like a force of nature that happens with its own logic and sense of timing. The recent drive to war in Iraq provides a good example. President Bush began preparing for war with Iraq long before he invaded in March of 2003, perhaps even before September 11, 2001. It is impossible to say what the real reason for this war was: whether it was a sincere fear of Saddam Hussein's weapons of mass destruction,

---

173. Gray, *The Warriors* (New York: Harcourt, Brace, and Co., 1959), 24.
174. Gray, *The Warriors*, 24.

a desire to assert American power, a personal vendetta, interest in oil, compassion for suffering Iraqis, a misguided desire for revenge for September 11, or something else. But once the troops were moving toward the Gulf, once they were poised on the border, there was no pulling back. And there was no way that Saddam Hussein could have done anything to avert the war. The logic of war takes over, with its concern with power, mastery, and the game of saving face. At that point it is too late to ask about "real reasons" behind the war. Rather, war has reasons of its own. And these are reasons that in peacetime we work hard to ignore.

Wars happen to individuals without their choosing, just as violent forces of nature suddenly rise up and destroy human dreams. Sartre's series of novels, *The Roads to Freedom*, written as reminiscences of the Second World War, contain numerous descriptions of the way in which war erupts as a destiny that overshadows every other human hope and dream. "In making war we all join in making it; I raise my hand, I draw at my cigar, and I make war... The war takes and embraces everything, war preserves every thought and every gesture, and no one can see it, not even Hitler. No one. He repeated: No one — and suddenly he caught sight of it. It was a strange entity, and one indeed beyond the reach of thought."[175] In wartime, war dominates every thought and action. It is no wonder that war was thought of as a God in ancient cultures. And yet, as Sartre indicates, despite the fact that those who live with war make war all the time during wartime — that is despite the fact that during wartime we are all consumed with war and consumed by it — none of us has freely chosen war. War chooses us. It acts upon us despite the fact that war is a human creation. Thus war is a sort of inhuman destiny that is enacted by the collective failure of humanity's higher ideals. As Sartre's character Mathieu recognizes this, he despairs: "I didn't choose this war, nor this defeat; by what phony trick must I assume responsibility for them? He was conscious within himself of the panic fury of the trapped beast, and looking up, saw the same fury in the eyes of his comrades."[176] From this existential crisis it is easy to lose oneself and give up in despair on one's highest aspirations. Thus individuals can easily be caught up in the frenzy produced by war because war can be affirmed as, in Chris Hedges' words, "a force which gives us meaning."[177] But the affirmation of war is also an affirmation of violence and of the other forms of extreme human experience that

---

175. Jean-Paul Sartre, *The Reprieve* (New York: Vintage Books, 1973), 325.
176. Jean-Paul Sartre, *Troubled Sleep* (New York: Vintage Books, 1973), 59.

are encouraged by the hedonistic focus on the present moment without regard for the future.

What is worse is that Americans for the most part get to *play* at war. With the exception of September 11, we view war from a distance. Although many of us have closely followed our troops in Afghanistan and Iraq — on TV, that is — we have the luxury of changing the channel, leaving wartime to return to peacetime. But this is perhaps a worse and more subtle horror. Our soldiers dwell in wartime, haunted by the specter of their own deaths, as they kill thousands of poorly armed adversaries whose entire world is suffering catastrophe. And we observe, comment, go to dinner, and soundly sleep the sleep of "the just." This disconnect from the killing we do is the luxury of our power. But it is despicable and appalling. How dare we sleep soundly when our fellow Americans are asked to kill and be killed in our names?

Although war has been lionized as a sanctifying force that brings out the best in us in terms of virtues such as loyalty, courage, and self-sacrifice, the virtues of war run contrary to those of genuine moral and intellectual development. We have yet to transcend the virtues of the "war spirit" in order to arrive at a broader form of what American philosopher Josiah Royce called "loyalty to loyalty." The "virtues" of war are often habits of conformity, callousness, and self-deception. Genuine philosophically grounded virtues are virtues of individuals. This is not to say that genuine virtues cannot be social or active and cannot include ideas about loyalty and courage. Rather, it is to say that the virtues of war are merely simulacra, or false appearances, of genuine virtue. It is important to bear this in mind because thousands of years of human culture have combined to valorize the attitudes and behaviors of the warrior. We have been taught to admire the strength, courage, loyalty, and cleverness of heroes such as Achilles and Odysseus. And yet these virtues are only good in the limited context of a warrior culture, where victory at war is the predominant cultural value. Hence, as Royce says, "we all think too often of loyalty as a warlike and intolerant virtue and not the spirit of universal peace."[178] The trick is to find a way to develop virtues such as loyalty and courage in peacetime.

---

177. Hedges writes, "many of war's most fervent adherents are those atomized individuals who, before the war came, were profoundly alone and unloved. They found fulfillment in war, perhaps because it was the closest they came to love. If we do not acknowledge such an attraction, which is, in some ways, so akin to love, we can never combat it" (Hedges, *War is a Force that Gives us Meaning*, 161).

178. Royce, *Philosophy of Loyalty* (Nashville: Vanderbilt University Press, 1995), 100.

The courage and loyalty of war are forms of self-sacrifice that run counter to the moral individualism of modern ethical life. These values are tied to a more ancient ethical tradition that emphasizes the insubstantiality of the individual in comparison with the social or metaphysical whole. This is why the values of war are tied up with religious and patriotic world-views. It is also why the tendency of individuals to sacrifice themselves for the cause has been so successfully manipulated by totalitarian ideologies, such as those that dominate the current strain of Islamic fundamentalism against which we are fighting.[179] The individual's "interest" in self-sacrifice might be connected with what Freud described as the death-drive or Thanatos and what Fromm described as the escape from freedom.[180] However, it is antithetical to the highest ideals of liberal society. Oddly enough, religions and states that emphasize the sanctity and autonomy of the individual — as in Christianity and in modern liberalism — nonetheless celebrate the virtue of self-sacrifice. As Glenn Gray writes: "The limits of free will and morality are transgressed, and man is forced to seek religious and metaphysical justification for self-sacrifice, even when committed in an evil cause... What our moral beliefs tell us is abhorrent, our religious self and our aesthetic self yearn for as the ultimate good. This is part of the riddle of war."[181]

The celebration of the virtue of self-sacrifice is one side of the value system of wartime. The other side is the willingness to kill. Ironically, this willingness is more widespread than the self-sacrificial virtue of the soldier. The soldier alone is asked to make the ultimate sacrifice; but the whole of society is asked to mobilize for killing. Modern war leads us away from the concrete reality of life. It may make sense for an individual to want to kill someone. It is possible to imagine being enraged by a neighbor, a lover, a trespasser, or some other individual up to the point of wanting to lash out at him, perhaps even kill him. Anger is a normal social reaction; and anger can lead to violence. Thankfully, for most of us, experiences of rage are few and far between. Moreover, it is rare that any of us becomes angry enough to consummate anger with violence. Even fewer of us have the urge actually to kill. And fewer still actualize our murderous urges. Wartime is different. In wartime, we methodically plan to kill. And in the modern world, war mobilizes a whole society to kill, asking individuals to

---

179. Paul Berman, *Terror and Liberalism* (New York: Norton, 2003).
180. Sigmund Freud, *Civilization and its Discontents*, Chapters 6, 7, and 8; Erich Fromm, *Escape from Freedom* (New York: Avon Books, 1969), especially Chapter 5.
181. J. Glenn Gray, *The Warriors*, 49-50.

support the political movement that aims at killing other individuals whom they have never met. It is a bizarre perversion of social morality when even school children are taught to cultivate a certain bloodlust aiming at defeating an enemy they have never met. This is a radical break from normal life, where the willingness to kill is far below the threshold of possibilities. And it is a radical break from the violent urges that individuals feel in their normal lives. War violence is singular because it asks individuals to cultivate the desire to kill others, but not individual others whom we see and know; rather, war asks us to cultivate the desire to kill abstract others whom we have never met. It might be different in the trenches, where soldiers must kill or be killed in face to face confrontations with enemies, but modern methods of war tend to allow for abstract mechanized killing. And yet, we must personify our enemies. Thus the war on terrorism has been aimed at Osama bin Laden and Saddam Hussein. This personification of the enemy gives a name to our cause, while allowing us safely to ignore the fact that we kill thousands of nameless soldiers and civilians in pursuit of the evil one. We must not be deceived: Osama and Saddam are themselves abstractions, created by the government and media. No one man runs a government or a terrorist organization; and yet it is convenient to speak of these abstractions because it allows us to abstractly justify the blood that flows from the bodies of those nameless ones who we kill.

War mobilizes a whole society. At all levels, individual members of a society are asked to support the killing of the enemy. Grandmothers, garbage collectors, and gardeners are all asked to agree that "yes, 'we' should be killing 'them.'" This identification with the "we" is subtle and insidious. Most of us do not realize that even with tacit consent, we are caught up in the "we" and that the "we" in wartime is dedicated to the proposition that "they" should be killed.

In other words, war is not directed at individuals; rather it is directed at abstract entities called "nations" or "peoples." However disturbing an individual's murderous urges might be, they are, for the most part, understandable: person X knows and hates person Y and his anger and hatred leads to violence. But in modern war, individuals do not know the others who they propose to kill enough even to hate them genuinely, for hatred involves at least some knowledge. It is quite odd both psychologically and morally to claim to hate and want to kill someone whom one has never met. However, in times of war, individuals allow themselves to be drawn into the political rhetoric in which their own individuality and the individuality of the enemy is effaced. Ordinary violence is at least on the continuum of interaction in which individuals are connected to one another. War represents another sphere of human possibility, one in which the group is primary and the individual is lost. Undoubtedly there is something satisfying about this loss of individuality. Durkheim analyzed this under the rubric of the solidarity of collective consciousness.[182] Individuals have a desire to come together with others. The most moving form of solidarity occurs when there is communal outrage directed toward enemies. Psychoanalysts tell us that this is satisfying because it satisfies the narcissistic urge to identify oneself with a larger whole while also fitting with both sadistic and masochistic tendencies: sadism directed toward the enemy and masochism discovered in what one must sacrifice in identifying with the group.[183]

Others have made this point in more detail; I want to emphasize both the strangeness of this phenomenon and its anti-liberal consequences. Liberal advances during the last two centuries have worked to create increased respect for the autonomy of the individual. We have struggled to break down the idea that individuals are fully defined by the category to which they belong, whether this category is nationality, race, or gender. Liberal values, moreover, focus on peaceful, tolerant, and rational means for resolving conflict. The struggle for liberal values is far from over and our tendency to succumb to the desire for war shows us that the struggle will continue. The illiberal tendencies of war show up most obviously in the many ways that individuality is lost in war. The most obvious loss of individuality happens when we demonize the enemy group. Members of the enemy group cease to be individuals with differences. Rather, they are all alike insofar as they are targets for our hatred and violence. Another loss of individuality happens on the part of those who support war through patriotism. Instead of thinking for themselves, patriots stifle their questions and objections in order to show a united "home front." This loss of individuality is linked to the first insofar as "our" group solidarity is reciprocally related to the fact that "their" group is out to do violence to our group. There is no denying that the solidarity produced by violence is profoundly moving, which is one of the reasons that war and patriotism persist. However, it is odd that proponents of liberal values and the importance of individuality should be willing to support the subversion of individuality that comes with patriotism. Wartime also undermines individuality by inverting the values that we normally hold dear,

---

182. Emile Durkheim, *The Division of Labor in Society* (New York: The Free Press, 1997), Chapter 2.
183. Erich Fromm, *Escape from Freedom*, Chapter 5.

alienating us from any sense of control we might have over political forces, and by focusing us exclusively on the hedonistic present. Finally, the most troubling loss of individuality happens when war leads us to force others to sacrifice their own individuality in the name of the cause. This happens when we ask soldiers to sacrifice themselves for the group and when we stifle dissent in order to create solidarity. The stifling of dissent is important — especially for those of us who want to hold on to our individual voices. However, the sacrifice of the soldier is perhaps the most troubling of all.

It is extremely odd that, in a liberal society, anyone would be willing to demand or even allow another to make the ultimate sacrifice for them. When we ask soldiers to go into battle on our behalf, we ask them to violate their individuality in two ways. First we ask them to risk being killed, the most obvious and the most permanent of sacrifices. But we also ask them to become killers, which represents a potential sacrifice of moral integrity. This is not to say that all soldiers are immoral or lack integrity. Rather, we ask soldiers to cultivate a set of dispositions and practices that are not acceptable outside of wartime. And we know how difficult it can be for soldiers to reintegrate themselves back into normal society. This has been a recurrent theme in literature and film since Odysseus took his long journey home from the Trojan war.

It is useful to consider the process by which violence is alienated within contemporary society. Our ordinary intuitions about violence and courage tell us that we should each fight our own battles. If I were in a conflict with my neighbor and our struggle led to violence, it would be bizarre to ask someone else to defend me. I am not saying that it is good to fight — there are often alternatives to violence. However, in the case when a fight is inevitable, and when it is a matter of self-defense, we feel as if we should each fight our own battles. After all, it is my integrity, property, or other values that are threatened by my neighbor. I must defend myself. It would be odd and impractical to ask someone else to take the risk of self-defense on my behalf. Indeed, one might call me a coward if I paid a proxy to fight my battles. And the proxy would be regarded as a dangerous and immoral individual, both because he was willing to fight for money or other inducements and because he deliberately cultivated viciousness and a desire to fight. Indeed, this theme has been seen in many Western movies: the cowardly townspeople make a deal with a dangerous outlaw for their own self-protection.

In general, it is strange and possibly immoral to ask someone else to take the physical and moral risk for you. However, we can see that there is something odd about modern warfare and the division of labor in society. Each individual who feels compelled to fight should fight, when that fight is justified. However, what happens in modern war is that we pay some young men and women to fight our battles for us, often (increasingly) including non-citizens and members of underprivileged classes. Our social system is set up so that we never have to fight our own battles: when I am in conflict with my neighbor, usually the best thing to do is call in a proxy, i.e., to call the police. This use of proxies might be cowardice on the part of the vast majority. But it is more likely that this is an essential part of the division of labor in society. In complex societies, we all develop special skills and some specialize in the use (or implied threat) of violence. But even though the division of labor is, in a sense, inevitable, it is often not comfortable. The division of labor creates problems of alienation and disconnection. In the case of war and military force, this disconnect often allows us — we who do not fight — to adopt a cavalier attitude toward war. We who stay at home will not suffer in the same way that our soldiers will: we will not be asked to kill or to be killed. And so we tend to ask our soldiers to do things that we ourselves would not be willing to do.

Moreover, this alienation and disconnection is part of the problem of fully knowing whether our leaders are being honest with us about the reasons for war. We must be careful with war because of the alienation that occurs as a result of the division of labor. We can never be sure that our leaders are telling us the truth. This point is a significant component of the epistemological problem that leads to practical pacifism. And, by delegating the activity of war, we ask some of our friends, relatives, and neighbors to pervert their souls for us. We pay soldiers and ask them to risk their lives. But we also ask them to become killers. Not only should they be reluctant to prostitute themselves in this way, but we should also refuse to pimp them and ask them to take this risk for us, especially when we are not certain of the justness of our cause.

CHAPTER 6. TERRORISM AND THE PHILOSOPHY OF HISTORY — Liberalism, Realism, and the Supreme Emergency Exemption

Practical pacifism is an approach that should be adopted by citizens of liberal regimes. Citizens should resist militarism because it is antithetical to liberal values: a democracy cannot become a military empire without sacrificing important liberal values. However, the new era, the age of terrorism, brings up a difficult problem for citizens of liberal democracies. Terrorists — both domestic and foreign — are opposed to some, if not all, of the principles of liberalism.[184] Most obviously, those who are willing to resort to violent force to get their messages across have lost faith in the peaceful and tolerant processes of democratic liberalism. Even worse, some terrorists, such as those who attacked symbolic targets in the United States on September 11, 2001, are explicitly anti-American and anti-liberal. And some terrorists have expressed a willingness to utilize weapons of mass destruction, the use of which might pose a threat that could destabilize our very society.

---

184. Although recent events tend to focus our interest on the September 11th attacks on the United States, we can include among terrorists not only Osama bin Laden but also Palestinian suicide bombers, the Irish Republican Army, Ted Kaczynski (the Unabomber), Timothy McVeigh, and others who utilize certain tactics designed to subvert domestic or international order by way of terror. The use of terror tactics indicates an implicit hostility to liberal ideas and to the idea of the just war tradition. In some cases, as with bin Laden, this hostility to liberalism is explicit. The anti-liberal views of Islamic terrorists are brought out forcefully by Paul Berman in *Terror and Liberalism*.

The question of the present book is how we ought to respond to such threats. My answer is that liberal states have the right to defend themselves with military force when directly threatened. However, such a response ought to be constrained by respect for the principles of the just war doctrine. In addition to terrorism's obvious threat to life and limb, the further danger of terrorism is that it can incline liberal democracies to employ illiberal means in order to combat it. This might happen, for example, when our leaders invoke the rhetoric of war and supreme emergencies in the face of terrorism and use this to push for methods of war that exceed the proper limits of the just war theory. Michael Walzer and John Rawls have discussed just such a policy under the rubric of "the supreme emergency exemption" to just war doctrine. This chapter will focus on Rawls' account, as found in his recent *The Law of Peoples*, since Rawls is arguably the most influential advocate of liberalism in the 20th century. But Rawls may be too quick to lose faith in liberal means toward liberal ends. We must be careful, as we respond to terrorism, that the response to terrorism does not become terroristic. Practical pacifists must see through the rhetoric of war and remain committed to those values that are under attack by anti-liberal forces. We must avoid employing terrorism in our response to terrorism.

The problem, of course, is that such restraint is entirely one-sided. Those who utilize terror techniques in attacks against liberal states are not constrained by liberal ideas about justice in war. Indeed, many terrorists are intent on attacking liberalism itself because they view it as a rival "comprehensive doctrine," in Rawls' sense. One wonders, then, whether liberalism should be constrained by its own principles in responding to such attacks. Much of this depends upon whether we conceive of liberalism as a comprehensive doctrine that articulates a vision of human flourishing, whether we view liberalism as merely "political" in Rawls' sense, or whether liberalism is merely a *modus vivendi* that allows for peaceful coexistence among people who ultimately disagree about the good life. If liberalism is merely "political" in Rawls' sense then it has no firm principles to prevent the slip toward the use of terror tactics when it is under threat. This returns us to the question of the burden of proof. While we may not claim that liberal values are absolutely good, they are the best values that we have — not only because they work politically to deal with pluralism (as Rawls' formulation has it) but also because they fit nicely with an idea of human flourishing that rates freedom and equality as important values. The Rawlsian formulation of liberalism is attractive; however, there is also a more comprehensive approach to liberal values that argues that freedom and equality are necessary for human happiness.[185] Since liberal values are so good, we must establish a very high burden of proof when we are asked to give them up.

Although Rawls' attempts to articulate an idea of international law that is "political" in his sense (i.e., that is not tied to any particular comprehensive doctrine and yet reasonable for adherents of a plurality of such comprehensive doctrines), his idea is tied to a specific philosophy of history that is potentially incompatible with other philosophies of history. This can be seen in his discussion of the "supreme emergency exemption," which is an idea about the historical necessity of violating liberal principles of justice in war in order to defend liberal values from some overwhelming threat. This indicates the limit of the political form of liberalism. The acknowledgement of supreme emergencies in history only makes sense from within a more substantive form of liberalism. Invocation of a supreme emergency might then justify those who view liberalism as a rival comprehensive doctrine, which must be destroyed by any means necessary.

Rather than avoiding this idea by trying to defend political liberalism, we should thus defend a more comprehensive commitment to liberal values such as liberty, democracy, and peace. This commitment is not neutral. When liberal values are confronted by illiberal terrorists, the non-neutral character of liberalism becomes obvious. Terrorists are wrong because they employ means that are wrong. This is true whether the terrorist pursues an end that is good or not. As Michael Walzer has indicated, discussion of ends to be attained is no excuse for terrorism.[186]

It is ironic that despite Walzer's critique of terrorism, he also defends the idea of a supreme emergency exemption to the rules of justice in war. This idea runs counter to the spirit of a more comprehensive commitment to the goods of liberty and peace. The idea that only liberal means should be used to promote liberal values is one that is based upon a more comprehensive faith in the power of democracy. As Chapter 9 will show, such a faith can be pragmatically grounded. Given this pragmatic method, a practical form of liberalism must recognize that in the real world occasionally force is necessary. Rawls and Walzer utilize the just war theory in order to justify the use of force; however,

---

185. For an approach of this sort, see Martha Nussbaum's "capabilities approach" as found "In Defense of Universal Values" in *Women and Human Development: The Capabilities Approach* (Cambridge: Cambridge University Press, 2000).

186. Michael Walzer, "Terrorism: A Critique of Excuses," in Steven Luper ed., *Social Ideals and Policies* (Mountain View, CA: Mayfield Publishing Company, 1999).

they go beyond the usual just war theory by allowing for supreme emergencies. Rawls admits that his theory is a hybrid that is both realistic and utopian. The realist component is seen in the very idea of a supreme emergency. In allowing for supreme emergencies, Rawls thus goes beyond the limits of liberalism. Although Rawls might claim that this is a pragmatic component of his theory, we must consider whether pragmatism can allow for the use of force that is "unjust" by definition. Pragmatic liberalism certainly allows for the use of force, even though force is a regrettable last resort. However, it is not clear that one who is committed to the value of liberal ideas can support the idea that in some cases it would be permissible to violate the idea of justice in war, even on pragmatic grounds. An obvious response is to recall that Dewey's liberal pragmatism was committed to the goal of unifying means and ends.

Before turning to this, however, I want to argue that the difficulty for anyone who is contemplating the use of terror tactics is epistemological. One can never know with certainty that the present historical juncture is really a supreme emergency, just as one can never know that terror is the only means of last resort. The idea of a supreme emergency exemption can only be invoked from within a philosophical interpretation of progress in history that sees the present moment as a supreme crisis. Weapons of mass destruction in the hands of rogue states or terrorists could, indeed, make a supreme emergency more likely. However, it is doubtful that mere mortals would be able to tell with enough certainty — while in the midst of the crisis — that the present crisis really was a supreme emergency.

While liberals certainly can defend themselves, peace and liberal values cannot ultimately be imposed by force. Rawls would agree, I think. However, he leaves open a door, which would allow violations of the principles of justice in war in cases of extreme self-defense. This approach thus risks opening the door to the use of terrorism in defense of liberalism, a result that we should struggle to avoid.

POLITICAL PHILOSOPHY AND HISTORY

Political philosophy is an ambiguous enterprise.[187] While it is concerned with questions of principles about justice and morality, this concern is connected with the changing nature of historical actuality. The connection between theory and practice in political philosophy is often made by way of a philosophy of history. Christian thinking about politics, for example, occurs within an eschatological view of history in which our concrete actions are crises to be judged in terms of the end of time. This has important implications for discussions of the justification of violence and of justice in war. As Stanley Hauerwas has stated, "the debate between pacificism and just war thinking is a theological issue about how we are to read and interpret history."[188] The political philosophies of Machiavelli and Hobbes, the two most famous proponents of political realism, can be understood in terms of a cynical view of history in which self-interested actions on the part of individuals continue to define political reality. Kant's political philosophy — his advocacy of liberal values — is understandable in terms of his hopeful philosophy of history in which progress is being made toward the establishment of perpetual peace. Hegel's political philosophy — more conservative, perhaps, but still liberal — follows from his faith that modernity represents the completion of the development of the idea of freedom. Rawls' discussion of international law can also be understood in terms of a certain view of history. For Rawls, history contains discrete entities called "Peoples" who act as political agents in the development of a "Society of Peoples" and who will agree to principles of peaceful coexistence under the "Law of Peoples."

The idea of a philosophy of history is a notoriously slippery one, since it involves making teleological judgments about the future based upon past events. Kant discussed the problem of such teleological judgments in his third *Critique*, claiming that they were regulative ideals of reason. He applied this idea to history and politics in his *Religion* book, in his *Rechtslehre* (part of the *Metaphysics of Morals*) and in *Perpetual Peace*. His interest in this venture in political philosophy and philosophy of history was to consider whether it is justified to hope for

---

187. I develop this idea in both "The Irony of Political Philosophy" [*Philosophy in the Contemporary World* 5:1 (Fall), 1999] and in *The Philosopher's Voice* (Albany, New York: State University of New York Press, 2002).

188. Stanley Hauerwas, *Should War be Eliminated?* (Milwaukee, WI: Marquette University Press, 1984), 52.

progress. He indicates that historical progress points toward the development of both liberal republican states and peace because liberal states do not go to war with one another, a claim that Rawls develops in *The Law of Peoples*. Kant's reflections in *Perpetual Peace* occur within a context of speculation about nature's plan for human endeavor. He states that nature herself indicates a "purposive plan of producing concord among men, even against their will and indeed by means of their very discord."[189] Kant recognizes that although this idea is "far-fetched in theory, it does possess dogmatic validity and has a very real foundation in practice."[190] Hope for progress is not grounded in a mere description of the facts of history. Rather, hope functions as an ideal, which ought to guide practice.

Like Kant, Rawls is hopeful that peace will prevail. This is what makes Rawls' idea "realistically utopian," as he describes it throughout *The Law of Peoples*. He shares Kant's hope for progress in history as a practical ideal. However, Rawls goes beyond Kantian liberalism by incorporating a less sanguine and more realistic (in the Machiavellian and Hobbesian sense) view of progress in history. This has important implications for the way in which a Rawlsian might deal with the problem of terrorism.

One wonders whether the fact of terrorism undermines hope for the completion of the liberal political project. The fact of terrorism seems to indicate certain limits to the idea that domestic and international politics can become stable and peaceful based upon either the domestic social contract or upon the international Law of Peoples. Unless one adopts a philosophy of history in which reasonableness (as Rawls defines it) prevails, it seems that strife and instability will continue because those who are not invested in the society of liberal and decent peoples will resist it. Those who are disenfranchised by the liberal system will struggle against it. Those whose religion is antagonized by liberal values will rally against it. And perhaps most insidiously, those who are disposed to anarchism and antinomianism (here I think of McVeigh and Kaczynski) will be opposed to it.

Kant is willing to make utopian claims about the trajectory of history because his liberalism is tied to a more comprehensive view of human nature and morality. For Kant, the bin Ladens and Kaczynskis of the world are immoral and

---

189. Kant, *Perpetual Peace*, in *Kant: Political Writings* (Cambridge: Cambridge University Press, 1991), 108. For more on Kant, see Michael Doyle's influential interpretation: Doyle, *Ways of War and Peace* (New York: Norton, 1997).

190. Kant, *Perpetual Peace*, in *Kant: Political Writings*, 109.

irrational. Kant's hope is that political peace will result as we all make progress toward enlightened morality and rationality. It is unclear, however, how Rawls can ground his realistic utopia in a philosophy of history that is not in some sense tied to a comprehensive doctrine about morality and rationality. Hope for the triumph of the Law of Peoples is not strictly a "politically" liberal idea because it must appeal to a philosophy of history in which "reasonable" peaceful coexistence triumphs over unreasonable fundamentalist or anarchist resistance. Thus Rawls' liberalism remains genuinely utopian and must be evaluated from the point of view of a more "comprehensive" metaphysics of human being.[191] Not that Rawls is wrong about his hope but, rather, his hope is more "comprehensive" than he wants to admit. He concludes, for example, with the following claim: "If a reasonably just Society of Peoples whose members subordinate their power to reasonable aims is not possible, and human beings are largely amoral, if not incurably cynical and self-centered, one might ask, with Kant, whether it is worthwhile for human beings to live on the earth."[192] The idea of "worthwhile" clearly points beyond political liberalism toward a more comprehensive view, which claims that peace is good and that human beings ought to strive for it.

MEANS AND ENDS

Terrorists are criminals who use unjust means to attain political ends. As such they are criminals who ought to be condemned, captured, and incarcerated (some might add executed — but this points us to a further conversation). Terrorists are known by the acts they commit. In other words, terrorists commit criminal acts including kidnapping, hijacking, and murder. Thus, as a RAND corporation analysis states: "an act of terrorism was first of all a crime in the classic sense."[193] Although such acts are politically motivated, they are still criminal. What makes them criminal is the fact that they harm and violate the autonomy of innocent individuals.

---

191. This chapter thus connects to other critiques of Rawls, which indicate that his form of liberalism is not as non-metaphysical as it claims to be. For example, Michael Sandel, *Liberalism and the Limits of Justice* (Cambridge: Cambridge University Press, 1982).

192. Rawls, *The Law of Peoples* (Cambridge, MA: Harvard University Press, 1999), 128.

193. Ian O. Lesser, et al., *Countering the New Terrorism* (Santa Monica, CA: RAND Corporation, 1999), v.

The problem with this definition is that "crime" is often thought to be defined merely by positive "law," while terrorists use political violence in part to contest positive law. We might be sympathetic to terrorists when we recognize that, in Robert Fullinwider's terms, "they appeal to morality without appealing to the law."[194] Terrorists might defend their crimes by claiming either that the law is corrupt or that there is a higher law which transcends the limits imposed by positive criminal law. For this reason, we must look to a more comprehensive moral scheme in order to condemn terrorism. Terrorists are wrong because the means they use are morally wrong. Liberal political systems should not tolerate the use of such means, not because they are not effective or illegal, but because they are morally wrong. A more comprehensive moral liberalism — even one that is pragmatically grounded — should be committed to means that are not terroristic and in most cases non-violent.

Even if we accept the fact that the terrorist is at war with us and with our shared system of positive law, the terrorist's acts are, according to standard definitions of justice in war, war crimes: they go beyond the means that are allowed even within war. "Terrorist tactics, in most cases, violated the rules that governed armed conflict — for example, the deliberate targeting of noncombatants or actions against hostages."[195] Finally, it is important to remember that terrorism uses its activities (its crimes) as a means to the further end of creating fear in the target population. Indeed, the identity of the immediate victims of terrorism is usually irrelevant, and the pain and deaths caused by terrorism are merely means for creating social anxiety in a sort of "systematically unsystematic" use of violence.[196] Again, this is why terrorism is ruled out by liberal principles.

If we deal with terrorism as merely a criminal matter, then law enforcement activities will be the preferred response. This raises certain practical difficulties, however, insofar as terrorism is often an international problem involving international victims and perpetrators as well as targets such as airliners and embassies. Domestic law enforcement is constrained by the political reality of borders and treaties. On the other hand, if we define terrorism as an act of war,

---

194. Robert K. Fullinwider, "Understanding Terrorism," in Steven Luper, ed., *Social Ideals and Policies* (Mountain View, CA: Mayfield Publishing, 1999), 652.

195. *Countering the New Terrorism*, v.

196. This notion comes from Michael Baur, "What is Distinctive about Terrorism and What are the Philosophical Implications," a paper presented at a conference on "Understanding Terrorism" at Loyola Marymount University in September 2003.

we run into other ethical and political problems such as a lowered burden of proof in establishing the culpability of the "enemy" and the ethical and political problems associated with a concern for justice in war. In more concrete terms, if Osama bin Laden and the others thought to be responsible for the September 11 attacks are "criminals," then we will have a difficult time apprehending them and prosecuting them in US courts. If they are "enemies" engaged in war, then our pursuit of them will require that we pay attention to the importance of preserving some idea of *jus in bello*. In both cases — whether we use law enforcement or whether we use military force — liberal states should recognize that certain means are ruled out by a basic respect for human rights as codified in either domestic law or in the principles of the just war doctrine as found in something like Rawls' Law of Peoples. For example, we ought not target innocents in retaliatory bombing and we ought not incarcerate and torture innocents.

The difficulty is that terrorists do not respect this limitation on means. For example, they do not discriminate between the innocent and the guilty. Timothy McVeigh blew up civilians, including children, to make his point. Osama bin Laden's fatwa of 1998 explicitly urged his followers to kill Americans, without regard for innocence or classification: "The ruling to kill the Americans and their allies — civilians and military — is an individual duty for every Muslim who can do it in any country in which it is possible to do it... We — with God's help — call on every Muslim who believes in God and wishes to be rewarded to comply with God's order to kill the Americans and plunder their money wherever and whenever they find it."[197] Should we adhere to principles of justice in war against an enemy who does not? — that is a difficult question.

Terrorists are not crazy. Terrorists utilize a calculus of terror that is a negative caricature of a utilitarian or hedonic calculus. The calculus of terror is designed to bring about certain ends. It is a rational decision procedure based upon the insight that terror disrupts social structures. Terrorists are not interested in causing pain per se: terrorism as an organized force is not simply aimed at causing pain or killing. Rather, international terrorists such as al-Qaeda are interested in using the threat of pain in order to antagonize a people and destabilize a social structure. Terrorism is evil insofar as it aims at destabilization and disruption; but it is also evil because the means for creating

197. Osama bin Laden, Fatwah ca. 1998, from International Policy Institute for Counter-Terrorism (http://www.ict.org.il/articles/fatwah.htm).

this disruption are themselves evil. Liberalism, on the contrary, is committed both to the end of stability and peace and to respect for the proper means for creating stability and peace.

Terrorism is insidious in that it destabilizes and disrupts by creating an atmosphere or mentality of fear. It is significant, for example, that the September 11 terrorists succeeded in disrupting the lives of hundreds of millions of people in the Western world by the "mere" hijacking of four airplanes resulting in the deaths of over 3,000 people. In strictly utilitarian terms, if terrorism were effective it would be an economical means of political activity. In this sense, political agents who use terrorism are not pathological at all, but are quite rational: they know how to do cost-benefit analysis in order to maximize the results of their activity. Of course, terrorism is not actually effective, in part because most of us refuse to negotiate with terrorists.

Despite the possible practical benefits of terroristic means, liberal values preclude us — we who are committed to liberal values — from using such means. Torture, for example, might be a useful interrogation technique. However, liberal principles preclude the use of pain as a means for producing information. Recent reports indicate that liberal states such as the United States have used torture — or have at least knowingly employed client states who use torture — in prosecuting the "war on terror."[198] While such means might be justified by something like the supreme emergency exemption, such a realist expedient should be avoided for the same epistemological reasons that we should avoid declaring supreme emergencies.

It is possible, for example, to imagine formal criteria that would justify the use of torture to extract information that could be used to prevent further terrorist attacks: if the person to be tortured were in fact guilty of preparing terror attacks; if there were no other way to extract the information; and if the danger of the terror attack were imminent.[199] However, there are many skeptical questions that could be posed. For example, how certain are we of the terrorist's guilt or of the "fact" that he has potentially life-saving information? Despite such formal criteria, torture is, in practice, almost always unjustifiable. As with the general argument of practical pacifism, we must establish a high burden of proof

198. See "Ends, Means, and Barbarity," *The Economist*, Jan. 9, 2003 and "The Dark Art of Interrogation," *Atlantic Monthly*, October 2003.
199. This discussion was informed by Fritz Allhof, "Terrorism and Torture" and William D. Casebeer, "Torture Interrogation of Terrorists." Both papers were presented at "Understanding Terrorism" at Loyola Marymount University in September 2003.

138

and be acutely aware of the limits of our knowledge in such cases. More importantly, however, we must remember that liberal states prohibit torture because of a suspicion that torture would be abused by those in power. This suspicion is also a key component in the argument against war and the supreme emergency exemption. States and politicians are often tempted to use more face that is necessary. And they are easily tempted to retreat to the realist perspective found in the idea of the supreme emergency. That is why we should be extremely reluctant to assent to such a realist exception: history shows us that states are all too ready to make exceptions when it comes to the use of violence.

It would be a trite exaggeration to claim that, when liberal regimes resort to torture, terrorists have in some sense "won" (because the terrorists have forced liberals to transgress their own principles, thus disrupting the liberal system of justice). However, liberal states ought to resist resorting to means that directly violate the principles of liberalism. Resistance to such resorts can be strengthened if we remind ourselves that liberalism's *raison d'etre* is to limit power. It can also be strengthened if we hold on to the melioristic hope that we can make the world a better place using nonviolent means.

This discussion of means and ends, of course, ignores the fact that patriotism and religion are often involved and that terrorists and suicide bombers are committed to a calculus that transcends the calculus of ordinary political advantage. Recent manifestations of Islamic fundamentalist terror reflect an ideology that rewards the martyr's death in an afterlife and that valorizes the martyr in a culture of martyrdom. It is significant that suicide bombers actively embrace their deaths and that, for example, their family members view them as heroes. It is important to note that this is not only a problem of Islamic fundamentalism. Patriots and religious believers of all nations and creeds have routinely been willing to kill and be killed for their causes (more on this in Chapter 8). We must see, then, that terrorism is not simply a belief in terror for its own sake. Rather, it is fostered by what Rawls would call a "comprehensive doctrine" that is antithetical to the values of the just war tradition and the values of peace and stability found in Rawls' formulation of the Law of Peoples. Such a view — whether it is religious or nationalistic — comes from a philosophy of history that runs counter to the progressive humanistic ideal of liberalism.

RAWLS AND THE PHILOSOPHY OF HISTORY

Theories of war are usually articulated in the context of a philosophy of history. Machiavellian realism comes from recognition of the precarious nature of fortune. Christian just war theory occurs within the context of an eschatological view of history and the demands of justice. Kant's thoughts about the Law of Peoples, perpetual peace, a league of nations, and the necessity of consent for going to war is located within his progressive enlightenment ideal. Rawls' theory of international law and justice in war is also connected to his implicit philosophy of history.

This poses a difficulty for Rawls because his ideal social contract is supposed to be a model of the way in which reasonable beings would come to agreement about principles of justice, despite disagreement about metaphysical ideas about progress in history. Likewise, his view of justice in international relations attempts to avoid historical concerns by focusing on ideal agreement among "peoples" who are abstracted from their previous historical interactions. Nonetheless, Rawls claims that his theory is tied to actuality insofar as it is "realistically" utopian. Rawls' discussion of the distinction between liberal and decent peoples, for example, recognizes that concrete historical differences among peoples are inevitable and ineradicable. However, Rawls maintains the hope (hence the utopian aspect of this theory) that liberal and decent peoples can come to agree about the Law of Peoples. This hope derives from an implicit philosophy of history in which diverse peoples will come to agreement about reasonable principles of justice. This process (what Rawls calls the second original position) is, arguably, less ideal and more historically situated than the analogous process that occurs in the first original position (the domestic social contract). This is so because the parties in the second original position are engaged in real political struggles that are guided by memories of past wars and fear of future war in a world that is fortified and armed. As we shall see, Rawls acknowledges the importance of concrete historical facts both in his recognition of differences between liberal and decent peoples (as well as outlaw states and burdened societies) and in his discussion of the supreme emergency exemption to the principles of justice in war.

It would be easy to interpret Rawls' idea of a Law of Peoples, if it were simply a restatement of the more substantive liberalism of Kant, whose hope for moral progress is a postulate of practical reason. However, one wonders what could justify Rawls in such a hope, especially in light of events such as

September 11 and the subsequent invasions of Afghanistan and Iraq. Liberal optimism has been criticized, for example, by John Kekes who calls it "the liberal faith" or "the enlightenment faith." Kekes links this explicitly to what he sees as a naively optimistic philosophy of history and the inability of liberalism to deal with the problem of evil.[200] In *The Law of Peoples*, however, Rawls responds to this criticism by acknowledging atrocities such as the Holocaust while defending what he calls "reasonable hope."[201] Rawls' discussion of hope has two prongs. On the one hand, hope is needed in order to combat evil forces, "otherwise, the wrongful, evil, and demonic conduct of others destroys us too and seals their victory."[202] On the other hand, hope is reasonable because the ideals of liberalism are already supported by liberal and decent societies. From this we can derive the basic idea of Rawlsian philosophy of history. Hope for progress toward international adoption of liberal values is supported by the idea that liberal values have triumphed in the past. This hope then serves as a mechanism for further progress in liberalization. Indeed, Rawls bases this account on the historical fact that an international community of liberal societies has tended toward peace and stability. He states, following Michael Doyle, that "absence of war between major established democracies is as close as anything to a simple empirical regularity in relations among societies."[203] He concludes that this historical generalization is the basic "hypothesis" that "underwrites the Law of Peoples as a realistic utopia."[204] Finally, he realizes that the hypothesis itself will serve to stimulate progress.

> Thus our answer to the question of whether a reasonably just Society of Peoples is possible affects our attitudes toward the world as a whole. Our answer affects us before we come to actual politics, and limits or inspires how we take part in it. Rejecting the idea of a just and well-ordered Society

---

200. "The name for this pipe-dream is the Enlightenment Faith. It is the illusion of an epoch that stretches from Rousseau to contemporary liberalism. It is the secular equivalent of the religious faith of Christianity, which it is intended to replace. It is fueled by a groundless optimism that substitutes wishes for facts, refuses to face reality, ignores history, and radiates a moralistic fervor..." [John Kekes, *A Case for Conservatism* (Ithaca, New York: Cornell University Press, 1998), 211]. Kekes links his own "pessimistic conservatism" explicitly to the political realism of thinkers such as Thucydides, Machiavelli, and Hobbes (*A Case for Conservatism*, 90). For further discussion of the liberal faith, cf. Kekes, *Against Liberalism* (Ithaca, New York: Cornell University Press, 1997), Chapter 7.
201. Rawls, *The Law of Peoples*, 23.
202. Rawls, *The Law of Peoples*, 22.
203. Rawls, *The Law of Peoples*, 52.
204. Rawls, *The Law of Peoples*, 54.

of Peoples as impossible will affect the quality and tone of those attitudes and will determine our politics in a significant way.[205]

Thus Rawls admits that the progressive interpretation of history is itself a powerful stimulant toward further progress. We must believe that liberalization is possible in order to reasonably continue to support it. As we shall see in subsequent chapters, this point of view is ultimately pragmatic: we should hope because hope is practically effective.

Kant (and Hegel) made similar claims about progress in history. However, these claims were articulated within the context of a more broadly construed substantive liberalism that tied political progress to moral progress and general enlightenment. A Hegelian account of history, as fleshed out by Francis Fukuyama for example, claims that all human beings are struggling toward mutual recognition.[206] From the perspective of political liberalism, however, claims about progress are fallible generalizations, not metaphysical truths. All that Rawls' philosophy of history can conclude is that "a Society of Peoples is indeed possible."[207] He cannot conclude, however, that it is inevitable or necessary. This theoretical limit has important implications for the practical implementation of the Law of Peoples, as we shall see in the next section.

THE SUPREME EMERGENCY EXEMPTION

One sees the limits of Rawls' philosophy of history in his discussion of the supreme emergency exemption. The very idea of a supreme emergency is derived from a philosophical account of progress and crises in history. A supreme emergency is one that confronts a people with the impending fact of their own annihilation. The example that Rawls borrows from Walzer is Great Britain in the early 1940s. Certain historical facts are important for understanding this situation. At this time, Britain was the only liberal European state unconquered by the Nazis; the United States had not yet entered the war in support of Britain; and there was a credible Nazi threat to destroy the British government and way of life. If these facts were accurate, then the British would have been justified, under the supreme emergency exemption, in utilizing any means necessary to

205. Rawls, *The Law of Peoples*, 128.
206. Francis Fukuyama, *The End of History and the Last Man* (New York: The Free Press, 1992).
207. Rawls, *The Law of Peoples*, 124.

preserve their liberal society including the deliberate targeting of non-combatants, sabotage, and other acts of "terrorism."

This idea, as it is discussed by both Walzer and Rawls, draws upon Winston Churchill's rhetorical flourish in which he called Britain's predicament in 1939 a "supreme emergency." The idea is that the danger posed by Nazism was so great that it justified violations of the standard principles of *jus in bello*. As Walzer describes this, it is the "back-to-the-wall" argument: "when conventional means of resistance are hopeless or worn out, anything goes (anything that is 'necessary' to win)."[208] When a supreme emergency is recognized, we are thrown back upon the laws of necessity and, as Walzer indicates, "necessity knows no rule."[209] Walzer then indicates that one must make a concrete judgment about the necessity of action, about the imminence of the threat, and about the immensity of the danger. This judgment is, however, undertaken in the dark and Walzer calls it a "wager." We wager that the determinate crime of killing innocents can be justified in light of the immeasurable evil that would result if we did not act (an evil such as the triumph of Nazism).[210] Walzer's discussion of the supreme emergency indicates a point at which utilitarian reasoning mixed with a dose of political realism overrides other principles of justice.

Rawls' discussion of the supreme emergency exemption picks up on Walzer's idea in both substance and detail (including critiques of the allied bombing of Germany and Japan). Thus Rawls seems to indicate that he is, at the limit, a consequentialist of sorts who is willing — in certain extreme emergencies — to sacrifice principles for consequences. This may sound like a sort of realism. But Rawls tackles the question of realism directly in *The Law of Peoples*, where he attempts to distinguish his point of view from a strain of realism that stretches back to Thucydides. Rawls' argument with the realist who interprets history as ceaseless struggle and war (and who then justifies expedience in war at the expense of principle) amounts to a different interpretation of the facts of history. As we have seen, Rawls claims that progress toward peace is possible because liberal peoples do not willingly go to war with one another. The more overtly realist interpretation of history, in opposition to this, is not so sanguine about the prospects for perpetual peace. But Rawls' emphasis on consequences nonetheless points to a form of realism.

---

208. Michael Walzer, *Just and Unjust Wars* (New York: Basic Books, 1977), 252.
209. Walzer, *Just and Unjust Wars*, 254.
210. Walzer, *Just and Unjust Wars*, 259-60.

There is no metaphysical guarantee that liberal values will triumph, which is why the supreme emergency exemption is needed.

An interpretation of the historical facts — coming from a more general philosophy of history — is required in order to make the determination that a current crisis is a supreme emergency. How can we ever be sure that a current crisis is a supreme emergency? Could the British know for sure that a Nazi invasion was imminent or would be successful? Can we be sure that the terrorism of September 11 is part of a global pattern of violent anti-American activity that will stop at nothing to destroy us? Such questions point toward concrete empirical analysis but also toward a perspective on history as a whole. A realist would note that history shows us that aggressive states continue to expand unless resisted and would view aggression as typical, while a liberal would emphasize that we have made progress toward a Society of Peoples and that continued progress was in some sense inevitable. The realist views aggression as the rule of history, while the liberal views it as an increasingly rare occurrence.

It is not surprising that a realist would allow for practical exemptions to the principles of justice in war. Indeed, the very idea of a supreme emergency points toward a realist interpretation of history, one that is willing to sacrifice principles to preserve the power that enforces those principles. It might be surprising, however, that liberals like Rawls would be open to the idea of a supreme emergency exemption. However, we must remember that Rawls describes his position as both "realistic" and "utopian." Rawls' approach is pragmatic and can be understood in connection with American pragmatism.[211] The realistic aspect of this utopia is precisely what opens the door to the supreme emergency exemption. From Rawls' point of view, the historical goal is the triumph of the Law of Peoples. For liberal peoples, the "long-run aim is to bring all societies eventually to honor the Law of Peoples and to become full members in good standing of the society of well-ordered peoples."[212] A supreme emergency undermines the possibility of the creation of a Society of Peoples. In this rare case, liberal ideals must be defended by any means possible.

This, however, seems to push Rawls in a direction that could undermine an overlapping consensus about the principles of justice in war. A Kantian liberal, for example, would agree to the terms of the Law of Peoples but would reject the

---

211. I discuss the connections between Rawls, Walzer, and American Pragmatism in "Toleration and Pragmatism," in the *Journal of Speculative Philosophy* 16:2 (2002), 103-116.
212. Rawls, *The Law of Peoples*, 93.

idea of a supreme emergency exemption because the Kantian philosophy of history remains hopeful and the Kantian moral philosophy prohibits the deliberate violation of principles of justice in war. Similarly, an absolute pacifist would maintain that violence is never justifiable. In both of these cases, a larger metaphysical view prohibits the deliberate violation of the principles of justice that Rawls allows. Indeed, Rawls recognizes this in his discussion of the Christian just war theory. He acknowledges that the Christian theory would reject the supreme emergency exemption.[213] The idea of the supreme emergency exemption, then, is controversial in a way that most of the rest of Rawls' just war theory is not. It is thus not clear why Rawls includes the supreme emergency exemption in his discussion. One explanation is that Rawls is afraid that his ideas would be too utopian without this realist exemption.[214] Another explanation is that Rawls is not fully committed to the hopeful view of history that he defends throughout the book. In either case, Rawls' just war theory is linked to a certain philosophy of history, which requires this realist exemption. This is troubling to the extent that it might undermine the possibility of overlapping consensus about the Law of Peoples among those who have alternative historical points of view.

PRACTICAL PACIFISM AND THE RHETORIC OF WAR

Walzer and Rawls appeal to pragmatic concerns in their defense of the supreme emergency exemption. This returns us to the question of practical pacifism. Is it more pragmatically useful to uphold the principles of the just war doctrine, or not? Walzer and Rawls admit that in some cases practical concerns override those principles that restrain the use of force. This question requires a concrete analysis in each and every situation. I am not absolutely opposed to the idea of a supreme emergency exemption. However, it is highly unlikely that we would ever confront a "supreme emergency" that could justify disregarding the principles of justice in war. We ought to set the bar quite high before we are willing to employ means that are prima facie immoral. The case of torture is a good one, here.[215] If we agree, based on liberal principles, that torture is prima facie immoral, then it will be up to the proponent of torture to make a strong

---

213. Rawls, *The Law of Peoples*, 103-105.
214. This is suggested by Rawls' discussion of utopianism in *The Law of Peoples*, pp. 6-7.
215. For a "liberal" defense of torture, see Alan Dershowitz.

argument that torture could be used in a particular exceptional case. If there is a ticking bomb that will kill innocent persons, if we have captured the bomber, if the bomber can in fact help us de-fuse the bomb, and if we can be sure that torture would be an effective way to discover the truth, then torture might be useful. However, it is important to note that such cases are extremely rare — each of the conditions would, in fact, have to obtain. Rather, it is more likely that violence will beget further violence and that the authority to torture or to violate principles of justice in war will be abused. Liberal theory since Locke has been worried about the abuse of power;[216] and history has shown us that our authorities find it too easy to resort to extreme measures. By admitting the possibility of a supreme emergency exemption or of a justified use of torture, we open the door to abuse.

In practical terms, one wonders whether the present "war on terrorism" constitutes a supreme emergency, which would justify attacks that harm innocent Afghani or Iraqi civilians. The rhetoric uttered by President Bush and others following the September 11 attacks did tend to sound the alarm of an all-out assault against our way of life. Almost immediately after the destruction of September 11, politicians and the media began speaking of America's "new war." These events were compared with the events at Pearl Harbor on December 7, 1941. We began preparing for war and soon we were dropping bombs on foreign soil, resulting in what one hopes is the "inadvertent" killing of innocent civilians. Such inadvertent killing could be justified by a realist theory, by the Christian just war theory or by Rawls' just war theory. The realist, of course, allows killing in pursuit of power. The traditional Christian point of view grudgingly accepts civilian casualties if they are indeed inadvertent effects in pursuit of justice (and thus the result of "double effect"). Rawls and Walzer, like most just war theorists, accept a version of the doctrine of double effect. However, they also open the possibility that such killings could be justified if they constituted a legitimate response to a supreme emergency. Rawls does not directly state

216. Locke's theory of toleration is itself based upon a claim about the efficacy of coercion. Locke holds that orthodox belief cannot be coerced. It is not exactly clear that this applies in reverse to torture (i.e., that the truth cannot be coerced out of a suspect). See John Locke, "A Letter Concerning Tolerance," in Steven M. Cahn ed., *Classics of Modern Political Theory* (New York: Oxford University Press, 1997); for discussion of Locke's theory, see Jeremy Waldron, "Locke: Toleration and the Rationality of Persecution" in John Horton and Susan Mendus eds., *John Locke: A Letter Concerning Toleration in Focus* (London: Routledge, 1991). For a reply to Waldron that focuses, in part, on the epistemology of belief, see Susan Mendus, "Locke: Toleration, Morality, and Rationality," in Horton and Mendus, *John Locke: A Letter Concerning Toleration in Focus* and Susan Mendus, *Toleration and the Limits of Liberalism*, Chapter 2.

whether the supreme emergency exemption would apply to terrorists, although the problem of terrorists who possess weapons of mass destruction points in this direction. If the threat to our liberal way of life were severe enough, the supreme emergency exemption would justify deliberately targeting civilians, using torture, or whatever it took to preserve our way of life.

We must be extremely careful with such an idea and the rhetoric of "supreme emergencies" that justifies it. Although we certainly must defend ourselves, we must err on the side of peace and resist the tendency to sound the alarm of total war. Indeed, we should be highly skeptical of "the war on terrorism" for its risks to non-combatants. One wonders whether any of the civilian casualties caused in Afghanistan or Iraq can be justified as an *unavoidable* consequence of the war on terrorism. The question is whether such casualties were in fact "unavoidable." Would it have been possible to eliminate the infrastructure of al-Qaeda without a full-scale assault on Afghanistan? Would it have been effective to beef up existing law enforcement personnel and procedures in order to prevent further attacks and apprehend some of the suspects? Would a more restrained attack on al-Qaeda bases have been just as effective? The same sorts of questions can be brought to the rest of the war on terror, including the invasion of Iraq.

A practical pacifist is suspicious of the resort to armed conquest, especially when it puts innocent civilians at risk. A practical pacifist questions whether in fact such violence and its unintended effects were unavoidable. The same arguments used against the terrorist apply to us as we respond to terrorism. Terrorists often seek to justify (or at least excuse) their use of terrorism by claiming that it is a "last resort" or "the only means available." But, for the most part, such claims are ideological: the terrorist is simply unwilling to employ other means or is impatient with the slow pace of democratic change.[217] A practical pacifist should point out that the rhetoric of war, supreme emergencies, terrorism, and the supposed necessity of unintended consequences is usually ideological. That is, the use of terror tactics, either by terrorists or in wars against terrorists, is usually not necessary and is thus morally indefensible.

We should carefully guard against the rhetoric of war because as soon as we begin invoking war rhetoric we begin the gradual slide toward militaristic solutions, realist strategy, and the slippery rhetoric of "supreme emergencies" and what Jonathan Glover calls "military drift."[218] As Glover has argued, one of

---

217. See Walzer, "Terrorism: A Critique of Excuses" for a similar discussion.

the problems is "the trap of Hobbesian fear": "war can result from the fear of being attacked as well as from the actual attack."[219] As politicians brandish the rhetoric of war, people actually begin to feel as if they are at war. And if it is a war against those who we think would like to eliminate our way of life, we may feel as if our "backs are against the wall" (as Walzer has described it). This can lead to a premature invocation of the supreme emergency exemption and a violation of our own most cherished principles. The Bush administration's national security policy now includes the possibility of pre-emptive attacks and the use of nuclear weapons on countries that are perceived to be antagonistic. This saber-rattling defensive posture might be useful to deter would-be attackers; but this policy ratchets up the fear factor and pushes us toward the Hobbesian trap, and must be used with extreme care.

Language and rhetoric are important. The "war on terrorism" is a new kind of war. Indeed, the idea of a war on terrorism stretches the idea of war in new ways insofar as this is not a war between nation states. One might argue that "war" here is used metaphorically, although this metaphor has brutal consequences. This should not be surprising. Over fifty years ago, George Orwell brought to the public's attention the fact that metaphors can disguise all sorts of political brutality. "Political language is designed to make lies sound truthful and murder respectable, and to give an appearance of solidity to pure wind."[220] This is not to say that those who invoke the rhetoric of the "war on terrorism" are murderers and liars. Rather, it is to say that we can be misled by the rhetoric of war into thinking that bombing campaigns, invasions, and the death of innocents can be justified as a last resort. The practical pacifist questions the rhetoric, doubts that such radical remedies are justifiable, and denies that finite mortals can know, in most cases, when the "last resort" has been reached.

The "war on terrorism" does not conform to normal ideas about war. It is not a conflict with another state. It is not even a conflict between "peoples," as Rawls defines this.[221] The terrorist networks that we are currently pursuing consist of small sets of private individuals without a geographical base and

---

218. Jonathan Glover, *Humanity* (New Haven, Conn.: Yale University Press, 2000), 75.

219. Jonathan Glover, *Humanity*, 131.

220. George Orwell, "Politics and the English Language" in *George Orwell: Essays* (New York: Knopf, 2002).

221. Rawls' idea of a "people" focuses primarily on "liberal peoples" who have common sympathies, a moral nature, and a representative government (Rawls, *The Law of Peoples*, 23-24). Terrorist networks may have common sympathies. But their illiberal tactics serve to undermine that claim that they have a moral nature. And they are not represented by any government.

without the other trappings of political sovereignty. Thus the current "war on terrorism" is a metaphorical war. It is a "war" in the same sense that we have been engaged in a "war on drugs." This means that "war" in the present sense has been extended beyond its customary usage in traditional just war theory. The "war on terrorism," because it is not a war between peoples or states, would be better understood as a law-enforcement concern that should thus be conducted within the normal limits established for law-enforcement — including restraint of force, due process, and certain conventions about the burden of proof. This means that the bombing campaign against Afghanistan, for example, could not be justified solely on the basis of pursuing Osama bin Laden and his network.[222]

The issue of classification is important for a number of reasons.[223] One issue has to do with the rhetoric of war. Islamist terrorists see themselves as engaged in a war. They may thus want to be afforded a certain status as warriors whose actions could be dignified by the idea of a just or holy war, despite the fact that they do not have the power or authority of a state agency. More importantly, the question of criminality brings up issues about proof, jurisdiction, and due process. The Bush administration's policy is to use military tribunals to prosecute terrorists, treating terrorists as war criminals. This approach has been adopted in order to ensure easier trials and convictions and in order to keep open the possibility of the death penalty. Those who object to this approach might insist that we ought to try suspected terrorists in non-military courts, whether domestic or international. This more liberal position is attractive for two reasons. We should not let the terrorists make us lose faith in the fairness and efficiency of the domestic legal system. And we should use this opportunity to strengthen the incipient international legal system. Nor should we support the use of military tribunals, because we should not set a precedent that encourages their use in other cases. Without in any way condoning acts of terror, we ought to protect liberty from the expansion of the military and the security state. Moreover, open criminal proceedings are important political

---

222. It might be justified on some other basis, such as the fact that the Taliban regime was illegitimate and dangerous to the people of Afghanistan or to international stability. Thus, the Taliban regime was an "outlaw state" in Rawls' sense. This would be especially true, insofar as the regime could be distinguished from the people it governed. Rawls' discussion of justice in war indicates that the prosecution of a war against such an outlaw state must be careful to distinguish between the regime and its people (Rawls, *The Law of Peoples*, 94-96). This consideration would then prohibit the indiscriminate bombing of civilian targets as a means for removing the regime.

223. This paragraph builds on some ideas defended by Mark A. Drumbl in his "Judging the 11 September Terrorist Attack," *Human Rights Quarterly* 24 (2002), 323-360.

strategies aimed at legitimizing the condemnation of terrorism by disclosing the truth. Terrorist should be tried as openly as possible in order to show the world the atrocity of terrorism. Unbiased prosecution is essential to eliminate the misconception that "might makes right," a thesis which undergirds terrorist strategy. At the very least we need to work to ensure the appearance of impartial justice — perhaps only available in an international court that includes at least some Islamic jurists — in order to get the message out that the vast majority of the world condemns such actions. Finally, an appeal to universal principles of justice that go beyond the law of the sword is crucial if we want to show potential terrorists that what they propose to do is wrong based on principles that they themselves would accept.

We should always be careful about using the indiscriminate destructive force of modern warfare. And we must be judicious about using the rhetoric of war, lest we become too willing to sacrifice principles of justice for success in killing. The rhetoric of war tends to incline us toward a realist point of view where supreme emergencies loom. The events of September 11 were horrible. It is doubtful, however, that they constitute a supreme emergency. One must note again that such judgments are always made within the context of a philosophy of history. An outright realist might indeed see September 11 as an act of war and a supreme emergency. However, for a practical pacifist, the burden of proof that would invoke the supreme emergency exemption must be set quite high: a realist exemption that would justify total war on terrorists and the states that harbor them could only be invoked in the most dire of circumstances.

Indeed, if liberal states must resort to violence in response to terrorism, they must be careful not to sacrifice their liberal principles in the name of realism. I hope that Rawls would agree. Rawlsian political liberalism's highest aspiration is for a reasonable pluralism in which those who adhere to divergent comprehensive doctrines can agree to certain basic principles of justice, which ensure stability and peace. Agreement on such principles cannot be imposed by force if they are to be genuine. This indicates the way in which political liberalism slips toward a more comprehensive sort of liberalism that holds that liberty cannot be imposed by force. A more comprehensive commitment to the value of liberty should, I think, be shared by all. And we should have enough faith in the human spirit's pervasive aspiration for liberty to avoid resorting to imperialism. Liberal states such as the United States are often guilty of violating liberal principles in order to attain political ends in the international arena, in what looks like oxymoronic liberal imperialism. Such political maneuvers can further antagonize those terrorists who are opposed to liberal values and who are not constrained by respect for human rights and the law of peoples. A liberal response to terrorism should demonstrate its commitment by holding on to its liberal values, while resisting the urge to slip toward realism in practice and a war on terrorism which itself becomes terroristic. Moreover, we must remain true to our own commitments: if we value liberty and justice for all and if we agree to the just war theory as found in the Law of Peoples, then we cannot violate these commitments without a very good reason.

CHAPTER 7. ALIENATION, INFORMATION, AND WAR

> Bureaucratic administration always tends to exclude the public, to hide its knowledge and action from criticism as well as it can.
> — Max Weber[224]

In order to judge whether any war is just, we need to have enough information about the cause of the war, about the means to be employed, and about the potential consequences of the war. The thesis of practical pacifism holds that most of us do not have enough information to judge in practice whether any given war is just. From this, one can conclude that citizens should err on the side of peace and should resist the drive to war.

The difficulty of this approach is that our militaristic culture encourages us to form judgments that support war, without sufficient evidence. In other words, the military nation wants conformity, not critical thinking. When Kant hypothesized that representative democracy would bring an end to war, he assumed that democracy and enlightenment would develop together.[225] But Kant was not aware of the problems of alienation, manipulation, and conformism that occur in mass democracies such as ours. From the point of view of those who lead militaristic nations such as our own, serious democratic

---

224. Max Weber, *Economy and Society* (New York: Bedminster Press, 1968), 3: 992.

225. Kant, *Perpetual Peace* in *Kant: Political Writings* (Nisbet trans., Cambridge: Cambridge University Press, 1991) and *Metaphysical Elements of Justice: Part 1 of the Metaphysics of Morals* (Ladd trans., New York: Macmillan, 1965), §§ 53-62. Also see Michael Doyle's interpretation of Kant's view in *Ways of War and Peace* (New York: Norton, 1997). Doyle's view is in turn adopted by John Rawls in *The Law of Peoples* (Cambridge, MA: Harvard University Press, 1999).

debate about militarism must be avoided. Although we are, hopefully, well past the days when anti-militarists such as Eugene Debs (in the US) or Karl Liebknecht (in Germany) could be charged with treason for criticizing the military state, anti-militarists are still marginalized, albeit in much subtler ways. For example, the mainstream American media virtually ignored those who wondered whether the military force of the "war on terrorism" and the recent invasion of Iraq were justified. Although there was some coverage of anti-war protests, the media rarely mentions those who systematically question military spending or the morality of stockpiling weapons of mass destruction. Anti-militarist positions are absent in mainstream American politics. Democrats and Republicans both wholeheartedly supported all of President Bush's militaristic proposals, from the USA Patriot Act to the invasion of Iraq. There are no major politicians who call for dismantling the military state. More insidiously, we are subjected to subtle forms of militarist propaganda in advertisements for military service, in the now ubiquitous posters that say "United We Stand," and during the war in Iraq in the great rallying cry, "Support Our Troops." President Bush has been quite adept at employing military imagery to inspire support for the policies of militarism.

The problem is not merely this or that president or administration, however. The fact is that the US is a militarist nation. Almost any president would deploy military power as President Bush did. Pacifists will be marginalized, no matter who is in power. Those who question the militaristic status quo are treated like, and are made to feel like, outsiders; they are rattling the bars of a cage that no one else sees. This is true despite the fact that, even during the Iraq war, polls showed that 20-30% of the population did not support it.[226] While this is a minority, it is not insubstantial: one-fifth to one-third of Americans were opposed to the war. Yet the propaganda campaign depicted members of this minority as outsiders. In general, the military state will work to preserve itself by preventing those who question militarism from being taken seriously. Pacifism appears to be absurd when it is viewed from within the perspective of militarism.

The question of the present chapter is two-fold. On the one hand, we might wonder why it is so difficult to resist the military state. The easy answer is that the military state practices some form of what Marcuse called "repressive

---

226. See, for example, see lists of polling data (Newsweek polls, ABC News/Washington Post polls, Pew Research Center for People and the Press, etc.) about the war in Iraq at PollingReport.com (http://www.pollingreport.com/iraq.htm).

toleration."[227] This is a situation in which the appearance of freedom becomes a way of producing conformity: we are led to believe that we have chosen militarism, when in fact we have not. On the other hand, we might wonder whether this general claim about the difficulty of resistance is itself rational. The problem with the claim of "repressive tolerance" is that it can take the form of a paranoid conspiracy theory: as if some ruling cabal were manipulating the government and the media. I do not think that the conspiracy theory approach is right. Rather, the tendency toward conformity is a systematic problem and is not a matter of the overtly malicious intentions of a ruling clique. The system-problem stems in part from the alienation of information that occurs in mass bureaucratic societies. This alienation is exacerbated in the militaristic state, which uses propaganda to convince individuals that war and militarism are needed, while also maintaining secrets about strategies, goals, and intentions. Understanding this problem helps to support the thesis of practical pacifism because it helps clarify the fact that ordinary citizens usually are not able to judge whether any given war is just. Indeed, when we begin to understand how our culture supports the militarist status quo, we can also begin to understand how most of us can believe that certain wars are just, even when we really have no way of making this judgment. In general, our culture encourages us to trust the military system, while discouraging us from asking questions that are critical of the status quo. This — our dedication to militarism — can be seen throughout our culture. It is found in silent support for our enormous military budget. It is found in the holidays and national symbols that commemorate military power. It is seen in the awe and pride we feel before military technology. And it is seen in the glorification of military power that is found in film. Given the fascination we have with our own military power, it is not surprising that those who question it are viewed askance.

Two Sides of Toleration and Dissent

The military state deliberately uses propaganda and the media to make its case. Particular wars must be sold and a general commitment to militarism must also be heavily marketed. My basic assumption is contentious. I begin with the assumption that despite our fascination with military power and hardware,

---

227. Herbert Marcuse, "Repressive Tolerance," in Robert Paul Wolff, Barrington Moore, Jr., and Herbert Marcuse, *A Critique of Pure Tolerance* (Boston: Beacon Press, 1969).

ordinary citizens of democracy are not interested in militarism or in war. With this assumption I maintain that the military state must deliberately work to overcome the basic pacifism that is found in human beings, in family structures, and in the pacific culture of mainstream religious belief. While I do not claim that human beings are inherently peaceful, I do maintain that ordinary citizens of democracies must be convinced to sacrifice themselves, their tax money, and their religious or ethical consciences to the war system. From the point of view of those who support the military establishment, this propaganda function is a natural and normal part of the military state: ignorant citizens who do not know what is in their own self-interest must be educated about the necessity of preparing for and waging war. But from an anti-militarist perspective, this "education" looks like indoctrination. This is especially troubling because the military establishment is so powerful. While military recruiters can come into our schools and homes (by way of T.V.) to "sell" the excitement and glory of military service, there is no "equal time" for the message of peace. Where are the exciting ads for pacifism and disarmament? The military establishment sees its advertising campaign as a normal and necessary part of recruiting. Perhaps this is so because very few people would support militarism if it were not glamorized and marketed.

American political leaders admit that wars must be marketed. Andrew H. Card, the Bush Administration Chief of Staff, openly admitted in September of 2002 that the Bush administration was using a marketing strategy to sell the war in Iraq (including the fact that they waited until the end of summer to introduce their "new product", i.e., the war).[228] The problem with this is that the government possesses firm control of the means of persuasion as well as funding from the federal budget. It is much, much easier for the government than for anyone else to get a message out. As a result, the anti-militarist perspective is effectively marginalized.

It is difficult for Americans to admit that this process of marginalizing occurs, because we have a long tradition that prides itself on freedom of speech and open debate. This tradition, indeed, extends beyond the history of America and includes the history of liberalism in general. The standard story says that the interrelated ideas of toleration, freedom of speech, and freedom of the press follow from ideas expressed by John Milton in his *Areopagitica*, developed by John

---

228. "Traces of Terror: The Strategy; Bush Aides Set Strategy to Sell Policy on Iraq," *The New York Times*, September 7, 2002.

Locke in his *Letter concerning Toleration*, and institutionalized by Jefferson and the Framers in the US Constitution and its First Amendment. Locke did argue that "the truth would do well enough if left alone."[229] However, like Milton, he was not as open-minded and tolerant as we are often led to believe. Milton and Locke both allowed for censorship of unorthodox religious views, such as, in Milton's case, Catholicism, and in Locke's case, atheism.[230] And it is important to note that the ideal of free speech has always been haunted by a worry about "seditious libel" as articulated in views that call into question the legitimacy of the state. Although we like to celebrate our tolerant institutions, critics have argued that tolerance itself can be an ideology that serves the interests of power and reaffirms the status quo. In the middle of the 20th century, critics of American democracy such as Walter Lippmann and C. Wright Mills argued that in mass society, there are only power interests and propaganda.[231] In the 1960s, this problem was identified by Herbert Marcuse as the problem of "repressive tolerance," the idea that dominant political forces will tolerate all views except those that call the social and political status quo into question. Noam Chomsky has made a career out of discussing the ways in which institutions of power work to "manufacture consent" while marginalizing dissent.[232] We have been led to believe that our nation was founded on a commitment to dissent and toleration in the name of genuine democratic deliberation; but we know that those in power seek to manipulate information in order to sustain themselves in power. As Liebknecht and other anti-militarists have argued, this is especially true of militaristic states, which must convince individuals to sacrifice themselves for military power. The interest of power does not include dismantling the military state.

---

229. Locke, John. *Letter Concerning Toleration,* in Steven M. Cahn ed. *Classics of Modern Political Theory* (New York: Oxford University Press, 1997).

230. For discussion of Locke and Milton, see Leonard W. Levy, *Emergence of a Free Press* (Oxford University Press, 1985), Chapter 4. Also see Stanley Fish, *There's No Such Thing as Free Speech* (Oxford University Press, 1994), Chapter 8 and Noam Chomsky, *Deterring Democracy* (London: Verso, 1991), Chapter 12.

231. Walter Lippmann, *The Phantom Public* (New Brunswick, NJ: Transaction Publishers, 1993), C. Wright Mills, *The Power Elite* (Oxford University Press, 1956), Chapter 13. For a response to Lippmann, see Dewey, *The Public and Its Problems* (Denver: Swallow, 1954); for a synthetic discussion, see Peter Manicas, *War and Democracy* (Cambridge, MA: Blackwell, 1989).

232. For example, Edward S. Herman and Noam Chomsky, *Manufacturing Consent* (New York: Pantheon Books, 1988) and Chomsky, *Media Control: The Spectacular Achievements of Propaganda* (New York: Seven Stories Press, 2002).

Our tendency to be suspicious of the honesty and motivation of our leaders is at once both rational and disconcerting. It is rational because history shows us repeated examples of the ways in which political power abuses information. Moreover, the very nature of the division of labor in society leaves us alienated from sources of information. We have good reason to be suspicious of those in power but we lack access to the sorts of information that would either alleviate or confirm our suspicions. As such, the suspicion of power can begin to seem like paranoia. The problem of the dissident view is that its suspicion of power undermines the feeling of solidarity that most of us want from membership in a political community. We want to belong. We want to identify with and trust our leaders; and thus we find ourselves easily seduced by the rhetoric and propaganda of patriotism. Critical thinkers are at the same time, however, repelled by the very same rhetoric and propaganda. As critical thinkers, we want the truth and are reluctant to assent when we lack evidence. As citizens and members of society, we trust our leaders and we believe the images we see on TV, just as we identify with the nation and its cause. But let's not be naïve: politicians and advertising executives make good use of our desire to trust and our need to belong. This is precisely why we should resist the easy path of complacency and acquiescence: we know they are trying to manipulate us in part because we know that we are willing to be manipulated. This is a bipartisan tendency: Americans are willing to believe their leader, whether the leader is Bill Clinton or George W. Bush. The conclusion is that we must question the rhetoric and propaganda that the government and the media disseminate daily. This is not to say that everything we see on TV or hear from our politicians is false. Rather, it is to clarify the task of critical questioning: we must ask ourselves exactly what we know and keep an eye open toward manipulation.

During wartime, rhetorical strategies and propagandistic media campaigns are at once more and less obvious. They are more obvious because during wartime the government uses the media directly to campaign for its war. Presidential addresses, press conferences, and speeches made by members of the Administration serve to explain the war in order to rally the people behind it. More than in times of peace, during wartime we see the government and hear its voice. During peacetime, it is perhaps easier to see and hear the voices of the Administration as offering a partisan opinion about what should be done. The emotional intensity of war and the demand to "be patriotic" during wartime serves to befuddle our critical perspective. During wartime we do not see our leaders as partisans with limited perspectives. Rather, we look to them as father figures who transcend bias and opinion. The discord over the invasion of Iraq should serve as a reminder of the problem. It should be obvious that the government uses its access to the media during wartime to put forward a specific agenda and to rally public opinion behind its policies. In the debate over the war in Iraq, we were persuaded into thinking that to be a good American one must support the President in his struggle against "irrational" forces in the international community (i.e., the French and others). Once the war began, we were supposed to fall in behind the troops. Once the war was declared over, we were supposed to forget whatever questions about its justification we might have had. During the run up to the war, most of the mainstream media ignored the fact that there was dissent at home and that this dissent continued through the war. In this way, the dissenters were marginalized and the dominant view was reinforced. To note this is not to pass judgment on the just-ness of the war on Iraq. Rather, it is to point out that most of us lack an objective standpoint from which we could judge the government's arguments about the necessity for war.

No citizen has access to the sources of information that Secretary of State Colin Powell and others used when making the case that war was necessary: information that was supposed to show that Iraq was a terrorist regime that posed an imminent threat to American security. We have now discovered that some of the information presented as a justification for war in Iraq was false or exaggerated. Dissenters tried to point this out before the war. However, those who asked critical questions about the government's claims were called unpatriotic. Now, the same questions are ignored as irrelevant, since the rationale for the war has shifted from the claim that a preemptive war was necessary to a claim about the importance of spreading democracy in the Middle East. Both of these might be good reasons to go to war, but ordinary citizens were asked to support the war on the basis of one rationale and when that was found inadequate, another was filled in. Either way, Americans lacked the concrete information that would allow them to form responsible judgments of their own. This experience should teach us to retain our skepticism about claims made in defense of war.

The techniques of propaganda may seem less obvious during wartime because we tend to ignore the fact that the government and the military control the flow of information about war and about militarism in general. Most of the information we receive about war, its causes, and its prosecution, is controlled by the government and the military. Moreover, the media, which finds war to be a thrilling and useful opportunity, supports war by creating images of patriotism and heroism, by stimulating our fascination with war, and by subtly biasing the news in the direction of support for military action. One of the main tasks of government during war is to consolidate public opinion behind the war effort. This effort is made easier by the common refrain of wartime: that despite our internal disagreements, the nation must show a united home front. Once the bombs begin to fall, we must rally behind the president and support the troops. Once the war begins, it is unpatriotic to ask whether we should support troops who are engaged in a war whose justness is still in doubt. Nor can the question be asked whether the best way to "support the troops" is to end the war immediately and bring them home. During wartime, dissenting opinions and serious moral questions can be stigmatized as unpatriotic or even treasonous. At the very least, our leaders and the media refuse even bring them up. No political leader could even ask — let alone argue — whether the best way to support the troops (that is, the best way to care for their consciences as well as their physical well) is to ask them not to fight in a war whose justness is in question.

The military state has become quite sophisticated in its use of the media. Critics have detailed the way in which news was sanitized and censored during the Gulf War of 1991.[233] Visceral pictures that showed the horror of war were deliberately not used by American news editors. The military censors did not allow photographs of the war dead on "our" side to be shown to the public. And the military managed the flow of news by keeping reporters contained within a "pool system," by asking reporters to identify with a specific group of soldiers, and by preventing them from seeing the action until it had been sanitized (by, for example, bulldozing the dead bodies of Iraqis under the sand). This approach continued in the recent Iraq war with the "embedding" of reporters and the ubiquity of retired military brass serving as advisors on major networks. And the media loved to play uplifting stories such as the tale of the rescue of Jessica Lynch. The military propaganda was perhaps most obvious when President Bush landed on an aircraft carrier in order to declare the "end of major combat." The awesome power of military hardware and our fascination with uniforms and military command structure can all be used for propaganda purposes.

In a recent work of media criticism, John MacArthur shows how, during the lead-up to the Gulf War, news was in fact manufactured in order to

---

233. Rodney A. Smolla, *Free Speech in an Open Society* (New York: Alfred A. Knopf, 1992), Chapter 10, Jonathan Glover, *Humanity*, Chapter 20; Chris Hedges, *War is a Force that Gives Us Meaning* (New York: Public Affairs, 2002), Chapter 6.

stimulate the public's support of the war.[234] MacArthur catalogues ways in which the press eagerly utilized a provocative analogy that compared Saddam Hussein to Hitler, and he discusses how the media worked to design music and graphics to accompany the war. But more disturbing than this is the fact that the press credulously published false reports about atrocities committed by Iraq in Kuwait. One of these had Iraqi soldiers removing 300 babies from incubators and leaving them to die. MacArthur shows that this story was a fabrication and also that the dissemination of this story was conveniently timed to fit the first Bush administration's drive to war. MacArthur shows that other stories — about forced deportation of Kuwaitis and about Iraqi raping, looting, and pillaging in Kuwait — were either fabricated or greatly exaggerated by the press. One wonders whether other more recent stories about Saddam and Iraqi atrocities have been exaggerated to serve the purpose of fanning the flames of war.[235] The point is not to argue that Saddam Hussein was a good guy; rather, this all shows that we must be skeptical about what the truth is when we are talking about foreign policy, politics, and war. Anyone who followed the debate at the United Nations leading up to the invasion of Iraq must realize that there were serious questions about who was telling the truth about Saddam's weapons of mass destruction. Since the declared end of the war, Americans have continued to debate the rhetoric that surrounded claims about weapons of mass destruction and Saddam's supposed links to the September 11 terrorists. But the insidious nature of military power is seen in that — once our troops were in Iraq — it was inconceivable that we should not support the policy that sent them there. Once military power is deployed, it demands support. We are often manipulated into supporting the deployment beforehand, while not really understanding the nature of the deployment or the supposedly just reasons for the use of military force.

Lest we think that the media are simply duped by the manipulations of the government and its military forces, we should remember that American reporters are people just like the rest of us. That is, they are patriotic and interested in "supporting the troops." Chris Hedges, who was a reporter during the Gulf War, has described it as follows. "The notion that the press was used in

---

234. John A MacArthur, *Second Front* (New York: Hill and Wang, 1992), especially Chapter 2.

235. For example, the claim that Saddam attempted to assassinate George H.W. Bush is based on sketchy evidence that was used by the Clinton administration in order to justify a missile attack on Baghdad in 1993, which itself was motivated by Clinton's desire to seem tough (see Seymour Hersh, "A Case Not Closed," *The New Yorker*, November 1993).

the war is incorrect. The press wanted to be used. It saw itself as part of the war effort."[236] From Hedges' perspective, the press is a loyal arm of the nation that aims to use the myth of war — the mythic story of the virtues and necessity of war — to sustain the morale of the troops and of the rest of the populace. Moreover, the press has a vested interest in this form of loyalty. Jingoism sells; or, at the very least, uncritical reportage sells better than self-critical and complex reporting that fully displays the horrors of war. As Hedges writes, "Mythic war reporting sells papers and boosts ratings. Real reporting, sensory reporting, does not, at least not in comparison with the boosterism we witnessed during the Persian Gulf War and in the War in Afghanistan."[237]

Of course one might object that modern means of communication could solve this problem somewhat both by allowing for a greater range of coverage and by providing visual images that allow us actually to "feel" war and to establish an empathic connection with its victims. Advocates of the Internet have long argued that citizens have access to information, by that means, that would otherwise have been ignored by the mainstream media. Nonetheless, the vast majority of citizens do not pursue alternative forms of information simply because this takes quite a bit of work and because the mainstream media does what most of us think of as a "good job." It is a fact that most of us get our information from the mainstream media, especially from television. Television poses an interesting problem. On the one hand, it is a ubiquitous source of information available to almost everyone. On the other hand, its visual imagery can be used to sway us one way or another. The persuasive power of television is found in the nature of its presentation, which is a combination of sound, visuals, and motion. The aesthetics of television make it much more powerful than the print media (whether traditional newspapers or the Internet). Michael Ignatieff has made much of the form of television, even linking the visual connection with victims of violence created by television to the development of a universal moral conscience.[238] He even speaks of "television's conscience," something which has developed in the last few decades. He claims that television aims at the following values: "to pay attention to the victims, rather than the pieties of political rhetoric; to refuse to make a distinction between good corpses and bad ones

236. Chris Hedges, *War is a Force that Gives Us Meaning*, 143.
237. Chris Hedges, *War is a Force that Gives Us Meaning*, 22-23.
238. For a similar interpretation of the importance of electronic communications, see John Lachs, "Both Better Off and Better," in *A Community of Individuals* (New York: Routledge, 2003), Chapter 10.

(though this was notoriously not the case in American coverage of Vietnam); and to be a witness, a bearer of bad tidings to the watching conscience of the world."[239] And yet, Ignatieff recognizes that the voyeuristic connection with horror that is facilitated by the visual media is both limited and pernicious. It is limited because it is so sensationalistic: images of horror must compete with each other in the "market in images of horror."[240] We find it interesting to watch mass violence on TV. In a recent discussion, Slavoj Zizek has described our fascination with the images of September 11 as connected with our love of spectacles and our interest in "reality TV."[241] The September 11 attacks and the war on Iraq are, quite simply, fascinating spectacles, especially when they are viewed from the safety of our living rooms. This spectacular approach to terrorism, war, and indeed to militarism in general is pernicious because it defuses critical thinking. The mere imagery of horror, despite its ability to move us, does not lead us directly to analysis and commitment. It is easy to be moved for a moment by images of horror, bewildered by the strange beauty of explosions; but it is also easy to change the channel and ignore these images without thinking about them, their causes, their consequences, and possible alternatives to militarism.

The vision presented by the media is self-authorizing: the importance of an event or an idea is judged not by its intrinsic worth but by the amount of attention that the news media pays to it. Perception is primary and it tends to override good judgment. Thus, we have been made fearful and have agreed on the need for increased security, when in fact most of our lives are relatively untouched by terror. It should be noted that, even in the year 2001, the risk of death from terrorist attack was well below the risk of death from ordinary murder. And it was quite a bit below the risk of death from highway traffic accidents. Indeed, "even in that year, the probability of being killed by terrorism in the United States was less than that of being run over by a car while walking."[242] There is something irrational about the fact that we have declared war on terror, when we are much more likely to be killed by being run over while we walk along the side of the road than we are to be killed by a terrorist. We can make sense of this response, however, if we recognize that the spectacle of terrorism and its repetition (both by the media and by the constant reference to it by our political leaders) is what fosters our sense of un-ease and authorizes our

---

239. Michael Ignatieff, *The Warrior's Honor* (New York: Henry Holt, 1997), 23.

240. Ignatieff, *The Warrior's Honor*, 28.

241. Slavoj Zizek, *Welcome to the Desert of the Real* (London: Verso, 2002).

fear. It is our fascination with the spectacle of terror and the media's use of this spectacle that makes us feel unsafe. It is hard to deny that the media barrage, which turned September 11 into an icon and a rallying cry, did a great service for militarism.

It is not my intention to ignore the suffering caused by September 11. Nor do I want to downplay the unimaginable horror that could be created if terrorists were to employ weapons of mass destruction. But I do want to point out that our judgments about potential risks and appropriate countermeasures are often based upon limited perspectives and partial knowledge. Quite a bit more suffering is caused on a yearly basis by auto accidents than by terrorism; and yet we are not declaring war on unsafe driving or spending billions of dollars to make roads and cars safer. A social decision was made to dwell on terrorism. One wonders what interests were served by this decision. The most obvious candidates are hawkish politicians who can take advantage of fear to keep themselves in power, as well as defense industries who profit from militarism. This is not to say that there was a *conscious* decision on the part of political and industrial leaders to manipulate us toward militarism by exploiting our fear of terrorism. The process is probably much more subtle than any deliberate collusion or attempt at overt manipulation. It has to do with the media focusing on what is easy to report and what sells (i.e., the spectacle of terrorism and war) and with politicians reacting to this to increase their own advantage. All of this may occur without any conscious decision. But this is still a problem: lack of conscious decision makes us all susceptible to the irrationality of the spectacle. Although the risk of death from auto accident is significantly higher, that story is not flashy; it is difficult to rally political will around traffic safety; and the automakers and oil companies would probably lose money if auto safety became a public focus. It is important to realize that the relation between the media and political and industrial power is a self-catalyzing feedback loop. The media sells spectacular stories. Politicians use the stories to sell themselves. And these approaches reinforce one another.

242. Roger D. Congleton, "Terrorism, Interest-Group Politics, and Public Policy," *The Independent Review* Vol. 7 (Summer 2002), p. 59. Congleton's analysis is based on the following data. The yearly average during the 1990s for highway traffic deaths was over 40,000 deaths per year; the yearly average for pedestrian deaths was 5,500. This is compared to the number of people killed in the attacks of September 11th 2001, which was less than 2,500. The average yearly death rate from terrorism in the 1990s was around 100 per year. But this decade-long average number can be misleading: in 1993 over 1,000 people were killed but in most other years there were no deaths from terrorism in the US.

The press likes to think of itself as a critical outsider to politics. But, when the nation is at war or is under terrorist attack, the media adopts a fawning attitude toward authority, in part because television is the source of community through which communal rituals are broadcast to the nation. The media's function is not, primarily, critical; rather, it functions to sustain whatever sense of community there is in our vast nation. After the September 11 tragedies, televised events including speeches by President Bush, patriotic ceremonies of commemoration, and the wars in Afghanistan and Iraq, became part of the process of mourning and served to create a sense of communal solidarity. It would be inappropriate to offer criticism at moments such as these, in part because such criticism would have to indict the uncritical media for its own role in making such things possible. The media is glad to contribute to this process as part of its obligation as a good citizen. And indeed, we do need the media to fulfill this function; but this function also serves to undermine whatever critical distance the media might have had.

The conclusion from this consideration of the media is that we must be skeptical of the power of the media to shape our experience of the world. This is especially true in wartime, when the media is willingly used by the military and the government to disseminate the patriotic and militaristic message. We should be skeptical; and yet precisely because it is the media which we are skeptical of, we do not have access to the kinds of information that would confirm our skeptical fears. This ambivalence in modern political life sets the stage for the difficulty of knowing whether any given war is just.

For the most part, ordinary citizens do not and cannot know whether any given war is just. This is the result of the division of labor in society and the necessity of secrecy in the name of security (the military can't, after all, tell us its secrets, its battle plans, etc., without undermining its efficiency). This alienation of information is also the result of the way in which the media plays its part in the division of labor, and willingly refrains from divulging secret information or criticizing the need for secrecy. This analysis may sound like a conspiracy theory. I do not want to go so far as to claim that the media is in cahoots with the government, although some have argued this based upon the shared interests and monopolistic tendencies of the media when it is considered as a business aimed at profit.[243] A more moderate point of view has been defended by G.

---

243. For this point of view, see John Nichols and David McChesney, *Our Media, Not Theirs* (New York: Seven Stories Press, 2002).

William Domhoff, who sees the media as merely a tool of power and not as, itself, a part of the power structure. [244] Nonetheless, this does make a critical understanding of the media an important part of our understanding of the power of the military state.

PARANOIA AND TERRORISM

An objection to the analysis presented here is that it is a paranoid conspiracy theory. Conspiracy theories abound these days, disseminated by the mainstream media, public access television, and the Internet. Ironically, as sources of information proliferate, so do conspiracy theories that worry about the information that we are not getting. The problem of conspiracy theories arises especially in wartime, in part because we demand explanations and information that are inaccessible to us because of the nature of military secrecy. Even worse, governments themselves can foster a belief in conspiracies as part of the war effort.[245] We all look for explanations, especially when important values are at stake, such as during times of war. When we do not find the information or explanations we seek, it is easy to propose an explanation that sees conspiracy behind the scene. And almost always, those who conspire have malicious intentions.

Richard Hofstadter has linked the propensity of people to believe in conspiracies to a "paranoid style" of politics. This style occurs as people seek to explain their own powerlessness by ascribing it to the evil machinations of some secret cabal (the Illuminati, Freemasons, and Catholics in the 19th century; Jews and Communists in the mid-20th century; and more recently, Liberals, the FBI and ATF, the Trilateral Commission, the military-industrial complex, or religious fundamentalists). Hofstadter indicates that this paranoid style appears when social forces are in conflict, when fundamental issues are in doubt, and when fear of impending catastrophe is great. People become paranoid when they feel that they "cannot make themselves felt in the political process." Hofstadter continues: "Feeling that they have no access to political bargaining or the

---

244. Domhoff writes, for example, "Media can amplify the message of the powerful and marginalize the concerns of the less powerful, but I do not think they are a central element in the power equation" [G. William Domhoff, *Who Rules America* (Mountain View, CA: Mayfield Publishing, 1998), 192].

245. For discussion, see Daniel Pipes, *Conspiracy* (New York: Free Press, 1997), Chapter 9.

making of decisions, they find their original conception of the world of power as omnipotent, sinister and malicious fully confirmed."[246] The paranoid style is well suited to describe the post-September 11 world: terrorism and fear of terrorism have made us all somewhat paranoid.

We may wonder what justifies Hofstadter in calling such theories "paranoid." The word literally means "thinking (noesis/nous) gone astray (para)." At best, the paranoid thinker is not rational; at worst he is crazy. Hofstadter does not think that conspiracy theorists are crazy. Rather, he says that they are, if anything, too rational because they demand a coherence from political reality that it can never possess: "In fact, the paranoid mentality is far more coherent than the real world, since it leaves no room for mistakes, failures, or ambiguities."[247] The paranoid approach looks for reasons for events, when in fact there may be no obvious reason at all to explain them.

Terrorism lends itself to the problem of paranoia and conspiracy theories. Because we are rationalists, we want to know who is to blame for terrorism. Because we like to think in simple terms, we want to be able to identify a few villains on whom we can pin the blame. Thus, after the September 11 atrocities, public will was mobilized against Osama bin Laden. A few of the more "paranoid" wondered whether the Bush administration had secretly allowed these horrors or had known about them in advance. We tend to think that there must be some reason that the terrorists were successful. We are not content to admit that perhaps they got lucky that day. We fail to recognize that the United States has been relatively free from terrorism and that the September 11 attacks represent an anomaly rather than a pattern. But such anomalies bother us. We search for patterns and reasons. We are not content with probabilistic explanations and statistical analyses. We demand to know what happened, in part because we want to know what can be done.

But this demand for knowledge may itself be unreasonable: we cannot predict and prevent terrorism with certainty. Richard Rorty has argued that the fact of the matter is that we do not know how to cope with the age of terrorism. "Nobody has yet explained how the government might hope to take effective precautions against, for example, the arrival of nuclear or biochemical devices in shipboard freight containers. One suspects that the officials of our government are well aware that no precautions are likely to eliminate, or even substantially

---

246. Richard Hofstadter, *The Paranoid Style in American Politics* (New York: Knopf, 1965), 39.
247. Richard Hofstadter, *The Paranoid Style in American Politics*, 36.

lessen, the chances of further terrorist attacks. But these officials are not about to tell the public that their government can think of little more to do than to tighten security at airports."[248] Even if we severely curtail civil liberties in promulgating a war on terrorism, we can never be certain that terrorism will end. And this is the problem that promotes both paranoia and conspiracy theories, while also lending support for increased militarism.

We are comforted by the illusion that someone out there is actually doing something intentionally to cause things to be the way they are. This is quite ironic, since those who espouse conspiracy theories are usually suspicious — in good liberal fashion — of those who wield power. But if the conspiracy theory is correct, then the conspirators really are somehow better, stronger, and wiser than we are. Thus, beneath every conspiracy theory is a bit of hope that our leaders really are in control. We hope that they know what they are doing, even if we do not agree with it. We are afraid to admit that there is really no one in control. It is more likely that Foucault was correct in arguing that power is diffuse and complex. Political power is a complex auto-catalytic process in which media, politicians, industry, and the public are caught. Conspiracy theorists hope that this is not so, perhaps because they fear the a-rational nature of social and political life. There must be something going on in the depths of the government that we simply are not privy to. We think this because we can't bear to admit that perhaps no one person or group is fully in charge.

An analysis of the rationality of conspiracy theories is important to help us understand contemporary political life in general. Liberals and conservatives often accuse each other of conspiracy. At the same time, they reject their opponents' conspiracy theories as irrational paranoia. Robert Bork, to cite one example, espouses a theory about a conspiracy of liberal politicians, intellectuals, and federal judges who want to overthrow Western civilization as we know it. According to Bork, liberals have an inordinate influence on society because of "a conscious effort on the part of intellectuals to alter American's perceptions of the world and of themselves, an effort, among other things, to weaken or destroy Americans' attachment to their country and to Western civilization."[249] Bork blames the hegemony of "radical liberalism" on a conspiracy of liberal elites who run the media, the courts, and the academy. And yet, Bork dismisses the conspiracy theories of black Americans as "paranoia"

---

248. Richard Rorty, "Fighting Terrorism with Democracy," *The Nation*, 275: 13 (October 21, 2002), p. 11.

249. Robert H. Bork, *Slouching towards Gomorrah* (New York: HarperCollins, 1996), 89.

which is fed by "race hustlers" and "university professors of Black studies."[250] Unfortunately Bork gives us no criteria with which to distinguish the "paranoia" of the black studies professors from his own supposedly rational suspicions about the liberal elite. The same sorts of debates fuel the "culture wars" and debates about whether atheistic humanists are staging a cultural coup or whether right-wing fundamentalists such as John Ashcroft are taking over the government. This sort of discussion culminates in the question of whether the media is biased toward the right or the left.[251]

This sort of debate continues in discussions about the war on terrorism. Civil libertarians are worried about the Bush Administration's plan to roll back civil liberties in the name of anti-terrorism, while pro-security conservatives worry that those who oppose the USA Patriot Act and the militarism of the war on terror are committed to completely subverting the American system. At issue is the question of trust. But this question cuts in two directions: conservatives tend to trust the government more than they trust individuals, while civil libertarians tend to trust individuals more than they trust the government. Both of these approaches to trust are based upon weak generalizations. Conservatives worry that we cannot trust individuals because some individuals might be terrorists. Civil libertarians worry that we cannot trust the government because some leaders might be tyrannical. It is difficult to say where the evidence points with regard to this conversation, although I tend to agree with the civil libertarian point of view. History shows that those in power have often used their power to gain more power at the expense of liberty. Statistical analysis of terrorism does not support the need for radical measures. A few extra precautions in the name of security might be justified at this moment. However, if we think that liberty is both a primary human aim and the primary means to other forms of human flourishing, we should err on the side of liberty unless a strong case is made for further repressive security measures. The problem with making this sort of judgment is that they are made in conditions of uncertainty. Does any of us really know what the risk of terrorism is? We all have opinions about this, but our opinions are based on uncertainty.

Many critics of American foreign policy claim that the US is aimed at creating global hegemony through both overt and covert action. In the opinion of those who argue from this perspective, since World War II, the US has become

---

250. Robert H. Bork, *Slouching towards Gomorrah*, 229.

251. See Bernard Goldberg, *Bias* (Washington, DC: Regnery Publishing, 2002) and Eric Alterman, *What Liberal Media?* (New York: Basic Books, 2003).

an imperial power with the Executive Branch siphoning off more power in the form of "blank checks" from Congress, which support the expansion of US power in the name of national security. As part of this process of working to ensure national security, the government aims to, in Chomsky's phrase, "manufacture consent" for its policies, including those policies through which the US supports undemocratic regimes and terroristic activities throughout the world. Critics like Chomsky contend that the government and the media mobilize information in order to create the conditions for consent that make these imperial policies look like they have broad democratic support. Of course, Chomsky's critical approach can fan the flames of a conspiracy theory which holds that elites control and manipulate the masses in pursuit of power. It is, however, difficult to know whether this conspiracy is true. In fact, if it were true, it would be impossible to know it in any straightforward sense. Thus we should admit that such a critical perspective is tinged with uncertainty. However, if such opinions are at all plausible, they point to the problem of alienation of information that is the source of practical pacifism. We do not need to believe that there is a full scale conspiracy aimed at "manufacturing consent" for US imperialism in order to be suspicious of militarism; rather, we simply need to acknowledge that the means of information are biased in the direction of support of the militaristic status quo. Given this, it is rational for the practical pacifist to question and resist the dominant forces that argue for military power.

Bureaucracy and Alienation

Bureaucratic institutions leave individuals alienated from decision-making processes which impact all aspects of their lives. Those who follow Weber's analysis of bureaucracy are especially inclined to see the secretive nature of bureaucratic specialization. If one accepts this claim about administrative secrecy, then the argument of practical pacifism follows fairly easily. Weber indicated that a proliferation of "administrative secrets" would be the necessary result of expanded bureaucracy. "Every bureaucracy seeks to increase the superiority of the professionally informed by keeping their knowledge and intentions secret."[252] More recently, Iris Young has followed Weber's analysis to indicate the bureaucratized welfare state results in a loss of the political sphere

---

252. Max Weber, "Bureaucracy," in *From Max Weber* (New York: Oxford University Press, 1946), 233. This is from Vol. 3, Chapter 6 of *Economy and Society*.

of public deliberation, producing what she calls a "depoliticized" society.[253] Developing ideas introduced by Weber, Young points to three conditions of alienation from bureaucratic institutions. (1) Bureaucratic decisions are made by finite individuals and are thus not impartial, despite an abundance of rules and procedures. Thus, individuals find themselves dominated by arbitrary authorities whom they did not elect. This results in "an experience of personal dependency and necessary submission to arbitrary will."[254] (2) Individuals are unable to challenge these bureaucratic rules and procedures because, in bureaucracy, experts with specialized knowledge control institutional power. Individual citizens cannot adequately possess the expertise necessary to challenge authority: "It is therefore difficult for people to challenge the doctors, social workers, engineers, statisticians, economists, job analysts, city planners, and the myriad of other experts whose judgments determine their action or the condition of their actions."[255] (3) Careerism produces compliant individuals who seek to preserve the status quo in order to preserve their own career opportunities: "Subordinates accept the hierarchical structure and the authority of their superiors because they themselves have legitimate hopes of rising to positions of greater authority."[256]

These three conditions result in what Young calls "depoliticization," as individuals are excluded from decision-making, unable to challenge this exclusion, and often unwilling to do so. As individuals become depoliticized in the face of alienating bureaucratic institutions, they become apathetic and cynical. This may not be paranoia, if, in fact, the institutions in question are indeed bureaucratic institutions prone to keeping what Weber called "administrative secrets." Indeed, Weber indicated that military bureaucracies are prime examples of institutions based on "administrative secrecy." Thus, it is no wonder that in our militaristic society, we feel a certain degree of alienation. Of course, one should wonder, however, at the fact that despite our alienation from information about military power, the vast majority of us nonetheless continue to support military power. The theory of propaganda and our desire to trust our leaders — as discussed above — can begin to help us make sense of this.

---

253. Iris Young, *Justice and the Politics of Difference* (Princeton: Princeton University Press, 1990), Chapter 3.
254. Iris Young, *Justice and the Politics of Difference*, 78.
255. Iris Young, *Justice and the Politics of Difference*, 80.
256. Iris Young, *Justice and the Politics of Difference*, 80.

One need not be a Weberian to accept such conclusions about administrative secrecy and alienation. John Dewey follows Emerson in complaining about our lack of self-reliance in the face of those institutions that want conformity. Dewey noted, as early as the 1920s, that "Americanization" represented a process of "quantification, mechanization, and standardization" that, when combined with our tendency toward "mass suggestibility," prevented Americas from genuine critical thinking.[257] Since Dewey wrote, the conformism of mass culture has continued to grow. American philosopher John Lachs has followed Dewey's lead to reach similar conclusions about contemporary mass society. Following Dewey's discussion of the difference between means and ends, Lachs concludes that the modern problem is that in large bureaucracies we find ourselves being used as means to ends which we do not ourselves understand. Alienation is the result: "We find agents in our highly mediated society experiencing themselves as instruments of causes they do not adopt and may not even approve."[258] Lachs has argued that violence itself can be an understandable response to this sort of alienation, both because violence is an expression of the frustration of our hyper-mediated social existence and because violence returns us to a form of active immediacy that we desire precisely because of our mediated existence.[259] One should note, however, that for Lachs, although violence is understandable as a response, the best response is to work to understand the fact of mediation and alienation.

These discussions of alienation should help to clarify the basic problem of practical pacifism: that we cannot know whether proposed uses of violence are justifiable. A further factor should be noted, in conclusion: our tendency toward self-deception. It may be the case that human existence is characterized, as Sartre has argued, by a tendency toward self-deception. This general claim is instantiated explicitly when we are asked to judge the goodness of our political institutions. Most of us do not want to admit that we have been deceived. Those who are interested in creating and mobilizing public opinion find a natural ally in the self-deception of patriots. Since the time of Socrates, philosophers have known that critical self-knowledge and social criticism are unpopular. As Chomsky writes, "Fame, fortune, and respect await those who reveal the crimes of official enemies; those who undertake the vastly more important task of

---

257. John Dewey, *Individualism Old and New* (New York: Prometheus Books, 1999), 12.

258. John Lachs, *A Community of Individuals* (New York: Routledge, 2003), 68.

259. John Lachs, "Violence as a Response to Alienation," in *The Relevance of Philosophy to Life* (Nashville, TN: Vanderbilt University Press, 1995), Chapter 10.

raising a mirror to their own societies can expect quite different treatment."[260] We are eager to point out the gullibility of others but we fail to admit it in ourselves. Indeed, the idea of patriotism has been expressed as "my country, right or wrong," which is an attitude that admits a lack of concern for self-critical analysis of one's commitments. A problem for political criticism is that individuals do not want to admit that they might have been wrong to support their country's policies.

If critics such as Chomsky are right, we must be cautious of the very idea of "democracy," since those who manufacture consent are quite good at convincing us that we have democratic control even as they manipulate us through such cleverly-named means as "USA Patriot Act" and "Operation Iraqi Freedom." When the President insists that "they" hate us because of our liberty, he ignores more substantial reasons for their hatred of us based in the history of Western intervention in Middle Eastern affairs. But this claim also serves to reassure us that we are free, despite the fact that the militaristic state is opposed to free and open debate about militarism. We "support our troops" in the name of freedom without wondering whether the very idea of a military society is one in which self-critical enlightened freedom can occur. Again, one need not go so far as critics such as Marcuse and Chomsky do to see that the military state makes criticism of militarism difficult. If we admit this, then practical pacifism begins to make sense.

Conclusions

One of the conclusions of the analysis presented is that ordinary citizens are alienated from the information that we would have to have if we were to judge whether the government was operating honestly. This is not to say that a secret cabal runs the government. Indeed, the inefficiencies of large bureaucracies and the ineptitude of government officials make it unlikely that any large scale conspiracy could be successful. The thesis of practical pacifism is not that we should resist militarism because there is a militaristic conspiracy in power. Such a claim concludes more than is warranted without a much more extensive empirical analysis. And it concludes more than is necessary to support the idea of practical pacifism. All that is needed for this thesis is a sufficient

---

260. Noam Chomsky, *Deterring Democracy*, 372.

amount of alienation of information. Since we have reason to doubt the motives of our leaders — and indeed since we cannot know the motives of our leaders — we should err on the side of pacifism. The use of violence is a terrible thing that should only be sanctioned in clear and compelling situations. If the case for alienation as discussed is plausible, then we should be reluctant to trust our leaders. When they present arguments for the necessity of war, we should question, protest, and resist, while demanding evidence of their good faith effort to adhere to the principles of justice in war.

One objection against this position is that its skeptical basis would result in anarchy, chaos, and disorder in society. In reply, one can recall that the skeptical approach to power lies at the heart of the liberal tradition from Locke to Jefferson and Paine to Mill. The liberal tradition begins with the suspicion that power tends to become tyrannical when not checked by skeptical questions about its legitimacy. More simply put: skepticism is healthy for liberal democracy. Locke makes it clear that the right to question the government is based upon the fiduciary nature of government: government is supposed to be based upon the consent of the governed. Thus the citizens have a right to demand information, so that they can decide whether to give or withhold their consent. With regard to important social and political questions such as war, it seems obvious that the consent of the people must be emphatic and explicit and that it must be based upon adequate information. Since it is citizens who will pay for the war both in terms of suffering and taxes, citizens should have a say about whether any given war is to be undertaken.

Along the lines articulated by Locke, Kant thought liberal regimes would rarely go to war because it would be difficult to get citizens to consent to war, especially when they realized that their own self interests were at stake. Michael Doyle and John Rawls have turned this idea into something of a principle of history: liberal states do not go to war with one another. The limit of Doyle's claim is found in the fact that liberal regimes do go to war with non-liberal regimes. The Gulf War and the current war in Iraq are examples of wars fought by self-proclaimed "liberal" states against so-called "rogue" nations. Unfortunately, the problem of alienation makes even the limited version of Kant's claim a bit more vague than it initially appears. It is not clear that citizens of liberal regimes have enough information actually to decide whether to consent or not. Thus, it is not clear that the US went to war as a fully "liberal" state in which enlightened citizens actually consented. Citizen consent is based, for the most part, upon what the government and the media tell them. And, for the most part, citizens want to believe what they are told. The propaganda machine works overtime to manufacture consent during wartime. This is not what Kant had in mind. In order to stimulate democratic deliberation and critical thinking about war, information is needed; but the government and the media often prevent citizens from fully knowing everything they would need to know to fully deliberate on the question.

The conclusion of the present chapter is that, since we do not have enough information, we should resist war. One might object that since our military and civilian leaders know more than we do, we should trust them; but resistance to power is healthy for a liberal regime. The American system was founded in defense of the right to dissent. Thus it is patriotic to question and resist. However, the real question is why we should not trust our leaders. The answer lies in the history of militarism. History shows that those in power and those who fight wars are not as much interested in the question of justice in war as they are interested in victory and power. Those in power deliberately use rhetoric and propaganda to manufacture consent. These reasons alone are sufficient grounds to question military power. Moreover, the very practice of dissent is crucial in wartime. Both morality and the truth tend to suffer under war. The practical pacifist dissenter reminds his leaders of the common interest in truth and morality. Although at some point we must trust our leaders to defend us, we must also demand that they honestly endeavor to provide for our defense within the limits established by the idea of justice.

CHAPTER 8. THE MYTH OF THE SUICIDE BOMBER: DESPAIR AND ESCHATOLOGY

> And Samson said, "Let me die with the Philistines." Then he bowed with all his might; and the house fell upon the lords and upon all the people that were in it. So the dead whom he slew at his death were more than those whom he had slain during his life.
> — *Judges*, 16:30

Suicide terrorism is not new. Samson is celebrated for bringing the walls of the Philistine hall crashing down, killing himself and some 3,000 Philistines. This story has been repeated for millennia and continues to be taught in American Sunday schools; but we fail to notice that this is an act of suicide terrorism. The biblical text tells us that the 3,000 victims included both women and children, and shows that Samson's motive was vengeance against those who had abused him. Moreover, the biblical text appears to celebrate Samson's deed. Before this bloody climax, Samson has killed thousands of other Philistines; and when this killing is done, Samson's prowess is described by claiming that "the spirit of the Lord came upon him." His final act of destruction is preceded by a prayer: "O Lord God, remember me, I pray thee, and strengthen me, I pray thee, only this once, O God, that I may be avenged upon the Philistines for one of my two eyes." Samson's motive is vengeance fueled by faith that the Philistines are evil enemies who should all die. Samson's vengeance makes no discrimination among its victims and he is not afraid to destroy himself in the process of exacting his revenge.

Samson's state of mind must have been similar to that of modern suicide bombers, who are motivated by hatred and faith to destroy themselves and their enemies. Analyses of the state of mind of Palestinian suicide bombers, for example, clearly link violence to a kind of religious elevation. An interview with a failed suicide-bomber reveals this: "By pressing the detonator, you can immediately open the door to Paradise... We were floating, swimming, in the feeling that we were about to enter eternity. We had no doubts. We made an oath on the Koran, in the presence of Allah — a pledge not to waver."[261] What is left out in this account of ecstatic religious devotion, of course, is the fact that it occurs within the context of hatred and indiscriminate violence. Just like Samson, the suicide bomber wants to kill as many of his enemies as possible out of hatred and vengeance. And like Samson, this violence is connected with religious belief. It is obvious, however, that this sort of hatred and revenge go beyond the limits of morality and of a morally acceptable religion. Some violence in pursuit of justice might, on rare and tragic occasions, be justifiable. But indiscriminate violence motivated by hatred can never be morally acceptable.

The present chapter seeks to understand the peculiar evil that is found in recent outbreaks of terrorism. Our tendency to over-generalize in such cases serves, in part, to keep us ignorant. It is obvious that the terrorism of Al-Qaeda or Hamas is not the same as the terrorism of Timothy McVeigh, the Unabomber, or Eric Rudolph; yet politicians favor gross generalizations. After September 11, President Bush named Iran, Iraq, and North Korea as the "Axis of Evil" and linked these nations to the war on terrorism, despite the differences among them. This misunderstanding was fostered and used to help drum up support for the invasion of Iraq. Political language is full of convenient abbreviations which confuse critical thinking. Indeed, this process of abbreviation and generalization underlies the process that results in hatred toward groups and indiscriminate violence toward members of these groups.

One could go too far in the opposite direction and claim that terrorists are beyond comprehension by any single idea. Yet, there is something in common in what terrorists do that is evil — there is some "family resemblance" characteristic. This is why it makes sense to call these people terrorists and to condemn them for their terrorism. Still, critical thinking about the evil of terrorism can be stymied when we view the terrorist is an "Other" who must be

---

261. Nasra Hassan, "An Arsenal of Believers: Talking to the 'Human Bombs.'" *The New Yorker*, November 11, 2001.

eliminated, while ignoring our own tendency toward terrorism. It is too easy to focus on a caricature of the terrorist as a mad suicide bomber motivated by an evil religion or irrational patriotism, while failing to be self-critical of our own ideologies and our own uses of unjustified violence. For this reason, the prima facie pacifism described in this book demands a more honest and self-critical view. The position of practical pacifism holds that all uses of violence are under suspicion until they are justified. Those whom we will eventually call "terrorists" (including, potentially, ourselves) are those who have failed to pass the test of justification.

ESCHATOLOGICAL HATRED AND SUICIDE BOMBERS

Despite this warning, the present chapter will deal in generalizations. It is useful to identify points in common among terrorists, even while recognizing that there are individual differences underlying these generalizations. I will focus on two themes: hatred and eschatological belief. Most terrorists — not only al-Qaeda but also domestic terrorists — are motivated by hatred and by eschatological faith. Hatred and eschatological faith can be linked because both grow out of a certain lack of philosophical self-consciousness. The philosophical perspective I have in mind maintains that ethics is primary and that religion and politics must conform to ethics. This is a "humanistic" orientation, which has been championed by philosophers since the time of Socrates and Plato, who maintained that we should not believe stories that have the gods doing or sanctioning evil things.

The point is not to argue against religion in general or any religion in particular. Indeed, a bit of study indicates that all religions have multiple interpretations and diverse practitioners, so one should avoid generalization. The goal, then, is to seek to understand the dangers of a hatred that is combined with eschatological faith, as it occurs in specific circumstances. When combined with eschatological faith, hatred becomes intractable; when combined with hatred, eschatological faith becomes destructive. This consideration of "eschatological hatred" is important for practical pacifism for two reasons: first, because we are all susceptible to it; and second, because eschatological hatred might mark the limit of nonviolent action.

Eschatological hatred forms a closed system. It might be the case that such a closed system can only be responded to with force. However, we must understand eschatological hatred if we are to avoid becoming the evil we would fight. In understanding eschatological hatred we may be able to imagine nonviolent ways of combating it; and if we understand the way in which eschatological hatred works, we may be able to see it in ourselves and thus stop our own tendency to become terroristic.

The idea that all terrorists are suicidal maniacs and "mad bombers" prevents us from fully comprehending the nature of terrorism while also justifying a vigorous campaign against them. The myth of the mad bomber allows us to conveniently forget that our own use of military force can become terroristic; we do not view our pilots and soldiers as "mad bombers" when they kill innocents. This is not to say that our pilots and soldiers are terrorists. They would be so only if they deliberately targeted the innocents they kill, which, we hope, they do not. But we must recall that the supporters of those we call terrorists do not view the agents they support as "madmen." Indeed, they use the language of martyrdom — however perversely — to describe those we condemn. The difficulty here is that humans tend to view things from the limited perspective of self-interest. We tend to view Samson as a hero and not as a terrorist because we identify with him. As Noam Chomsky has routinely pointed out, we do not pay attention to the terrorism that we ourselves commit.[262] Our own use of violence is thus beyond reproach, while the violence of the "other" is viewed as being obviously evil or insane.

Chomsky's critique is an important reminder of the tendency to lack self-consciousness; but there clearly is a difference between the violence of al-Qaeda and the violence of American bombers. This difference is one of intention. This intentional difference marks the difference between what one might call the "pure" terrorism of al-Qaeda and what one hopes is the "unintentional" terrorism of the US military. Apparently, the al-Qaeda terrorist's intention is to kill as many Americans (or our allies) as possible; this intention is motivated by hatred. It is usually hatred that motivates someone to destroy his own life in pursuit of his enemy. Even though hatred can be caused by a number of factors — including poverty, despair, ignorance, and resentment — hatred is the passion to

262. For example, Noam Chomsky, *Power and Terror* (New York: Seven Stories Press, 2003). This lack of self-consciousness includes a lack of data, which would quantify the casualties (whether military or civilian) caused by "counter-terrorism" and the "war on terrorism." In raw numbers, the war in Iraq killed more "innocents" than the September 11th atrocity. The "body count" as compiled at http://www.iraqbodycount.net/ is somewhere around 4,000 civilians (as of May, 2003). This number does not include military dead, for which there is no estimate.

destroy the other, a passion that can be so strong that it is willing to sacrifice itself in order to accomplish its end.

Of course, it is possible that the American people and the American military are motivated by hatred in their prosecution of the war on terrorism. If so, then we should be critical of our war on terrorism and should recognize its tendency to become terroristic. A just war should not be motivated by hatred. Rather, it should be motivated by the pursuit of justice; and it might even be motivated by love and compassion.[263] It is quite possible that military power and militaristic nations easily risk falling into hatred. Militarism should be condemned for this tendency to obsess over and demonize enemies. Military force that would be justifiable should not be motivated by hatred. Violence motivated by hatred is evil because it leads to the goal of indiscriminately killing as many members of the enemy group as possible (whether soldiers or civilians) merely for the sake of killing them.

The suicide bomber has been presented as a metaphor for chaos and unstoppable evil. We have learned to be afraid of the idea of a terrorist strapping on a belt full of explosives and detonating himself (our image is usually male) in a crowded street. September 11 merely showed us another means that the suicidal terrorist could use to inflict civilian casualties. The suicide bomber is not stoppable by the ordinary means employed by law enforcement. The hatred and eschatological faith of the suicide bomber makes him immune to normal deterrent strategies. A bomber who is willing to die is not easy to deter.[264]

Since suicide terrorism cannot be deterred by the normal means of law enforcement, the suicide bomber provides us with the image of a sort of ultimate power of resistance against the forces of stability and order, which is why he is

---

263. The claim that just war is motivated by love is made by Paul Ramsey, *The Just War* (New York: Charles Scribner's Sons, 1968).

264. A pre-September 11th discussion of "Suicide Terrorism" by *Jane's Intelligence Review* makes this clear. "The traditional concept of security is based on deterrence, where the terrorist is either killed or captured. The success of a suicide terrorist operation is dependent on the death of the terrorist. The suicide terrorist is not worried about capture, interrogation (including torture), trial, imprisonment and the accompanying humiliation. Furthermore, in suicide attacks, there is no need to provide an escape route, or for the extraction of the attacker/attacking force. The group does not have to concern itself with developing an escape plan, often the most difficult phase of an operation. Therefore, a suicide terrorist could enter a high security zone and accomplish his/her mission without worrying about escape or evasion. The certain death of the attacker enables the group to undertake high quality operations while protecting the organisation and its cadres. As every prisoner has a point of breaking under psychological or physical pressure, the certain death of the attacker or attackers prevent the captor extracting information" ("Suicide Terrorism: A Global Threat" *Jane's Intelligence Review*, 20 October, 2000).

so frightening. This resistance can either appear to be a noble act of self-sacrifice against a totalitarian enemy — the usual interpretation of those who value the "martyrs" who make the ultimate sacrifice — or it can appear to be a deranged act of nihilism aimed only at destruction — the usual interpretation of those who brand terrorists as evil. The truth of terrorism is probably somewhere in between. This is not meant to downplay the evil of terrorism; however, we should consider the possibility that terrorism is not merely the result of nihilistic insanity. In other words, we would have to look beyond the "insanity" of terrorism in order to fully understand why it is wrong. Eschatological hatred is morally and epistemologically wrong, but this does not necessarily mean that it is insane. The suicide bomber is not necessarily an anti-social or sadistic psychopath who wants to kill everyone for the sake of killing. Rather, he has succumbed to the tendency to move from ordinary anger and outrage toward hatred.

It could be argued, of course, that hatred is always pathological. This is the approach taken by psychologist Willard Gaylin, who defines hatred as follows: "a sustained emotion of rage that occupies an individual through much of his life, allowing him to feel delight in observing or inflicting suffering on the hated one. It is always obsessive and almost always irrational."[265] The psycho-pathological component of hatred is found in its obsessive nature. The pathological hater is consumed by hatred of his enemy and will go to great lengths to ensure that his enemy is defeated. To this extent hatred is like any other obsession. The psyche of the hater is obsessively linked to the object hated in the same way that the psyche of the lover is obsessively linked to the object of love. While lovers want to see their loved one thrive, haters want to see the hated enemy suffer. Like love, however, hatred can be more or less rational and more or less pathological. Criteria for distinguishing pathological hatred from non-pathological hatred can be found in morality and epistemology. Pathological hatred is an obsession that focuses on causing the enemy to suffer despite moral and epistemological limits. The basic moral limit is one of desert. Bad deeds deserve to be punished. But the hater wants to punish the enemy beyond the limits of desert. Similarly, human relationships must be based upon knowledge. It makes sense to claim that you do not like someone whom you know fairly well; but it is irrational to say that you hate someone whom you have never met. What, after all, would be the

---

265. Willard Gaylin, *Hatred: The Psychological Descent into Violence* (New York: Public Affairs, 2003), 34.

ground for your judgment about the need to destroy the enemy, if you didn't really know anything about the enemy? Hatred of the sort that mobilizes terrorists is aimed at enemies that are only vaguely known. This can be seen in the fact that terrorists are willing to kill indiscriminately. The individuals killed are not considered as individuals at all; rather they are viewed as representatives of a group to be exterminated. The hatred of the terrorist can thus be quite "cold": it can be calm and deliberate, which is why it is so appalling. To kill in this "cold-blooded" way is pathological because the hatred of the enemy that inspires the killing is part of a closed worldview that does not bother to consider the individual person who is taken as a representative of the hated group. Such hatred can usually be traced to propaganda and ideological manipulation. Ideological propaganda deals in generalizations and can use these to create hatred. But this hatred is irrational because it is based upon a lack of knowledge. The hope is that education and critical thinking can begin to cure this.

Hatred is linked to normal emotions such as fear and rage, the basic instincts that make up the "flight or fight" response. Fear prepares us to run; rage prepares us to fight. It makes sense to run away from something that is immediately threatening: this response is a survival mechanism. Likewise, rage and the instinct to fight — violence in self defense — are sometimes appropriate, too. But that reaction easily slides into a kind of hatred it is both ideational and ideological, and that focuses on long-term pursuit and extermination of the enemy. Sometimes this is rational and morally acceptable: there are some evil persons whom we perhaps ought to hate. But often hatred exceeds the limits that are established by the pursuit of justice; and one of the questions we need to ask is: Whose perspective is the right one in defining evil?

Hatred is easily linked to eschatological thinking. Human judgments about the course of history are usually based upon little evidence and a lot of faith. Hatred of the enemy is often part of the eschatological scheme, if the enemy is thought to be preventing the completion of the eschatological story. Although this obviously happens in religious mythology, it also happens in ordinary life. One can be consumed with hatred for another who is thought to be preventing the completion of one's own life plans.

One explanation of hatred is that it is a result of impotence. Haters lack the capacity either to express their rage or to escape from unpleasant circumstances. Thus, in a classic Freudian process of symptom formation, these repressed drives manifest themselves as ideational disturbances. The feeling of impotence is thought to be the result of something that the enemy is doing. In ordinary life, we can come to hate those who seem to stand in the way of our plans. In the eschatological context, we can come to hate those groups who we suppose are preventing the completion of God's plan. The violence that results from hatred can seem rational, from this perspective, if it is understood as aiming at destroying the thing which is causing our impotence. If cultural and political manipulation are also taken into account, we can begin to see how hatred could be created and reinforced for political purposes: the enemy is supposed to threaten our power and satisfaction and so must be destroyed. This points us toward the moral problem of political and eschatological hatred: it tends to demonize hated groups and turn them into evil enemies to be eradicated. Such demonization of the enemy is immoral because it fails to take up the question of desert by looking at individuals within the group. It is often based upon a lack of knowledge about the enemy. And it is furthermore often based upon a lack of self-consciousness. Often the impotence and anxiety one feels is a result of psychological problems and is not, in fact, caused by the enemy we hate.

If we view terrorism as an act of insanity or illness, then it can look like a force of nature, which is somewhat unpredictable and totally unpreventable.[266] We can harden targets to make them less vulnerable but, if suicide terrorists are insane, then there is no stopping them. The irony of the idea of the insane suicidal terrorist is that this very characterization serves to further the purpose of terrorism, which is, after all, to terrorize. We are afraid of suicide terrorism because the mad bomber is, in a sense, unstoppable. At the very least, the madness of the terrorist is — for those of us committed to life, order, stability, democracy, and peace — an incomprehensible illness that must be eradicated. Thus we wring our hands, cringe in fear, and long for a "final solution" such as the war on terrorism, which would remove this plague from the earth. There is no negotiating with terrorists because in their madness, terrorists make it clear that is "us or them": we either kill them or they kill us. This dualistic way of thinking helps explain the rhetoric of the Bush administration, which soon after September 11 said, "either you are with us or you are against us." Such an approach serves only to exacerbate violence on both sides. The approach of practical pacifism is to resist violence unless it is necessary. This means that we must seek means other than violence to deal with terrorism. One way of beginning to imagine other means is to resist the dualistic language and vilifying imagery of the mad bomber. More importantly, we must mobilize humanistic

---

266. Richard Rorty, "Fighting Terrorism with Democracy" in *The Nation*, October 21, 2002

arguments against the eschatological beliefs and irrational hatred that ground terrorism. This critique is not only directed at the other — at the Islamic suicide bomber — it is also directed back home. We should be on guard against eschatological hatred that can occasionally be found in home-grown American terrorists and in the terroristic responses to terrorism that might be found in the very idea of a "war on terror."

SUICIDE, MARTYRDOM, AND SCAPEGOATING

We — that is, Westerner liberals — like to think that suicidal terrorism develops only in exotic non-Western (i.e., Islamic) societies; as if we do not practice, advocate, or support either terrorism or martyrdom. We tend to forget that Jesus and many early Christians were martyrs. We tend to forget the incomprehensible self-sacrifice of the Jews at Masada. We tend to forget the words of the great American martyr, Nathan Hale, who valiantly proclaimed that he regretted that he had only one life to give for his country. We also tend to forget that suicide attacks can form a standard part of war. The Japanese kamikaze pilots are one well-known example, although of course the kamikaze is another example of a non-Western religious/political ideal. Closer to home, those soldiers who launched themselves in human waves during the trench warfare of the First World War can also be understood as suicidal. Likewise, resistance fighters during the Second World War were occasionally willing to sacrifice their own lives to resist the Nazi regime. We tend not to consider these examples as forms of suicidal terrorism, either because they are part of "normal" military operations or because they are for a "good" cause, such as the defeat of Nazism.

The point is not necessarily to put Hale and the French Underground in the same camp as contemporary suicide terrorists such as Mohammed Atta. Rather, it is to indicate that the notion of self-sacrifice for a higher cause is pervasive even in Western culture. Two important distinctions must be made, however. We must distinguish among the causes for which self-sacrifice occurs; and we must distinguish among the means of self-sacrifice. Suicidal terrorists could be seen as "evil" either because their cause is not just or because their means are not just. But the question of just cause becomes immediately quite muddy when we realize that some terrorists conceive of themselves as freedom fighters who are fighting to end oppression. The question of means is more precise. Suicide bombers kill "innocent" people. Although the question of who is "innocent" is also a complex one, it seems safe to say that bombers who kill children kill innocent victims. The suicide bomber is not "evil" because he is a martyr who sacrifices himself for a cause. Rather, he is seen as "evil" because he kills civilian by-standers as part of his martyrdom. The "evil" of suicide terrorism is not its suicidal component but its homicidal intent. The reason for pointing this out is to indicate that, although the suicide bomber provides an interesting icon on which to focus our outrage, this outrage should be directed with equal vehemence against all — including our own forces — who kill innocents for a supposedly higher purpose.

Sinister forms of suicidal "terror" do occur in America. If we understand terrorism to mean murder and violence used against random innocents, then the acts of Dylan Klebold and Eric Harris, the Columbine, Colorado shooters are American suicide terrorists. One might go so far as to claim that every time there is a murder-suicide, this represents a form of suicide terrorism. One recent study by the Violence Policy Center estimated that in 2001 there were 1,324 murder-suicide deaths.[267] This appears to support the estimate made by epidemiologists that there are between 1,000 and 1,500 murder-suicides per year in the US One might further expand this discussion by bringing in the issue of so-called "suicide by cop," in which people rampage with weapons fully expecting to be killed by the police response.[268]

The reason we tend to ignore these varieties of violence in discussions of terrorism and the war on terrorism is that such violence appears to be unpolitical. Suicide by cop and murder-suicide are understood as the actions of deranged individuals without a larger ideological (political or religious) agenda. The terrorism of suicide bombers is organized and politically motivated. But this means that suicidal terror bombers are not necessarily either insane or nihilistic, as Scott Atran has shown in his recent psycho-social analysis of suicide bombers.[269] Rather, suicide bombers are often young men who are educated about both religion and politics and who view their action as a matter of service

---

267. "American Roulette: The Untold Story of Murder-Suicide in the United States" (Violence Policy Center, 2002), available on-line: http://www.vpc.org/studies/amercont.htm.

268. For a discussion, see Daniel B. Kennedy et al., "Suicide by Cop," *FBI Law Enforcement Bulletin* 1998 http://www.forensiccriminology.com/Suicidebycop.pdf.

269. Scott Atran, "Genesis of Suicide Terrorism," *Science* (7 March 2004), 299: 1534-1539. For a narrative description of the life and beliefs of suicide bombers, see Nasra Hassan, "An Arsenal of Believers," *The New Yorker*, November 19, 2001.

to their community and who understand their hatred as defensible from within a certain political or religious purview.

The service of such a "martyr" to his community only makes sense in a larger religious or political context, in which the sacrifice is justified. Islam, like Christianity, includes an idea of martyrdom, or *shahadat*. This idea is tied to the notion of *jihad* or just war. Although the Islamic religious context is somewhat different from the Christian context (as we shall see below), it is not so different as to be incomprehensible. The *shahid* or martyr is supposed to die for a good cause governed by principles that justify both the violence committed by the martyr and the martyr's own death. This is not nihilistic violence of the sort of Klebold and Harris. However, it is the sort of violence that has been justified by some who operate within the Western tradition. Timothy McVeigh thought that his violence was justified by a form of American patriotism; David Koresh though that his violence was justified by a Christian revelation; Eric Rudolph thought that his violence was justified by his views on abortion and homosexuality; and Ted Kaczynski thought his violence was justified by his ecological analysis of contemporary social life.[270]

The discourse of justification helps to show that the suicide bomber may not be an ordinary psychopath. Rather, the suicide bomber views himself as a warrior utilizing means that are justified by the context of his own tradition of warfare. It is perhaps too convenient for us to view the suicide bomber as a madman because we can then safely ignore suicidal "missions" that our own forces engage in, while also ignoring the terroristic destruction of civilian life that is caused by our weapons. From most people's perspective, the suicide bomber is immoral. And it is true that the suicide bomber is often motivated by a politicized form of eschatological hate. But it is also true that his immorality is part of the larger immorality of warfare in general and the practice of demonizing and hating enemies that is a standard practice in motivating soldiers to fight. The immorality of the suicide bomber is not a form of psychopathic madness. Rather, it is part of the larger madness of warfare and the insanity of seeking to justify the slaughter of innocents in the name of a higher power, whether this higher power is religious or political.

The US's "war on terror" is a geo-political struggle that is focused on pacifying certain rogue nations. It is not about ending violence in all its forms.

---

270. See Adam L. Silverman, "Just War, Jihad, and Terrorism: A Comparison of Western and Islamic Norms for the Use of Political Violence," *Journal of Church and State.*

But our tendency to dwell on international terrorism and the mythic form of the crazed suicide bomber while ignoring the fact that our fellow citizens kill each other and kill themselves tells us something about the way in which ideology and propaganda function in our society. We have been sold the war on terrorism, along with its geo-political implications, when possibly a greater threat — at least in terms of numbers of dead — can be found in our ordinary home-grown variety of suicidal murderers.

Although the risks posed by politically or religiously motivated terrorists are real and must be dealt with, one still wonders whether our fears are justified or whether the fear of terrorism has been "manufactured" by the political and media establishments who make up what Hermann and O'Sullivan call "the terrorism industry."[271]

One way of approaching this problem is to recognize that, in post-modern language, terrorists are "the Other." This label is convenient, as it allows us to ignore the fact that all cultures and religions can foster hatred and all can become terroristic, even including Western Christianity.[272] It is important to see through the simple ideology that places "them" against "us" in a perspective which sees current events as "clash of civilizations," as Samuel Huntington does. Huntington's analysis of Islam shows that there are various factors in Islamic violence, including a tendency toward militarism, lack of central political power, and proximity to non-Muslim groups.[273] However, Huntington also recognizes one factor that is ideological on his part: the idea of "indigestibility," by which he means the unwillingness of Muslims to assimilate and adapt to non-Islamic culture. Huntington states with regard to this problem: "Even more than Christianity, Islam is an absolutist faith."[274] Such an overstatement suffers from

271. Edward S. Hermann and Gerry O'Sullivan, *The Terrorism Industry: The Experts and Institutions that Shape Our View of Terror* (New York: Pantheon Books, 1989). The idea of the "manufacture" of terrorism parallels the view of Hermann and Noam Chomsky in their *Manufacturing Consent: the Political Economy of the Mass Media* (New York: Pantheon Books, 1988).

272. On rightwing Christian terrorism and eschatology, see Jonathan R. White, "Political Eschatology: A Theology of Antigovernment Extremism" in *American Behavioral Scientist*, 44: 6 (February 2001), 937-956. For a discussion of another form of American and Christian violence as found in the violence of American Mormonism see John Krakauer in *Under the Banner of Heaven* (New York: Doubleday, 2003). On Islamic terrorism, see essays by Lewis, Kedourie, and Vatikiotis in Benjamin Netanyahu, *Terrorism: How the West Can Win* (New York: Farrar, Straus, Giroux, 1986). For a more general discussion of the connection between religion and terrorism that also discusses Jewish terrorism, the Japanese Aum cult, and others, see Bruce Hoffman, *Inside Terrorism* (New York: Columbia, 1998), Chapter 4.

273. Samuel Huntington, *The Clash of Civilizations* (New York: Simon and Schuster, 1996), Chapter 10.

its own form of absolutism. Western conceptions of Islamic indigestibility and the idea of a clash of civilizations conveniently serve the interests of Western power. We must be careful of those who claim that "we" are the good guys, tolerant and amiable, while "they" are not. Such claims are often made in order to justify the expansion of Western power. This is not to say that American ideals are not good. Indeed, liberal humanism may be the best approach for human beings. Rather, liberal humanist ideals often can be used as cover for more Machiavellian interests. A dichotomizing view, which focuses on "our goodness" vs. "their evil," allows "us" easily to condemn "them" without ever thinking about our own misdeeds, responsibility, and tendency toward absolutism.

There are important conceptual problems within our understanding of terrorism and our ideas about suicide bombers. A structural analysis of this might follow someone like Rene Girard, who would point to the process of scapegoating and the sacrificial nature of violence.[275] Girard goes so far as to understand violence as a process of mimesis and sado-masochism: we desire what the other desires (and vice versa), and what we ultimately desire is violence (or power over the other). From this ultimately Hegelian point of view, our current dichotomizing view, which pits the insane terrorist against the disciplined war on terror, is another example of the classic clash between brothers since Cain killed Abel and since Bacchus destroyed Pentheus. As the struggle for recognition becomes violent, we anathematize the other over whom we want total control. At the same time, the other grasps at whatever means is available to him in order, in one last fiery moment of violence, to inflict as much harm as possible. This expresses the nature of hatred: the desire to cause the enemy to suffer no matter what the consequences. Girard's conclusion is that a religious sacrifice — a surrogate victim, i.e., the scapegoat — is necessary in order to achieve peace and unanimity: hatred and violence need to be deflected onto a fetish object. But without a shared object — as occurs in a clash between religions — there can be no mediation or displacement of violence. And the result is that violence and hatred will breed and grow. The war on terror can become terroristic if it is not deflected by a fetish object that we share with our opponents. Now, in the West, the fetish object is money. We might think, then, that we could buy terrorists off with money. But money may not function in this

---

274. Huntington, *Clash of Civilizations*, 264.

275. Girard, *Violence and the Sacred* (Baltimore: Johns Hopkins University Press, 1977).

way for members of some religious sects. Thus the only choice might be to fight terrorism with more terrorism.

Of course, practical pacifism rejects such a view. It begins from a humanistic belief that education about the nature of violence, about the nature of hatred, and about the nature of religious eschatology can produce an end to violence. If this fails, either because the terrorist's hatred is so intense or because the terrorist is not concerned with the humanistic philosophical critique of hatred and eschatology, then perhaps some violence will be necessary. Nonetheless, this violence should be used with restraint and should be motivated by justice rather than hatred.

Terrorism and Eschatology

The point is not to advocate a post-modern type of relativism, nor to say, "we all are terrorists," although terrorism is a means that has been utilized by all cultures, including our own, especially when eschatological hatred has flourished. We must recognize this if we are to find common human resources to argue against terrorism in all of its manifestations; but not all violence is terroristic and some violence, limited by the just war theory, may be justified as a response to terrorism. Still, we must be self-critical in order to avoid becoming terroristic ourselves. The religious, cultural, and political dichotomizing that grounds some recent discussions of terrorism is dangerous when it leads to a justification of terror tactics used in response to terrorism. In order to argue in general against those less careful thinkers who might advocate terror tactics in response to terrorism, one must look for what different cultures of terrorism have in common. To be honest, one must admit that there are probably several common themes among terrorists. One that is important and easily argued against is the eschatological component.

Most terrorism occurs within the context of faith in some eschatological construct, especially when this construct also contains a story about an enemy who is to be hated. Terrorism of all varieties can be linked to what Bernard Yack has called "the longing for total revolution."[276] Those who are willing to employ terror tactics are willing to justify violent means by appealing to some end that transcends the values or ordinary life. This is the basic idea of eschatological

---

276. Bernard Yack, *The Longing for Total Revolution* (Princeton: Princeton University Press, 1986).

thinking, linked to what J.L. Talmon has called "political messianism" and the "religion of revolution."[277] We saw this in a previous chapter in Walzer's and Rawls' willingness to allow terroristic means in pursuit of the historic goal of defending liberalism during a supreme emergency. Indeed, something like the idea of a supreme emergency is invoked by Islamic scholars who seek to justify martyrdom and suicide bombing, such as when the Islamic way of life is supposed to be at risk.[278] When this idea is applied to the case of Palestine, for example, the Palestinian suicide bomber might be seen as responding to a supreme emergency in the life of the Palestinian people. Recall, however, that in the previous discussion I argued against Walzer and Rawls. The same arguments apply to those who would argue for a supreme emergency in the case of an embattled Islamic people, namely that finite human beings lack certainty when it comes to a declaration that the present case is a supreme emergency.

Violence in the name of some transcendent goal will end only when human beings remember their epistemological limits and are thus taught to see the limits of eschatological beliefs, whether these beliefs are religious or more overtly political. Of course, one must be careful not to smudge together different varieties of thought. The idea of eschatology is primarily a religious idea, founded within a cosmological totality that includes a vision of the end of time.[279] Some varieties of terrorism can be understood in this strictly religious sense: the violence in the Middle East is at least partially caught up in ideas about the eschatological significance of power over the holy land and over the center of religious power — Jerusalem.

Most religious mythologies are based upon some account of the beginning and end of time.[280] Contemporary religious fundamentalisms are usually infused

---

277. J.L. Talmon, *Political Messianism: The Romantic Phase* (New York: Praeger, 1960).

278. Raphael Israeli, "Manual of Islamic Fundamentalist Terrorism," *Journal of Terrorism and Political Violence* 14: 4 (Winter 2002), especially pp. 33-34. Israeli provides a reading of the text *Qira'a fi fiqh al-Shahada* ("Readings in Islamic Martyrology"). Also see the discussion of this perspective in Islamic Fundamentalism in Paul Berman, *Terror and Liberalism*.

279. I have critiqued eschatological thinking from another direction in "Toward an Ethics of Time: Eschatology and its Discontents," in *Philosophy in the Contemporary World*, 7: 2-3 (Summer-Fall 2000), 33-41. Sources for this discussion include Jürgen Moltmann, *Theology of Hope* (trans. Leitch, Great Britain: Robert Cunningham and sons, 1967) and Nicolas Berdyaev, *The Beginning and the End* (London: Geoffrey Bles, 1952).

280. For discussions of eschatology in religious myth, see: Mircea Eliade, *Cosmos and History: The Myth of the Eternal Return* (New York: Harper and Row, 1959); Mircea Eliade, *Myth and Reality* (New York: Harper and Row, 1963); Norman Cohn, *Cosmos, Chaos, and the World to Come* (New Haven: Yale Nota Bene Books, 2001); also Henri Frankfort, *Kingship and the Gods* (Chicago: University of Chicago Press, 1978).

with an explicit eschatological component.[281] The human quest to find meaning in time is both natural and wonderful. We need to find meaning in time. However, if one undertakes this search for meaning in an uncritical fashion, then the process can give rise to terrible results. This happens when the ideas of mythic time identify enemies to be hated while making dogmatic demands about the religious need to destroy these enemies.

Implicit in eschatology is an idea of responsibility in time. Giorgio Agamben provides an interesting analysis of what he calls "messianic time." For Agamben, messianic time — for Christians, the time after the resurrection of Christ — is a time that occurs in the presence of the messiah, whose death and resurrection provide a rupture in ordinary time that marks the transition to messianic time. It is "the time it takes us to bring time to an end."[282] For those who understand the present time in this way, the presence of the messiah at each and every moment of time means that we are responsible in each moment to do God's will. It is this which creates the urgency with which the messianic believer is compelled to accomplish God's will. Most religious and mythic traditions share a concern for the end of time and this concern is meant as a guide for ethical and spiritual practice. According to Christian dogma, the *eschaton* of history is re-union with God in which God will judge our present deeds. Although the descriptions of the end of time in the book of *Revelation* are replete with horrors and death and destruction, the point of this whole story is the time that comes after the destruction: the time of peace that will prevail for the faithful. Some rightwing Christian fundamentalists have perverted and politicized this story such that the faithful are supposed to help carry out the process of destruction.[283]

---

281. As Marty and Appleby conclude in their study of religious fundamentalism: "Repudiating secular-scientific notions of progress and gradual historical evolution, for example, fundamentalists often see themselves as actors in an eschatological drama unfolding in the mind of God and directing the course of human history. Indeed, dramatic eschatologies shape fundamentalist identity and inform action in many, if not all, cases." [Martin E Marty and R. Scott Appleby, "Conclusion: An Interim Report on a Hypothetical Family" in Marty and Appleby, eds. *Fundamentalisms Observed* (Chicago: University of Chicago Press, 1991), volume 1, p. 819].

282. Giorgio Agamben, "The Time that is Left," *Epoché* (Fall 2002) 7: 1, p. 5.

283. White, "Political Eschatology," 947. For the connection with prophecy and violence see Krakauer, *Under the Banner of Heaven.*

THE ESCHATOLOGICAL SUSPENSION OF THE ETHICAL

Ironically, just as the eschatological perspective gives spiritual and ethical structure to the present moment, it can also lead to the subversion of ethical norms. At the end of time, most mythic traditions speak of a final battle between the forces of order and the forces of chaos. In this battle, ethical limits are suspended in order to ensure the victory of order. While this has links to the just war tradition's ideas about justified violence, the violence of the end of time is simply not constrained by the ethical norms that are supposed to guide us in time. With a nod to Kierkegaard, we may call this the "eschatological suspension of the ethical." In the eschatological context, the demands of ethics can be supervened by the higher demands of sacred history.

The gods themselves often override the ethical commandments. The flood story found in so many traditions provides a good example. In the Hebrew story, God floods the earth to destroy wickedness and create the world anew. In the Gilgamesh story of Mesopotamia, the god, Enlil, wipes out the human race because humans have become noisy and bothersome. In Greek mythology, it is Zeus who destroys mankind — except for Deucalion. According to Frankfort, the cosmogonic significance of these flood stories is to provide the mythic traditions with a sort of cosmological *tabula rasa* from which human history can emerge.[284] However, from the eschatological perspective, these stories provide a warning against the destructive power of the gods in their struggle against the forces of wickedness and chaos. Indeed, flood images return in stories about the apocalypse: the flood is seen to represent the origin and end of history. In *Revelation*, this flood becomes a lake of fire into which the wicked dead, including Satan, are thrown. The lake of fire is thus the "second death" or the final end of those not worthy of eternal life.[285] In the cosmogonic flood stories the destructive power of the gods ignores all subtle ethical discriminations: the god destroys all.

The idea of destruction without discrimination is linked to the emotion of hatred: when hatred consumes us, we want to destroy, without care for making subtle discriminations about who really deserves to be destroyed. In the Samson story, this is called vengeance. In the Old Testament, vengeance is celebrated again and again. The 94th Psalm, for example, is a prayer which calls for the

---

284. Henri Frankfort, *Kingship and the Gods*, 233 and footnote note 6.
285. Revelation 20.

"God of vengeance" who is asked to come and destroy the wicked: "He will bring back on them their iniquity and wipe them out for their wickedness; the Lord our God will wipe them out."[286] Of course, it is the Old Testament God, the God of the Hebrews, who is the God of hatred and vengeance. In a recent article entitled, "The Virtue of Hate," Rabbi Meir Soloveichik discusses the Samson story and others and reaches the conclusion that, "while Judaism believes that forgiveness is often a virtue, hate can be virtuous when one is dealing with the frightfully wicked."[287] This claim is made to contrast Jewish hatred with Christian forgiveness. But the Christian approach still allows for hate. Paul says, "Let love be genuine; hate what is evil, hold fast to what is good." This implies that one might be justified in hating the wicked. But Paul goes further and says that we must not actively pursue this hatred. Vengeance belongs to God alone. Thus, Paul concludes, "Repay no one evil for evil." And, "Do not be overcome by evil, but overcome evil with good."[288] In the eschatological story of Christianity, there is the hope that only the wicked will be destroyed: God will preserve the good. But Paul's message is that this destruction is up to God: mere mortals should not take the final judgment into their own hands. Nonetheless, the Old Testament and the prophecies of *Revelation* give ample warning of the fact that indiscriminate death and destruction are not beyond the capacity of a wrathful God. And many Christians continue to view it as their task to actively work to destroy evil, hated enemies.[289]

Of course, what is needed is an ethical critique of eschatological hatred. The difficulty is that this humanistic and philosophical approach can appear to be anti-religious. Socrates, who mounted such a critique, was accused of atheism. We may side-step the question of atheism, however, in order to focus on the question of ethics. My basic premise is that God would not command us to hate; nor would he sanction indiscriminate killing. I hope that religious believers agree with me; and I think that the Christian texts, at least, support this view. The problem is, of course, that some religious believers interpret their scriptures differently. Humanists have always worried about this hermeneutical problem, and they have claimed that the perspective of ethics must provide the touchstone for interpreting scriptures. In the 19th century, for example, Ludwig

286. Psalms 94: 23.

287. Meir Soloveichik, "The Virtue of Hate" *First Things* 130 (Fall 2003), 42.

288. Romans 12: 9, 12:17, and 21.

289. See Jonathan R. White, "Political Eschatology: A Theology of Antigovernment Extremism" in *American Behavioral Scientist*, 44: 6 (February 2001), 937-956.

Feuerbach followed Kant in criticizing religion from an ethical point of view. He realized that for religious faith, love and hate were both means to be employed by faith. The problem for Feuerbach was that faith alone was insufficient to tell us when hate or love would be appropriate. "The love which is bound by faith is a narrow-hearted, false love, contradicting the idea of love, i.e., self-contradictory, — a love which has only a semblance of holiness, for it hides in itself the hatred that belongs to faith; it is only benevolent so long as faith is not injured."[290] Those who are willing to hate in the name of faith are those who admit that there could be something like an "eschatological suspension of the ethical."

Eschatological doctrine gives meaning to the present, so it is not surprising that adherents of eschatologies are willing to suspend ethical norms in the service of the god: preparing the end by assisting the god in his destructive plan. Recalling Kierkegaard might help explain the eschatological suspension of the ethical. In *Fear and Trembling*, Kierkegaard describes the "knight of faith" as personified in Abraham.[291] Abraham's faith is found in his willingness to violate ethical commandments in the service of the God. Thus the knight of faith suspends ethics teleologically: religious commitment to God is higher than ethical commitment. Kierkegaard's idea of the "teleological suspension of the ethical" proposes the religious end as higher than the ethical end: obedience to God is higher than obedience to the moral law. Eschatological suspension of the ethical proposes the same thing. Moreover, in the eschatological context, this suspension of ethics is linked to the final climactic battle of cosmos vs. chaos. Since this is the final moment of human history, occurring in the presence of God, ethical norms are no longer sufficient as guides for action. Rather, eschatological norms prevail. These norms, norms that are only "known" by faith, are contingent upon the revealed will of the god: the eschatological demands are known only to the faithful. In this way, Abraham appears to be a murderer from the perspective of the uninitiated; but from the perspective of faith, he is a "higher man," one who has suspended the ethical commandments for a higher purpose.[292]

Eschatological thinking can be even more intricately connected with violence and hatred. The final purpose or the culmination of time provides us

---

290. Ludwig Feuerbach, *The Essence of Christianity* (trans. George Eliot, New York: Harper Torch-books, 1957), 265.

291. Kierkegaard, *Fear and Trembling* (ed. and trans. by Hong and Hong, Princeton: Princeton University Press, 1983).

with a task that is more important than the ethical commandments and in which an orgy of violence will finally serve to end all violence. In this way, faith and eschatology demand that we go "beyond good and evil."[293] The implication is that it might be justifiable to suspend ethical thinking in the present moment, provided that this suspension is done out of faith, on the model of Abraham, at the moment of eschatological crisis. This can appear to be justified when we think that the eschatological story requires hatred toward and destruction of the devil and his evil followers. Willard Gaylin writes in his analysis of hatred that "hatred for the devil has always been one hallmark of love of God."[294] The ethical question is whether there are limits to what one might do both in pursuit of evil and out of love of God.

This discussion of Abraham is linked to the thinking of the September 11 terrorists. In a discussion of some documents discovered by the FBI in one of the hijackers' cars after the September 11 atrocity, Kanan Makiya and Hassan Mneimneh make this connection explicit.[295] The terrorists were instructed to put their faith in God and prepare themselves for death. The instructions state: "Forget and force yourself to forget that thing which is called World; the time for amusement is gone and the time of truth is upon us." This temporal theme is eschatological: now is the time of crisis at which the end of time will begin. Makiya and Mneimneh focus their analysis of this document on the "sense of doom" found in it and the idea of the activities of the terrorists as part of a larger "sacred drama." Finally, they translate the Arabic word *dhabaha*, which was used in this document, as "slaughter." The terrorists were to slaughter their victims in an act that is connected to the idea of the ritual sacrifice of sheep. The authors point out that this word is the same word used to speak of Abraham's intended slaughter of Isaac and his subsequent slaughter of the ram. The use of this word and others makes it clear that the terrorists were to put themselves in the frame

---

292. And violence is justified in the name of religion. Rene Girard has discussed this at length in his *Violence and the Sacred*. It is significant, as Girard has pointed out, that Abraham's violent intention is in fact consummated — not by killing Isaac, but by killing the ram provided by God. From this perspective religion only directs and controls violence; it does not eliminate it.

293. This ironic allusion to Nietzsche is connected, in Judeo-Christianity, back to the beginning of time. In Eden, the first historical event was the eating of the fruit of the tree of knowledge of good and evil. The end of time will be an analogue to this: at the end of time, we will again be beyond good and evil in our direct relationship with God.

294. Gaylin, *Hatred*, 226.

295. The following is based upon Hassan Mneimneh and Kanan Makiya, "Manual for a 'Raid'" in *New York Review of Books*, January 17, 2002. Mneimneh and Makiya also quote and translate portions of the Arabic document found in the terrorist's car.

of mind found in Abraham: willing to suspend all other concerns for the demands of faith. What makes the terrorists' murderous act of faith even more shocking is the fact that they were instructed to sacrifice themselves as martyrs in the frenzy of destruction. The authors correctly conclude, "the idea that martyrdom is a pure act of worship, pleasing to God, irrespective of God's specific command, is a terrifying new kind of nihilism."

Such a conclusion flows from an attempt both to downplay the idea of martyrdom as it is found in the West and to confuse the idea of martyrdom or *shahadat* that is found in Islam with the idea of jihad.[296] It is not martyrdom that is the problem; it is the willingness to slaughter innocents as part of one's martyrdom. The document discussed by Mneimneh and Makiya mentions the promise of a martyr's reward in paradise. What is evil is the idea that any God would reward those who kill innocents.

RELIGION AND POLITICS

There is an ongoing dispute among scholars about the nature of Islamic terrorism, focused on the question of whether it is a religious movement or a political movement. One interpretation, forcefully argued by Paul Berman, argues that it is best understood as an Islamic appropriation of Western totalitarianism, inspired by Marx, Nietzsche, Mussolini, Hitler, and Lenin.[297] This approach is interesting insofar as it offers a connection between Islamic terrorism and other forms of Western terrorism that can be justified by that "longing for total revolution" described by Bernard Yack. The link is, again, eschatological: some idea about the end of history that allows for, even demands, a suspension of ethical principles in action in the present.

It is clear that the Palestinian terrorists, for example, have political ends in mind, even when these ends are tied up with religious eschatology. Indeed, one of the reasons that the violence in the Middle East is so intractable is that religion and politics are mixed together, along with oppression and poverty. Even a cursory reading of the ideas that are offered in support of terrorism shows the volatile mixture of religion and politics. In the thinking of Hamas, for example, the land of Palestine is a holy land that must be defended. The Charter

---

296. See Adam L Silverman, "Just War, Jihad, and Terrorism."

297. Paul Berman, *Terror and Liberalism*. Also see Ladan Boroumand and Roya Boroumand, "Terror, Islam, and Democracy" in *Journal of Democracy* (April 2002), 13:2, 5-20.

of Hamas states explicitly, "The Islamic Resistance Movement believes that the land of Palestine is an Islamic Waqf [holy land] consecrated for future Moslem generations until Judgment Day."[298] Moreover, it is also not surprising that, in Israel, this dispute is linked to land and access to holy sites. Such an interest in access to land cannot be understood solely in Marxist terms as an interest in land as capital. Rather, this is a religious interest linked to eschatology; and this religious interest is also a political interest in autonomy, self-rule, and access to resources.

The Hamas Charter makes it clear that "nationalism" is also a form of religious identity. Thus the religious motif predominates. Religious eschatologies are sacred histories, focused upon the establishment and maintenance of order in the present within a cosmography that locates certain places on this earth as holy sites with important eschatological implications.[299] The temple mount in Jerusalem is the *axis mundi*, the sacred point at which divine cosmology and temporal history meet.[300] The sacred history of Muslims and Jews demands defense of such holy places and thus justifies the eschatological suspension of the ethical that occurs in religious violence and terrorism.

This can all be found in the much-disputed idea of jihad.[301] The Hamas Charter states, "There is no solution for the Palestinian question except through Jihad. Initiatives, proposals and international conferences are all a waste of time and vain endeavors."[302] And: "The day that enemies usurp part of Moslem land, Jihad becomes the individual duty of every Moslem."[303] As is well known, Osama bin Laden used similar language in his Fatwa of 1998 declaring war on Americans.[304] A careful reading of the Fatwa shows the linkage among religious, political, and economic reasons for the war on Americans. Bin Laden says, for example, "the United States has been occupying the lands of Islam in the holiest

---

298. Hamas Charter of 1988, Article 11 (http://www.mideastweb.org/hamas.htm). The word *waqf* means holy land (see Silverman, "Just War, Jihad, and Terrorism," 86).

299. Cf. Eliade on "The Symbolism of the Center" in *Cosmos and History: The Myth of the Eternal Return*, 12-17.

300. The Hamas Charter states (Article 34) that "Palestine is the navel of the globe and the crossroad of the continents."

301. For an example of the disputed nature of this word, see Daniel Pipes, "Jihad and the Professors," *Commentary* (November 2002), 114: 4, 17-21 and the Letters to the editor that replied to his essay in *Commentary*, (February 2003), 115: 2.

302. Hamas Charter, Article 13.

303. Hamas Charter, Article 15.

304. Available on-line at the International Policy Institute for Counter-Terrorism: http://www.ict.org.il/articles/fatwah.htm.

of places, the Arabian Peninsula, plundering its riches, dictating to its rulers, humiliating its people, terrorizing its neighbors, and turning its bases in the Peninsula into a spearhead through which to fight the neighboring Muslim peoples." These political, religious, and economic causes then lead to the claim that America has declared war on Islam. This in turn leads to the famous proclamation: "We — with God's help — call on every Muslim who believes in God and wishes to be rewarded to comply with God's order to kill the Americans and plunder their money wherever and whenever they find it." These arguments are interesting in that the notion of jihad occurs within a totalizing worldview which links religion and politics, which is why the notion of jihad has such a volatile mobilizing force. However, as many experts have noted, jihad is part of Islamic just war theory and it does not — in its standard interpretation — sanction the slaughter of innocents.[305]

Most forms of violence are stimulated by the idea of "longing" for completion or transcendence. This longing, when stymied, can become hatred. We long to end oppression, to establish justice, or to bring about the end of history. Following Kant, Bernard Yack defines longing as an empty wish to obtain that which we know it is impossible to attain.[306] Such longing produces anxiety and uneasiness that is translated into an urgency to act. Action guided by longing aims to revolutionize present conditions in order to create new conditions that would make possible the actualization of the object of desire. Yack focuses his discussion on the secular revolutions since the French revolution, revolutions which have focused on transforming institutions so as to actualize the human spirit. Some contemporary terrorists still operate in such a context. However, religious terrorists are even more firmly embedded in eschatological thinking and messianic longing.

One cannot reason with a person who is possessed by a messianic faith, a longing for total revolution, and an obsessive hatred for evil enemies. Indeed, one who argues for patience, tolerance, and peace will be viewed as an infidel or apostate who lacks the faith that is required to understand the need for a suspension of ethics.

Yack is correct when he says that we must distinguish the humanistic longing of modern secular thinkers from the longing of religious eschatology.

305. See Bernard Lewis, "License to Kill: Usama Bin Ladin's Declaration of Jihad" in *Foreign Affairs* (November/December 1998), 14-19

306. Yack, *Longing for Total Revolution*, 5; Yack draws upon Kant, *Anthropology from a Pragmatic Point of View*, 155.

Religious longing is connected to a view which places infinite responsibility on each and every moment. Secular longing is connected to a view of history that shows that humans have the power to shape institutions according to our ideals. It cannot be denied, of course, that secular political revolutions have slaughtered millions, especially in the 20th century; but these secular movements went wrong when they violated ethical ideals for political aspirations, just as religious movements go wrong when they violate ethical norms for religious ends. . Religious eschatology almost by definition subordinates ethics to religion, understanding ethical commandments as originating with God. As such, religious terrorism inspired by messianic eschatology may prove to be more intractable than secular political terrorism because the religious sentiment that gives rise to eschatological terrorism is opposed to a perspective which would place ethics higher than religion. .

The idea of an eschatological suspension of the ethical can be found both in terrorists and in those who wage war against terrorism. A war against terrorism can have the same sort of eschatological hope as that which motivates the terrorist against whom the war is waged. The present war on terrorism offers us a "crusade" against those who hate us, with the hope that this war can be a war to end terror. Unfortunately, many of those who are engaged in the war on terrorism do see it as a crusade in the religious sense. Consider the case of Lieutenant General William Boykin, a deputy undersecretary of defense, who in 2003 was in charge of hunting down Osama bin Laden and other terrorists. In October of that year, he became the subject of media attention when it was revealed that he was giving speeches at Christian churches in which he claimed that the US had God on our side in the fight against Satan.[307] This does not mean that General Boykin would advocate going beyond the limits of the just war theory or that he would condone hatred for all Muslims. But there is a risk of slipping toward eschatological hatred when war is conceived in religious terms. Although the Bush administration has carefully guarded the language of crusade so as not to provoke a memory of medieval eschatological battles, the idea of war as a crusade is not easily avoided.

The idea of a climactic battle of historical significance can also be articulated in non-religious terms. American wars in the 20th century were fought under the idea of making the world safe for democracy.[308] Since the First

---

307. See, for example, Richard T. Cooper, "General Casts War in Religious Terms," *Los Angeles Times*, October 16, 2003.

World War, we have been inspired by the idea that the next war would be the final war that would end war. The danger of this type of thinking is that it can lead to the idea that the end justifies the means. We might attempt to justify the horrors of war in light of its anticipated historical outcome. Ironically, such thinking also fuels the ideas of terrorists who fight against us: terrorists justify their actions by appealing to some idea about the historical end, which they think justifies their terror tactics.

CONCLUSION

Theories about justice in war diverge along eschatological lines. As Stanley Hauerwas has noted, "pacifists and just war thinkers draw on quite different assumptions about eschatology."[309] An analysis of eschatological thinking is important for the argument of practical pacifism, because the practical pacifist rejects the idea that finite fallible human beings have access to the story of the end of time. The primary temporal claim made by a practical pacifist is that we must focus modestly on the present. Present suffering is the key problem to be confronted. This idea is grounded in a fallibilist and humanistic epistemology. We can be more certain of present suffering than we can be of a hoped-for final end to suffering. We can be more certain of the outcome of working to alleviate suffering now than we can be of the outcome of larger historical struggles. The implication of this point of view is that we should avoid causing suffering in the present, if possible, when such suffering is obvious. This leads to pacifism, because it is fairly certain that resort to violence causes suffering. But such pacifism is not absolute. Sometimes, present suffering must be alleviated by the

---

308. Woodrow Wilson made this claim in his "War Message" to Congress in April of 1917: "The world must be made safe for democracy. Its peace must be planted upon the tested foundations of political liberty. We have no selfish ends to serve. We desire no conquest, no dominion. We seek no indemnities for ourselves, no material compensation for the sacrifices we shall freely make. We are but one of the champions of the rights of mankind. We shall be satisfied when those rights have been made as secure as the faith and the freedom of nations can make them" (From the World War I Document Archive: http://www.lib.byu.edu/-rdh/wwi/1917/wilswarm.html). President Bush has made similar claims in his speeches. In his address to the nation at the onset of the war in Iraq he said: "My fellow citizens, the dangers to our country and the world will be overcome. We will pass through this time of peril and carry on the work of peace. We will defend our freedom. We will bring freedom to others and we will prevail," (http://www.whitehouse.gov/news/releases/2003/03/iraq/20030319-17.html).

309. Stanley Hauerwas, *Should War Be Eliminated?* (Milwaukee, WI: Marquette University Press, 1984), 9.

violence of something like humanitarian intervention. We must weigh unknowns without resorting to vague ideas about the end of history. We must compare the suffering caused by intervention against the suffering alleviated by intervention. Such an analysis must remain focused in the present and avoid eschatological rhetoric. Rhetorical flourishes about eschatological goals take us away from concrete suffering and point us toward a transcendent mode of justification in which suffering in the present — even suffering that we cause — will be redeemed. This tendency to look beyond present suffering toward ultimate redemption is not only a problem of religious fundamentalism. It can be seen in liberal claims about making the world safe for democracy, just as it could be found in those who argued for the need for a communist revolution.

There is a good reason that warriors and terrorists think in eschatological terms: they confront the possible end of time in a very palpable sense. Death is the end of time; war and terrorism deal in death. The very idea of wartime represents the opposite of peacetime. Wartime is an alternative temporality in which ordinary values are skewed, in part because death looms as a real presence. Warriors and terrorists must reconcile themselves with death — both their own eventual deaths and the deaths they cause. The eschatological impulse is to find death redeemed in some transcendent good — whether it is the triumph of liberalism, communism, Islam, or Christianity. This redemption of death goes in several directions. On the one hand, the soldier's death will be redeemed by his courage, fidelity, and self-sacrifice. On the other hand, the enemy's death is deserved because the enemy is evil. These two redemptive themes are comprehensible because they form the background of our long history of warfare and faith: the faithful are redeemed, while the hated enemy is not.

However, warriors in modern warfare must also believe that the deaths of innocent bystanders can somehow also be redeemed, just as those who are motivated by eschatological hatred are willing to kill people who are "guilty" simply by association with a group. The warrior's faith is that his act of killing — which would otherwise be immoral — can be redeemed because it is morally necessary. And he further believes that some deity will succor the innocent who are killed. This is the idea of the crass but telling motto, "Kill 'em all and let God sort 'em out." The idea is that if those who are made to suffer are truly innocent, their innocence will be redeemed in some other life.

Practical pacifism begins from a rejection of this mode of reconciliation and redemption. Transcendent schemes of justification provide ways of reconciling us with death; but the humanistic pragmatic approach is skeptical about such transcendent schemes. Thus, death is not redeemable, as far as we know; nor is killing. We each have only one life to live. Each moment of an individual's life is of infinite worth to that individual. Such a view results in a tragic view of death and killing: killing and death might be necessary for the pursuit of justice, but they are unredeemable in any transcendent world of value. The death of even one innocent bystander is a cause for regret and guilt, because such a death is unredeemable. The basic humanist idea is that transcendent schemes of redemption are at best ungrounded and speculative. At worst, transcendent schemes of redemption are misguided, ideological, obfuscatory, and possibly even malicious. Those who claim that the deaths of innocent victims can be redeemed state something that no human being could know. And those who claim that we should sacrifice ourselves for a cause are often attempting to manipulate us into sacrificing ourselves for a highly speculative good, which serves to empower others (i.e., those who do not themselves make the sacrifice). Those who claim that we should be willing to kill for a cause are likewise asking us to sacrifice our moral integrity for the same dubious purpose.

Those who spew eschatological hatred are driven by an obsessive connection to the evil other whom they hate. We can easily understand how certain conditions might make such hatred possible. Life in the Palestinian camps provides one obvious example of social conditions that can breed this form of hatred. And certain religious doctrines — whether fundamentalist Christianity or Islam — also seem to have a causal role. However, understanding the psychic, social, and ideological sources of eschatological hatred does not make it right. Terrorists are wrong and they should be opposed, perhaps with force when necessary. However, the long-term solution to the problem is not simply to oppose it with force. Rather, one must work to change the causal structure that supports terrorism. We must argue on epistemological grounds against the idea of eschatology. We must provide therapeutic and educational activities that can defuse psychopathology. We must work to change the social conditions that foster the sorts of hatred we have been describing. And we must self-critically examine our own tendency to slip into a form of eschatological hatred of our own.

CHAPTER 9. THE MELIORISTIC IMPERATIVE OF LIBERAL HOPE

> If there is a conclusion to which human experience unmistakably points, it is that democratic ends demand democratic methods for their realization.
> — Dewey[310]

We live in precarious times characterized by terrorism, war, neo-imperialism, and a potential clash of civilizations. Is it reasonable to hope for a liberal peace based on a commitment to democracy, international law, human rights, and education? Are we moving toward a liberal peace or are we mired in the never-finished business of war? A definitive answer to this question would require a historical vantage point that we simply do not possess. Nonetheless, despite our limited ability to draw final conclusions about history, we can still answer the question of whether we should continue to hope for progress because such an answer is ultimately a normative one. We should hope for progress toward a liberal peace because hope is a necessary practical attitude for those who would work for progress. This does not mean that we should naively "hope against hope." Rather, it means that we should hope because hope provides the motivational force that allows us to continue to work for progress. This hope is connected with practical pacifism because it is essential for the restraint and activism that is part of practical pacifism: the practical pacifist must hope that liberal means can be practically effective while restraining him/

---

310. John Dewey, "Democratic Ends Need Democratic Methods for their Realization" in *John Dewey, Later Works* (Carbondale: Southern Illinois University Press, 1981), 14: 367-368.

herself from resorting to those sorts of violence that result from hatred and despair.

Liberal hope is about both means and ends. To hope that we might achieve our ends is also to hope that certain means will be practically effective. If we are inspired by a melioristic faith in liberal values, then there are limits to the practical means by which we might work to actualize our ends. Liberal values are easily betrayed by those who rationalize the use of illiberal means as a necessary expedient for their dissemination. Liberal hope is connected with the belief that peaceful means, such as education, open opportunity, and freedom of choice will be effective to bring about the liberal peace. As Dewey writes, "A genuine democratic faith in peace is faith in the possibility of conducting disputes, controversies, and conflicts as cooperative undertakings in which both parties learn by giving the other a chance to express itself, instead of having one party conquer by forceful suppression of the other."[311] This is not to say that liberals or pragmatists must be absolute pacifists. Rather, pragmatically-minded liberals can support something like the just war approach, as long as the use of force is viewed as a regrettable last resort. This means that peaceful liberal means must be utilized with vigor, creativity, and intelligence, while violence and coercion must be viewed as temporary and regrettable expedients. To seek to preserve and to disseminate liberal values by coercive means often represents a form of despair and cynicism that is the demise of liberalism. Coercion is the method of choice for those who do not trust people to choose liberal values for themselves if given the opportunity. However, since the primary value of liberalism is liberty, to use force as a means is to undermine the entire project. Of course, a pragmatist should be careful in postulating absolute conclusions. In the real world, it might occasionally be necessary to use force to defend liberal values. And our evaluations might change depending upon the circumstances — as Dewey's own assessment of war changed over time in light of the means and the ends to be obtained. However, violence can never be the primary means of disseminating liberal values. Individuals must come to liberal values on their own. The basis of liberalism is a commitment to some variant of the claim that individuals cannot be forced to be free.

The interdependence of means and ends must be borne in mind when we consider current political trends that seem to move in an illiberal direction, including threats to civil liberties arising in the context of the war on terrorism

---

311. Dewey, "Creative Democracy — The Task Before Us," *Later Works*, 14: 228.

and the strategic shift toward the acceptance of pre-emptive and retributive military action. These two trends are linked insofar as they both result from a commitment to security and order that trumps a commitment to liberty. Although these policies are ostensibly designed to protect liberty, they protect liberty through illiberal means. This represents an instability in liberalism that arises from the outstanding problem of uniting means and ends in practice. Liberals hope — or, rather, they *should* hope — that liberal means can be effective for promoting liberty and peace, while cynics and conservatives doubt that they are. To combat a cynical retreat to military realism we must emphasize the fact that trust and hope are essential for a truly liberal peace. Leaders of liberal regimes should remain hopeful that liberal ends can be actualized by liberal means. To give up this hope is to retreat to a form of cynicism that feels that in the "real world" liberal values are incapable of defending themselves on their own terms.

CYNICISM, REALISM, AND VIOLENCE

It is easy to despair. The universe is cold and vast, the gods seem, at best, indifferent to suffering, and battlefields and industrial waste dumps bear witness to the destructive power of human beings. Even worse, the metaphysical comforts that soothed our ancestors have been subject to critiques that leave us without refuge. It is also easy to become cynical and suspicious of such basic human resources as altruism, compassion, love, virtue, and even the pursuit of truth. Cynicism leaves us without faith in either the means or ends that are essential to the liberal approach. From a cynical perspective, the best we can do is to impose liberal values in an illiberal fashion because without coercive force people will not accept these values for themselves. If we do not trust people to choose democracy and liberal values for themselves if given the opportunity, then we fall into the "Hobbesian Trap" which claims that "in the real world" it is necessary to utilize illiberal means, including an expanded surveillance state, a coercive education system, and ultimately police and military force. In international affairs this leads to what Jonathan Glover has called "military drift" and the tendency (criticized in Chapter 6) of liberal just war theorists to permit exemptions to the principles of justice in war.[312] To liberals committed to the interdependence of means and ends, such a cynical approach to the dissemination of liberal values is a disaster. As Dewey says, "resort to military force is a first sure sign that we are giving up on the struggle for the democratic way of life."[313]

Cynicism is a complicated phenomenon; it should not be reduced to mere psychological egoism. Refined cynics stress the fact that human beings are ignorant and incontinent: we don't know the good and, even when we do, we are unable or unwilling to actualize it. Peter Sloterdijk's *Critique of Cynical Reason* takes this even further. Sloterdijk indicates that cynicism is the result of the slow death of enlightenment ideals that we call post-modernity. Sloterdijk defines post-modern cynicism as "enlightened false consciousness."[314] Post-moderns who follow Marx, Nietzsche, and Freud have "seen through" all of the structures of ideology and have come to realize that the process of critique, the process of seeing an ideology as an ideology, is itself ideological. This leaves post-moderns without a ground upon which to stand. One response to this problem is to return to comfortable traditional ideologies, albeit with a cynical despair that recognizes that there is no hope of attaining transparency, truth, or progress. This is, in fact, the attitude that Richard Rorty — one of America's best-known living philosophers — has defended under the rubric of "liberal ironism" or "post-modern bourgeois liberalism."[315] Rorty's brand of cynicism is complex and sophisticated. It follows from careful analyses of epistemology, politics, and ethics. And yet it remains cynical. This can be seen in Rorty's rejection of the attempt to distinguish philosophy from politics and other arts of rhetorical persuasion.

> Nor is there much occasion to use the distinctions between logic and rhetoric, or between philosophy and literature, or between rational and nonrational methods of changing other people's minds. If there is no center to the self, then there are only different ways of weaving new candidates for belief and desire into antecedently existing webs of beliefs and desire. The only important political distinction in the area is that between the use of force and the use of persuasion.[316]

312. Jonathan Glover, Humanity: *A Moral History of the 20th Century* (New Haven: Yale University Press, 1999).

313. Dewey, "Democratic Ends Need Democratic Methods for their Realization," *Later Works*, 14: 367.

314. Peter Sloterdijk, *Critique of Cynical Reason* (Minneapolis: University of Minnesota Press, 1987), 5.

315. Richard Rorty, "Private Irony and Liberal Hope" in *Contingency, Irony, Solidarity* (Cambridge: Cambridge University Press, 1989) and Rorty, "Postmodernist Bourgeois Liberalism," *The Journal of Philosophy*, 80: 10, Part 1, (1983), 583-589. For a discussion of Rorty's conservativism and its difference from Deweyan progressivism, see Richard Schusterman, "Pragmatism and Liberalism between Dewey and Rorty," *Political Theory*, 22: 3 (1994), 391-413.

The cynicism present results from the inability or the refusal to distinguish various means of persuasion. There is a risk that the distinction Rorty draws at the end of this quote, between force and persuasion, is one that Rorty cannot support from his perspective. Rorty's position seems to be quite close to that of other cynics, such as Marx and Nietzsche, who have rejected the distinction between the force of words and the force of arms.[317] Although Rorty is reluctant to make this leap, without a commitment to some methodological values, without faith in the effectiveness of liberal means, it seems that there is no way to distinguish between persuasion and force. Without a commitment to the interdependence of means and ends, it seems that there is nothing to prevent us from using illiberal means to "persuade" people to accept liberal values. Rorty's cynical ironism is, he tells us, a *private* affair and he wants to defend a non-ironic notion of public or "social hope."[318] However, Rorty leaves us without any good reason to defend our values..

Such cynicism might stem from a mis-reading of Dewey's early comments on force, violence, war and peace.[319] Dewey does emphasize the fact that all means are forceful, and he also asks us to evaluate effectiveness and efficiency when choosing means. This might suggest that, for Dewey, "the end justifies the means," an idea dear to the hearts of cynics and realists. However, Dewey also emphasizes that for truly liberal ends, the best means are usually liberal ones, such as education, dialogue, and the use of intelligence. In his later writings he comes to the further conclusion that the interdependence of means and ends should lead us to be wary of violence, coercion, and war because, in actuality, these means undermine the ends of peace and progress.[320]

Rorty's conclusions are not new. Post-modernists derive their cynicism from Marx, Nietzsche, Freud and others, leaving us with that form of "enlightened false consciousness" described by Sloterdijk: we are enlightened enough to recognize that we suffer inescapably from false consciousness. The ironic conclusion of the last several hundred years of enlightenment and critique

316. Richard Rorty, "Private Irony and Liberal Hope" in *Contingency, Irony, Solidarity* (Cambridge: Cambridge University Press, 1989), 83-84.

317. See my discussion of Marx in *The Philosopher's Voice*.

318. Rorty, "Private Irony and Liberal Hope" in *Contingency, Irony, Solidarity*, 86-87.

319. See Dewey, "Force, Violence, and Law" *John Dewey, The Middle Works* (Carbondale: Southern Illinois University Press, 1980), 10: 211-215, "Force and Coercion" *Middle Works*, 10: 241-251.

320. See "Means and End" *Later Works*, 13: 349-354 and "Democratic Education in the World Today," *Later Works*, 13: 294-303.

Practical Pacifism

is that critical enlightenment has led us to believe that there is no enlightenment. Such a conclusion serves to undermine the idea of progress. In this sense, cynicism is self-fulfilling: by rejecting as ideological the idea of progress, the cynic undermines the project of progress, thus actually giving support to those regressive elements which are contemptuous of progress for less "enlightened" reasons. In this sense enlightened cynicism can actually become a form of conservatism, at least insofar as it has no basis from which to criticize the status quo.[321]

The post-modern cynic has a profound understanding of the critical process of enlightenment. Cynics are produced by advanced education; they are not born. And yet, critical education has failed to produce in the cynic faith in the process of education. Instead of recognizing the creative power of human intelligence, progressive possibilities for the increase in human freedom, and the potential for future improvement and more enlightenment, the cynic sees ideology, self-interest, and the potential for deeper disillusionment and violence. Part of this grows from a suspicion that education is actually indoctrination rather than self-development. And so the cynic sees no point in pursuing critical education or in participating in political activism, except possibly as a means of entertainment. Cynicism is, in Sloterdijk's words, "the end of the belief in education."[322]

One strategy is for the enlightened cynic to return to "life as usual." However, because of his cynical education, he returns to life with contempt for the superficial values and naïve beliefs of those who whole-heartedly embrace "life as usual." Zygmunt Bauman indicates that post-modern cynics who give up on the project of universal enlightenment become "vagabonds," unable to return to the comfort of home and yet unable to settle anywhere else.[323] The cynic is alienated from the life he inhabits but is unable to imagine or hope for the possibility of progressing beyond this form of "life as usual." So, the cynic's strategy for coping is to retreat to irony and sarcasm, as in the ploys of Kierkegaard's Aesthete or the deliberate contempt expressed by Diogenes, the

---

321. See Richard Schusterman, "Pragmatism and Liberalism between Rorty and Dewey," op. cit. As Leon Eisenberg has concluded, "Pessimism about man serves to maintain the status quo. It is a luxury for the affluent, a sop to the guilt of the politically inactive, a comfort to those who continue to enjoy the amenities of privilege" (Leon Eisenberg, "The *Human* Nature of Human Nature," *Science*, 14, April 1972, 123-28; quoted in Alfie Kohn, *The Brighter Side of Human Nature*, 40).

322. Peter Sloterdijk, *Critique of Cynical Reason*, xxix.

323. Zygmunt Bauman, *Postmodernity and its Discontents* (New York: New York University Press, 1997), Chapter 6, "Tourists and Vagabonds."

first and greatest cynic. One should note, however, that the cynic's own cynicism is made possible by critical educational advancement and indeed by the injustice that persists in society. Cynics are products of luxury and education. Nonetheless, the cynic is contemptuous of those who would claim that the privileged sort of education, which creates the conditions for the possibility of cynicism, is unjust. To the jaundiced eye of the cynic, questions of justice cease to be meaningful. Everyone is out to protect his own, and since there is no way out of this cycle of selfishness except through self-deception, the cynic gives up on the progressive hopes of liberal enlightenment.

Another variety of cynicism is found among so-called political realists such as Machiavelli, Hobbes, and more recently John Kekes.[324] Since Plato, political philosophers have been skeptical about the irredeemably dark side of human nature and about our tendency toward ignorance and self-interest. Machiavelli and Hobbes both thought that humans were greedy for glory and were motivated by base impulses. Machiavelli justified the immorality (or a-morality) of the prince as a response to the immorality of his subjects and his enemies. Hobbes justified a strong state as a necessary expedient to subdue the animal motives of human beings. This view is cynical to the extent that it holds that it is power, not reason or discourse, that matters as the engine of social change. Kekes' recent defense of "conservatism" comes from a critique of what he calls "the liberal faith" in the basic goodness of human beings. He sees this faith in philosophers such as Rousseau, Kant, and Rawls. "It is the secular equivalent of the religious faith of Christianity, which it is intended to replace. It is fueled by a groundless optimism that substitutes wishes for facts, refuses to face reality, ignores history, and radiates a moralistic fervor that leads the faithful to treat disagreement as a sign of immorality."[325] Kekes struggles to avoid slipping toward despair and cynicism and reaches, despite himself, a surprisingly melioristic conclusion. "Conservatives deny that what is warranted is severe enough to result in hopelessness. The ideal of a good society that makes good lives possible for those who live in it is unattainable, but it can still be approximated."[326] The problem is, however, that unless this conservative view is connected by way of hope to an imperative for action, it can easily slide toward cynicism and despair.

---

324. For a recent discussion of Machiavelli and Hobbes, see Michael Doyle, *Ways of War and Peace* (New York: Norton, 1997), Part One.

325. John Kekes, *A Case for Conservatism* (Ithaca, NY: Cornell University Press, 1998), 211.

326. Kekes, *A Case for Conservatism*, 218.

Cynicism and political realism thus give up hope in liberal means. For this reason, they easily advocate the use of political violence, which practical pacifism rejects. The practical pacifist holds that often there are nonviolent means to liberal ends. The cynic sees this as both naïve and ideological: naïve because the world of power requires the use of force and ideological because liberal values such as peace are no better justified than any other means. A defense of practical pacifism must thus work to show both that nonviolent means can be effective and that we have good reasons to believe that liberal values are good.

LIBERALISM AND MELIORISM

Liberal values such as nonviolence can be defended without making absolute claims about the essence of human nature or about the structure of reality. The sort of justification I have in mind is pluralistic: we have many good reasons to believe that nonviolence is good. Among these reasons are the following facts about human beings: individuals in all cultures seem to want to have their autonomy respected by others and legally recognized; most of us tend to enjoy and love one another; many of our cultural traditions have long argued that nonviolence is the goal of human development; nonviolent approaches to problem solving often produce non-zero-sum solutions; and we are developing toward global interdependence. None of these provides a definitive argument in favor of liberal values; however, there are so many good reasons on the side of liberal values, including the value of nonviolence, that the burden of proof rests on those who argue otherwise. My approach to this argument seeks to avoid making absolute claims based upon one argument strategy. Rather, I begin from the idea that finite mortal human beings usually do not know which argument is absolutely definitive. This does not mean that we cannot have very strong arguments in favor of the power and value of nonviolence and other liberal values.

This pragmatic approach is especially important when we consider questions about hope and history. We would be wrong, for example, to oppose cynicism and realism with a form of metaphysical optimism such as Leibniz defended.[327] Such optimism suffers from the ills of other metaphysical creeds: it tends to be absolutist and it tends to ignore the fact of suffering and death. We should also be reluctant to affirm a liberalism, such as Hegel's, that understands liberal values as the fulfillment of spirit's work in history, making the spread of liberal values the inevitable result of God's plan. Those of us who are inclined toward empiricism and humanism resist the Hegelian faith in the work of spirit. We admit, rather, that liberal democracy is an unstable human creation. From a pragmatic perspective, liberalism is not an inevitable component of "the best of all possible worlds." Rather, liberalism is the best system that we finite mortals have created for ourselves thus far in history and it is the system best defended by a plural set of arguments.

History shows that liberal values are late developments in human experience. Liberal values have been and continue to be contested by other visions of the good life. Despite this instability, we must hope that liberal democratic institutions can survive, flourish, and spread. While we would do well to shy away from essential claims about the historical progress of human being, the basic presumption of liberalism is the normative claim that we should be free to determine our own future. This normative claim requires faith in human potential. This is a pragmatic faith: it is supported by self-critical experience, inductive reasoning, and plural arguments; it is not derived from an abstract metaphysical theory. The metaphysical optimist believes that everything happens for the good without regard for the ambiguity of the empirical evidence. Ironically, this sort of optimism can be linked to the sorts of eschatological violence criticized in Chapter 8: if there is a plan for history, violent action aimed at actualizing this plan might be considered justifiable. Likewise, metaphysical optimism can be linked to the sort of impractical absolute pacifism described in Chapter 3: optimists can sometimes focus on keeping their own hands clean, while ignoring the demand of concrete suffering by claiming that all suffering will be redeemed in the next life. Rather than adopting optimism from a metaphysical vantage point, the pragmatic faith in democracy is an experimentally discovered fact that, if things are to become better, it is up to us to actively use inquiry, dialogue, and criticism to make them better. This idea is best described not as optimism but rather as meliorism.

Meliorists are committed to the liberal idea that human freedom can lead to human advancement. Melioristic faith in human potential fits with the two liberal values of freedom and equality. Hierarchical societies that deny the value

---

327. For a discussion of the history of optimism, see Brian Domino and Daniel W. Conway, "Optimism and Pessimism from a Historical Perspective" in Edward C. Chang, ed. *Optimism and Pessimism: Implications for Theory, Research, and Practice* (Washington D.C: American Psychological Association, 2001), pp. 13-30.

of freedom and equality have always been founded upon the idea that some people have better access to wisdom or virtue and thus are better able to choose for others. Liberalism rejects this idea and holds, rather, that individuals are to have as much freedom as possible and they are to be considered as equal, especially with regard to the capacity to judge autonomously. These liberal values are connected with the idea that human beings are in fact able to make progress toward actualizing their potentialities both individually and collectively.

Liberals believe that if individuals are allowed to actualize their own potentials, they will for the most part actualize them for the better. There are two closely related reasons of such a belief. One might believe that humans are innately good and that they will always develop their potential for good if not stymied by unsupportive environments. Or, one might believe that human potential is ambiguous, with progressive development requiring a nurturing environment. The first option can be derived from a view such as Rousseau's, which focuses on eliminating the corrupting influence of environmental conditions. The second version of the liberal belief fits better with Dewey's idea that we need to reconstruct supporting institutions so that they better enable us to actualize our potentials. Both views appear to run aground on the empirical fact that some human beings may not in fact actualize their better potentialities, despite nurturing environments. We have to take psychopaths into account. Indeed, if human beings are indeed free, then we confront the problem of radical evil. Environmentalism only goes so far to explain the development of human potential: at some point we must recognize the human capacity to choose either good or evil. Some nihilistic terrorists, like the shooters in Columbine, may deliberately use their freedom in order to do evil. However — contra Kekes — liberals do not ignore evil. Nor do they turn a blind eye to suffering. Rather, they choose for pragmatic and strategic reasons to focus on the hopeful positive outcomes of liberalization. Meliorism is not only a descriptive account of the possibilities for progress; it is also a *normative* claim that we *ought* to hope for progress. While some will choose evil, the vast majority will not — because the vast majority are repelled by evil. And rejection of evil can be fostered by proper education. This is the basic historical hope of liberalism.

One might begin with Rousseau in order trace the genealogy of the normative value of hope in liberal thinking, although Kant gives us the clearest indication of this approach. Rousseau's focus is on the fact that the ills of society "are of our own making."[328] While a cynic might draw from this conclusion the view that human beings are irredeemably fallen, Rousseau holds out the hope that since these ills are due to us, we should be able to remedy them through social reform and education. Indeed, for Rousseau, we *should* hope that we can make the world better.[329] However, Rousseau's educational theory emphasizes a return to nature that runs counter to the Deweyan approach to reforming social and educational institutions.

Building upon Rousseau's basic insight, Kant clarifies the normative approach to hope in both theory and practice, and links it to a reform of institutions.[330] Early in his career Kant explicitly rejected Leibnizian optimism as ungrounded metaphysical or theological speculation.[331] For Kant, hope is not to be grounded in a theodicy that explains away evil. Rather, it is a moral imperative with practical significance. Kant, or course, famously connected the issue of hope with epistemology by asking in the first *Critique*, "what may I hope?" [332] For Kant, the justification of hope occurs through a speculative attempt to unify theory and practice by asking the question of whether moral duty will have a reward. Kant's answer is that we have a *practical* interest in assuming that our moral hopes will be fulfilled. This is not metaphysical optimism. Nor is Kant naïve about evil. He explicitly considers the possibility of radical evil, late in his career, in his *Religion within the Limits of Reason Alone*, which is as much a book of political philosophy as a book on religion. He concludes, quite rightly, that neither the optimistic nor the pessimistic/cynical conclusion is warranted: "man as a species is neither good nor bad...he is as much the one as the other, partly good, partly bad."[333] Kant asks us to hope, not as the result of a descriptive theory of human goodness but as a moral imperative. With regard to

---

328. Jean-Jacques Rousseau, *Discourse on the Origin of Inequality* in *The Social Contract and Discourse on the Origin of Inequality* (ed. by Lester G. Crocker, New York: Washington Square Press, 1967), 183. Rousseau's Savoyard Vicar makes a similar claim: "O Man! Seek no further for the author of evil; thou art he. There is no evil but the evil you do or the evil you suffer, and both come from yourself" [Jean-Jacques Rousseau, *Emile* (trans. Barbara Foxley, London: J.M Dent, Everyman, 1995), 293].

329. Joshua Cohen discusses Rousseau's normative hope in "The Natural Goodness of Humanity" in *Reclaiming the History of Ethics* (ed. by Andrews Reath, Barbara Hermann, and Christine Korsgaard, Cambridge: Cambridge University Press, 1997), 102-139

330. For Dewey's discussion of the limits of Rousseau's approach to education, see John Dewey, *Democracy and Education* (New York: The Free Press, 1966), 112-118. For his more positive assessment of Kant's approach, see *Democracy and Education*, 95.

331. Immanuel Kant, "An Attempt at Some Reflections on Optimism" (from 1759) in Immanuel Kant, *Theoretical Philosophy: 1755-1770* (Cambridge: Cambridge University Press, 1992). Also see Kant's unpublished notes on optimism that accompany this essay ("Reflections 3705-5: AK 17: 229-39").

332. Kant, *Critique of Pure Reason* (New York: St. Martin's Press, 1956), B 333.

333. Kant, *Religion within the Limits of Reason Alone* (New York: Harper and Row, 1960), 16.

the moral postulates of freedom, God, and immortality, Kant says, for example: "the possibility of these conditions can and *must* be assumed in this practical context without our knowing or understanding them in a theoretical sense."[334] For morality to work, we must have some hope for its success: hope is a moral or practical necessity.

Kant ultimately links this to his thinking about war and peace. We must hope for peace for practical reasons. Moreover, we are entitled to hope, so long as the possibility or impossibility of peace is underdetermined in theory. Kant concludes with the following:

> We must act *as though* perpetual peace were a reality, which perhaps it is not, by working for its establishment and for the kind of contestation that seems best adapted for bringing it about (perhaps republicanism in every state)... Even if the realization of this goal were always to remain just a pious wish, we still would certainly not be deceiving ourselves by adopting the maxim of working for it with unrelenting perseverance.[335]

Although Kant allows for the use of violence and war, such use is always to be limited by a liberal commitment to respecting persons as ends in themselves. While this sounds paradoxical — that one could go to war and kill persons while respecting them as ends — this idea is firmly embedded in the just war approach. While absolute pacifists might reject this idea, the point of the just war approach is that we should be reluctant to use violence and that we should avoid the realist argument for total unrestrained war.[336] For Kant, the limits imposed on the use of violence are linked to the hope that these limited means can be practically effective.

Kant's ultimate hope is that philosophical ideals can stimulate progress. Thus public intellectuals, especially, must have hope for progress. According to Kant, the key moment in progress is the moment at which philosophical ideals become public. And it is the institutional connection that foreshadows the Deweyan idea of reconstruction. In the process of educating the world about progress and the hope for progress, philosophy serves to stimulate the world toward progress.[337] Kant believes that once the truth of progress has been

---

334. Kant, *Critique of Practical Reason* (New York: Macmillan, 1956), Preface, 4.

335. Kant, *Metaphysical Elements of Justice* (trans. Ladd, New York: MacMillan, 1965), sec. 62, p. 128.

336. For a discussion of the continuum between pacifism and just war thinking, see Richard Miller, *Interpretations of Conflict* (Chicago: University of Chicago Press, 1991).

337. See my discussion of Kant in *The Philosopher's Voice*.

publicly communicated, this truth will begin a chain-reaction which leads toward continual future progress. Thus the hopeful liberal approach has pragmatic effects. Future history is in part created by us as we work to bring our vision of the future into actuality. If this is the case, then the argument between meliorism and cynicism is decisive. Just as the meliorist will help to actualize the hoped-for outcome, the cynic's own cynicism will also be self-actualizing. This recognition of the prophetic and activist nature of the philosopher's voice changes the theory-practice relation. Enlightenment and freedom are not objects to be possessed at some point in time. Rather, they are processes of creative human activity. The liberal faith is thus a practical imperative based upon the fact that we must believe we can actualize the good in order to have any hope of success in the process of actualization.

A similar view has been defended by John Rawls in *The Law of Peoples*. As discussed in Chapter 6, Rawls defends what he calls a "reasonable utopia": an ideal liberal theory which is realistic enough to deal with unjust regimes, burdened societies, and outlaw states. Following Doyle's interpretation of Kant, Rawls bases his argument for an expansion of liberal values on the empirical claim that liberal democracies do not go to war with one another.[338] This fact gives us reason both to hope and to work for the expansion of liberalism. Rawls' hopeful philosophy of history claims that what he calls "burdened societies" and "outlaw states" can be dealt with by just wars and by the gradual expansion of democratic values. However, we must have faith in this form of progress in order to work to actualize it. Rawls concludes with a brief explanation of his melioristic view: "For as long as we believe for good reasons that a self-sustaining and reasonably just political and social order both at home and abroad is possible, we can reasonably hope that we or others will someday, somewhere achieve it; and we can then do something toward this achievement."[339] Melioristic faith about the prospects for liberalism is necessary for the creation of liberal institutions and indeed is a contributing factor in their success.

---

338. Michael Doyle, *Ways of War and Peace* (New York: Norton, 1997), Part 2.
339. Rawls, *The Law of Peoples* (Cambridge, MA: Harvard University Press, 1999), 128.

Optimism, Pessimism, and Pragmatism

Kantian and Rawlsian liberalism is thus closely related to pragmatic liberalism. Pragmatic liberalism requires self-confidence as well as other virtues such as open-mindedness, courage, determination, and hopefulness.[340] It is a way of life founded on a belief that human beings are good enough to solve our own problems.[341] One of the seemingly self-evident principles of liberalism is trust in the self and in the potential of all human beings to govern themselves. Of course there are many epistemological, psychological, and political assumptions underlying this claim, which is why liberalism continues to be a topic for debate. As mentioned above, cynics doubt that most individuals are actually able to judge their own best interests. Illiberal communalists and defenders of what Isaiah Berlin called positive liberty go further and claim that it is not in fact desirable for individuals to pursue a good that runs counter to the social good. And critical theorists such as Adorno and Horkheimer point out that subtle forms of domination haunt the ideology of progress.[342]

The contemporary global situation leaves us with a profound ambivalence about the question of progress. For each problem, one can imagine a solution, and for each success, one can imagine a downside. In discussing the question of progress, the radical and absolute nature of the disjunction between optimism and pessimism is obvious. The solution to such a disjunction is also obvious: it is

---

340. For a description of the "pragmatist faith" and its links to some of these virtues, see Gregory F. Pappas, Open-mindedness and Courage: Complementary Virtues" in *Transactions of the Charles S. Peirce Society*, 33: 2 (Spring 1996), 316-335. For further discussion of the virtues of liberalism, including other virtues such as tolerance and generosity, see James T. Kloppenberg, *The Virtues of Liberalism* (Oxford: Oxford University Press, 1998).

341. As Dewey says, "the foundation of democracy is faith in the capacities of human nature; faith in human intelligence, and in the power of pooled and cooperative experience. It is not belief that these things are complete but that if given a show they will grow and be able to generate progressively the knowledge and wisdom needed to guide collective action" [John Dewey, "Democracy" (address of February 1927), in Steven M. Cahn, ed., *Classics of Political and Moral Philosophy*, 1197 from John Dewey, *Later Works*, vol. 11]. For discussion of Dewey's melioristic faith in democracy, see Michael Eldridge, "Dewey's Faith in Democracy as Shared Experience" in *Transactions of the Charles S. Peirce Society*, 32: 1, 11-30; Hilary Putnam, "A Reconsideration of Deweyan Democracy" in Putnam, *Renewing Philosophy* (Cambridge: Harvard University Press), Chapter 9; Richard Schusterman, "Pragmatism and Liberalism between Dewey and Rorty" in *Practicing Philosophy* (New York: Routledge, 1997); John J. Stuhr, "Dewey's Social and Political Philosophy" in Larry Hickman, ed., *Reading Dewey* (Bloomington: Indiana University Press, 1998), 82-99; John J. Stuhr, "Democracy as a Way of Life," in Stuhr, *Philosophy and the Reconstruction of Culture: Pragmatic Essays after Dewey* (Albany: State University of New York Press, 1993), 37-57.

342. Max Horkheimer and Theodor W. Adorno, "The Concept of Enlightenment," in *Dialectic of Enlightenment* (New York: Continuum, 1997).

a pragmatic approach, which focuses on the question of what is good for us to believe. This follows from Kant's basic insight: when the facts underdetermine the conclusion, we are entitled to turn to the normative question of what we *should* believe. This is especially true when it comes to moral and political thinking.

It is useful to accentuate the positive. The idea that positive thinking produces its own results is one that was dear to the heart of American philosophers. Emerson, for example, celebrates hope in his essay, "Progress of Culture," where he says that "difficulties exist to be surmounted."[343] He ties this to liberal values, by holding out the hope that increased liberty will produce better men and a better society: "we wish to put the ideal rules into practice, to offer liberty instead of chains, and see whether liberty will not disclose its proper checks; believing that a free press will prove safer than censorship; to ordain free trade, and believe that it will not bankrupt us; universal suffrage, believing that it will not carry us to mobs, or back to kings again."[344] Emerson's faith is that an increase in liberty will result in a better life because it will stimulate individuals to take responsibility for their own actions so that they might become active and self-reliant. Such thinking obviously influenced James. In a popular essay entitled, "Is Life Worth Living?" James discusses the way in which attitude matters to the accomplishment of a task.[345] James looks at a concrete example. If you are going to jump from a cliff across a chasm to a ledge on the other side, your attitude is an important factor in the outcome. If you believe you will be able to clear the gap, it is more likely that you will be able to. A pessimistic evaluation of the situation will leave you with a nervous, half-hearted attempt that will probably fail. James concludes with the following practical advice: "believe that life is worth living and your belief will help create the fact."[346] This idea of the practical import of attitude has been embodied in "positive psychology," a recent trend in psychology led by Martin Seligman. Seligman's discussion of pessimism vs. optimism in a subject's "explanatory style" is linked

---

343. Ralph Waldo Emerson, "Progress of Culture" in *The Complete Writings of Ralph Waldo Emerson* (New York: Wm. H. Wise and Co., 1929), volume 2, 797-798. For a discussion of Emerson, hope, and the "American faith," see Stanley Cavell, "Hope against Hope," Appendix A of *Conditions Handsome and Unhandsome* (La Salle, IL: Open Court, 1990).

344. Emerson, "Progress of Culture," 797.

345. William James, "Is Life Worth Living?" in *The Will to Believe and other Essays in Popular Philosophy* (New York: Dover Publications, 1956). For a recent discussion of James and hope, see Phil Oliver, *William James's 'Springs of Delight'* (Nashville: Vanderbilt University Press, 2001), especially Chapter 5.

346. James, "Is Life Worth Living?" 67.

to outcomes in terms of life prospects: in general we do better when we describe things in a positive manner.[347]

However, for all its inspirational value, a focus on "accentuating the positive" simply pushes the question back to another level. After all, perhaps we should accentuate the negative in order to see what real problems continue to haunt us. If it is simply impossible to leap across the gap, we should devote our attention to building a bridge rather than hoping against hope, leaping and failing. Human decency also requires a recognition of the tragic side of life: it is inhuman and inhumane not to be profoundly affected by continued suffering. Thus, an overemphasis on positive thinking can be both self-defeating and insensitive. Likewise, too much faith in liberal democracy overlooks continued threats to liberal values both from the apathy of the citizens of liberal regimes and from the antagonism of external enemies.

What is required, then, is a synthetic melioristic approach. Such an approach, if it is to remain liberal, will hope that the lives of individuals can be made better by the liberal means of education, expanded opportunity, etc. However, this form of meliorism must not be naïve. Indeed it will be tinged by a recognition of the tragedy of being human. There are "evil" and recalcitrant individuals in the world; and we might have to employ violence as a tragic last resort in order to deal with them. However, we must struggle to avoid the quietism and despair that can result from acknowledging our tragic situation. Such a view has been described best by Dewey. Dewey recognizes that a metaphysical optimism that views this world as the best of all possible worlds "might be regarded as the most cynical of pessimisms" because it effectively ignores suffering and evil.[348] He goes on to say that "meliorism is the belief that the specific conditions which exist at one moment, be they comparatively bad or comparatively good, in any event may be bettered."[349]

Dewey's explicit and emphatic meliorism is connected to his faith in human intelligence, in democracy, and in education. Yes, this is an article of

---

347. Martin Seligman, *Learned Optimism: How to Change Your Mind and Your Life* (New York: Pocket Books, 1998). For a brief introduction, see "Optimism, Pessimism, and Explanatory Style" by Seligman, et al. in Chang, ed. *Optimism and Pessimism*. The connection between positive psychology and American pragmatism was pointed out in a paper by James Pawelski, "'The Energies of Men': A New Approach from Positive Psychology" in a presentation at the American Philosophical Association in December of 2001. I thank Professor Pawelski for providing me with a copy of his unpublished paper.

348. John Dewey, *Reconstruction in Philosophy* (Boston: Beacon Press, 1963), 178.

349. John Dewey, *Reconstruction in Philosophy*, 178. For a discussion of meliorism in Dewey (and G.H. Mead), see James Campbell, "Optimism, Meliorism, Faith," *History of Philosophy Quarterly* 4: 1 (1987), 93-113.

faith, but it is perhaps best understood as a practical presupposition that is revisable in light of the practical results of action.[350] Dewey says, for example, in *A Common Faith*: "all endeavor for the better is moved by faith in what is possible, not by adherence to the actual."[351] But Dewey strives to distance this pragmatic faith from the optimistic faith of idealistic philosophies and religions, what Kekes maligned as the "liberal faith." The pragmatic faith is best understood as the revisable claim that positive thinking and creative intelligence applied by intelligent beings in the world can lead to progress toward human flourishing. When Dewey says, famously, that "a pragmatic intelligence is a creative intelligence," we must take this to mean that intelligence can be used to accomplish the pragmatic task of melioration.[352] We must face problems as challenges to be overcome by avoiding that type of cynicism that often results when metaphysical optimism is rejected. The pragmatic challenge is to recognize the horrors of existence while working actually to ameliorate them. Pragmatic hope walks the line between positive thinking and recognition of the precariousness and tragic elements in life. We should affirm our confidence in the power of free intelligence, while acknowledging, in Dewey's words, our "littleness and impotencies."[353] This confidence is connected with a faith in liberal means. As Sidney Hook says, "to the meliorist, the recognition of the gamut of tragic possibilities is what feeds his desire to find some method of negotiating conflicts of value by intelligence rather than by war or brute force."[354]

The question of meliorism came to the fore in a debate stimulated by John Lachs in the *Journal of Speculative Philosophy* (vol. 15, no. 3, 2001).[355] Lachs concludes that although we could bemoan the negative elements in the world today — environmental crises, political injustice, terrorism, and evil — such a preoccupation with the negative can prevent us from acting positively. In other

---

350. See Michael Eldridge, "Dewey's Faith in Democracy as Shared Experience," *Transactions of the Charles S. Peirce Society*, 32: 1 (Winter 1996), 11-30.
351. Dewey, *A Common Faith* (New Haven: Yale University Press, 1960), 23.
352. Dewey, "The Need for Recovery in Philosophy" in *The Philosophy of John Dewey*, edited by John J. McDermott (Chicago: University of Chicago Press, 1981), 94.
353. Dewey, *Experience and Nature* (New York: Dover, 1958), 420.
354. Sidney Hook, *Pragmatism and the Tragic Sense of Life* (New York: Basic Books, 1974), 22-23. For a recent discussion of Dewey and tragedy, see Bruce Wilshire, *The Primal Roots of American Philosophy* (University Park, PA: Penn State Press, 2000), Chapter 7.
355. John Lachs, "Both Better Off and Better: Moral Progress amid Continuing Carnage" and replies by Denis Schmidt, Andrew Light, and Cynthia Willet, in *Journal of Speculative Philosophy* vol. 15, no. 3, 2001. Lachs' essay has been reprinted in *A Community of Individuals* (New York: Routledge, 2003).

texts, Lachs has echoed Rousseau in arguing that an affirmative attitude can combat those forms of cynicism and apathy that result from alienating institutions. To make these institutions better we must believe that our active participation can be effective. "If we see the modern world as of our own making, it will not seem so oppressive and alien."[356] Lachs is not a naïve Panglossian optimist, however. He concludes his article with the following: "We find throwbacks and face reversals again and again. The black holes of nastiness we continue to encounter set our tasks as educated human beings and especially as philosophers. But taking all of this into account, we still feel the tides of decency rising and see shafts of light to guide our actions and to feed our hope."[357] The pragmatic conclusion is that we need to remember that progress has been made in order to inspire our efforts to make further progress. But it is important to remember both sides of the argument: we must recall our failures in order to set the agenda for action; we should recall our successes in order to give us hope that our actions might be effective.

Such an attitude is well suited for the post-September 11 world. We have good reasons to question our faith in liberal values and our optimism about progress. However, we also need to believe that these values can prevail on their own terms. Moreover, in times such as these, it is important to recall the pragmatic idea of the interdependence of means and ends. Absolutists attempt to justify means in light of absolute ends. But a pragmatic approach that is humanistic and fallibilistic recognizes that we do not have access to these absolute ends. Thus we must focus on the question of means. If liberal values are to be defended, they must be defended by liberal means because liberalism is defined both by the ends it values and by the means it approves for actualizing these ends. Liberty, which is essential for liberalism, is a process, not an end in itself. If we are to be free, we must be free now, even as we work to secure more freedom. We should thus be extremely reluctant to sacrifice liberty for security and peace for war, while taking care to do what is necessary in light of a precarious and changing world.

The discussion of means and ends has concrete implications for the ways in which we are willing to defend ourselves from enemies domestically and internationally. The question is an open one and its solution depends upon an assessment of the practical implications of liberal hope. With regard to war, for

---

356. John Lachs, "Violence as a Response to Alienation" in *The Relevance of Philosophy to Life* (Nashville: Vanderbilt University Press, 1995), 111.

357. Lachs, "Both Better Off and Better," *A Community of Individuals*, 108.

example, pragmatic liberals should worry that the means of violence cannot produce the end of peace. I am not claiming that liberals and pragmatists need to be pacifists. There may be situations in which force might be necessary to protect liberal values. However, liberal pragmatists should have a strong presumption toward peaceful means, if only because they worry that it is difficult, if not impossible for fallibilistic or humanistic approach to justify resort to a means such as war, whose finality is absolute. Indeed, because peace and freedom are precarious, while death is absolute, we should struggle to preserve peace, freedom, and life against that form of cynical realism that risks these values in the name of security and stability.

CONCLUSION

Meliorism is ultimately not a descriptive claim but a normative claim with practical impact. Meliorists say that we should emphasize the possibilities for good in order to actualize them. It is good to look for positive possibilities because this emphasis will contribute to progress toward the good. Meliorists think that cynicism about human nature is self-affirming: if you dwell on the dark side, you will never overcome it. Of course, one cannot be so naïve as to ignore terrorism, alienation and the other ills of the contemporary world. And one cannot be so inhumane as to tell sufferers that their suffering and loss can be redeemed by positive thinking. Rather, the meliorist asks us to acknowledge the horror of suffering while looking at it as a problem for which we should imagine possible solutions. More importantly, meliorism asks us to hope that such solutions can be found and actualized by that form of creative intelligence that is stimulated by liberal values and that employs liberal means.

A cynic might object that there is no non-ideological way to establish the value of a direction for progress. The liberal meliorist might agree about the fallible nature of human knowledge. However, for the liberal, the burden of proof rests on those who would deny liberal values. This burden of proof is established based on the presumption that liberty is a good: it is up to the cynic to argue that it is not. Moreover, the liberal realizes the danger of the cynical conclusion in practical terms. If the cynic is right, then there is no reason to refrain from utilizing illiberal means to actualize liberal ends. The liberal meliorist strongly disagrees on this point. Since we do not have access to a transcendent scheme of justification that would justify the use of illiberal means, the best we can do is remain committed to liberal values in both means and ends. Despite terrorism, despite unrest and misery throughout the world, we still must hope that liberal values can be obtained by liberal means including nonviolent action and education. This hope is a normative imperative derived from the commitment to liberal values but also derived from the empirical fact that liberal means do in fact lead to liberal ends. Again, the burden of proof rests on the realist or cynic who would claim that illiberal means can in fact work to actualize liberal values. Coercive force might occasionally be necessary in both foreign and domestic affairs. However, this is a reluctant last resort that usually indicates a previous failure to creatively and vigorously disseminate liberty and peace through the liberal means of education, opportunity, tolerance, and respect. Rather than retreat to conservative or cynical realism, now is the time to renew our commitment to the interdependence of liberal means and end by creatively utilizing our intelligence to defend both peace and liberty.

Chapter 10. Democracy, Philosophy, and Peace

> Given human beings' love of truth, justice, peace, and freedom, creating
> a better, more compassionate world is a genuine possibility.
> — Dalai Lama[358]

The ideas presented in this book may be greeted with incredulity by those
who simply cannot imagine pacifism of any form, especially in the aftermath of
September 11. The topic of this book — war and peace — is not one that invites
easy consensus. Indeed, recent events show us how radical are our
disagreements about militarism, about the use of violence, and about the proper
interpretation of the global scene. These disagreements stem from divergent
ways of seeing or imagining the world and from different moral evaluations of
the use of violence. Our intuitive moral and political judgments are usually
colored by context and experience; but the philosopher's job is to scrutinize
these intuitive judgments by examining the principles and facts that support
them.

A philosophical consideration of the war on terrorism must ask basic
questions about what terrorism is, whether it is something we should be afraid
of, and what we should do in reaction to our fears. Philosophers have long
claimed that knowledge can be used to combat fear. Epicurus followed Socrates,
for example, in claiming that rational analysis shows us that there is nothing to
fear in death. Fear can be used to support irrational attitudes and behaviors; and

---

358.The Dalai Lama, *Ethics for a New Millennium* (New York: Riverhead Books, 1999), 217.

fear can be supported by cultural forces that want us to be afraid. Fear thus requires a long and patient practice of philosophical therapy; but this therapy is certainly worth the effort. We must work to overcome fear because fear is usually part of those psychological and political attitudes that lead to violence: fear leads to the flight or fight dilemma. Fear of our neighbors produces the attitudes found in the Hobbesian state of nature, which in turn leads to the creation of strong police and military states. Philosophical reflection can show us that fear is often a subjective reaction based upon a limited point of view. Our fears can be seen as irrational when we view the world from the more comprehensive perspective provided by philosophical reflection. Of course, not all fear is irrational. Fear is dependent on context and experience. This variability in our perception of the world explains the variability in our moral and political judgments. Statistical evidence shows that the risk of death by terrorism is quite small when compared with other risks we face on a daily basis.[359] However, we may feel a substantial amount of fear when we consider the possibility of terrorism. The amount of fear one feels will color the judgment made about the suitability of violence as a means for responding to the threat of terrorism. One's response to terrorism will thus be colored by the totality of one's values and the way these values interact with biographical, cultural, and even geographical contexts.

Divergent views, often fed by very real differences in life experiences, can be expressed and addressed through nonviolent means. This is the heart of philosophical dialogue. Although philosophical interlocutors may be angered by each other's remarks, they have the self-discipline to continue the dialogue, because they are committed to the values that ground the process of philosophical argumentation. Despite radical disagreements about the conclusions of their arguments, they agree that the process of philosophical critique is a primary value. Philosophers share a certain space of imagination that is grounded in a shared commitment to the value of dialogue. They imagine that in an ideal world, this commitment to reasonable argument would be the guiding force for all of us. In this philosophical utopia, there would be far less violence and much more effort to understand one another. When angered, we might take the time to understand the basic assumptions made by others, and make an effort to formulate reasonable arguments in reply.

---

359. See Roger D. Congleton, "Terrorism, Interest-Group Politics, and Public Policy," *The Independent Review* 8:1 (Summer 2002). Also see John Mueller, "Harbinger or Aberration: A 9/11 Provocation" *National Interest* (Fall 2002), 45-50.

Of course, many humans — terrorists and, occasionally, politicians — do not want to engage in dialogue. And occasionally we must use force. I do not claim that we should have done nothing in response to the September 11 attacks. Nor do I claim that we should learn to forgive these attacks: some crimes are unforgivable. Force might be justifiable in pursuing and apprehending the terrorists, and if apprehended and convicted, the terrorists deserve to be punished. However, a convincing case has not been made to justify the invasions of Afghanistan and Iraq on these grounds alone (I could imagine an argument from humanitarian intervention, but that was not the rationale used to convince the world before the war was begun). From the perspective of the practical pacifism I have defended here, the problem is that honest reflection shows we do not have enough information to say with certainty that these wars were justified. How, then, can we support them? Why did the US deviate from the procedures of international law for the apprehension and punishment of terrorists — which the US had supported, for example, in the case of the terrorist attacks on the Pan Am flight that was blown up over Lockerbie, Scotland.[360]

A commitment to a law enforcement approach is closely related to a commitment to philosophical argumentation. Law courts provide forums in which arguments can be heard and the truth can be exposed. For that reason, they are importantly like philosophical forums. Of course, law courts must make practical judgments that are to be enforced by legitimate authorities. But the commitment within the court is that all sides should have the opportunity to present their case. It is unfortunate that the war on terrorism has quickly leapt to the use of military force while avoiding the opportunity to construct genuine consensus about the crime of terrorism. If we were to use international courts that included Islamic jurists to condemn and punish terrorists, we would create a sense of global legitimacy as we fight terrorism.

Many will claim that the ideas set forth in this book are hopelessly naïve. Indeed, I have heard the claim before. But I want to make sure that I am not misunderstood. I am not advocating a form of absolute pacifism. Absolute pacifism is, in fact, naïve. Commonsense tells us that force is sometimes necessary to stop others from doing something. However, commonsense also tells us that force is usually both the first and only option considered. It is this feature of commonsense that my own practical pacifism rejects. Common sense

---

360. For more discussion of this approach, see Mark A. Drumbl in his "Judging the 11 September Terrorist Attack" *Human Rights Quarterly* 24 (2002), 323-360.

often asks us to assent to actions that are not clearly justified from the perspective of philosophical reflection. Much of what passes for commonsense represents a closed system that is unable to imagine alternatives to war. The media hammers us with worst-case scenarios that produce an irrational feeling of fear. Our historical education commemorates the use of military force. Our politicians tell us that we must take up arms to fight to defend our way of life. And movies and television celebrate the hero who grabs a gun and blows away the bad guys. Common sense teaches us that this is the best way to proceed. But philosophical reflection asks us to wonder if this is true by asking us to confront what we know about the need for violence, its risks, and its intended benefits. But such philosophical questioning runs counter to the sense of self-certainty found in the common imagination. Philosophical questions are thus viewed askance by most people, who want to be reassured that their immediate reactions are right. In the same way, pacifists, even practical pacifists, always have a hard time finding a sympathetic audience in cultures that are grounded in militaristic assumptions. We have to continually struggle to question the militaristic assumptions of the common imagination, because these assumptions are supported by our mainstream political and popular culture.

For this reason, one of the practical tasks of pacifists is to argue against the violent and militaristic ideology that underlies mainstream culture. And for this reason, pacifists are viewed as crazy and rebellious nonconformists. Thoreau, America's most famous anti-militarist protester, was jailed for his protests. We continue to be maligned. In the winter of 2003, before the US invaded Iraq, protesters were routinely cursed at and mocked. At one freezing cold event in February of 2003, in Wasau, Wisconsin, pro-war protesters waved American flags and chanted "USA, USA" so loudly that it was difficult to hear the messages of peace that were being spoken from the podium. The pro-war advocates displayed no hesitance or misgiving. They were not advocating war as a regrettable last resort. Rather, there was a blood-thirstiness to their position that was truly frightening.

It is true that pacifists who imagine a world beyond militarism are imagining something that is nowhere in sight. But is this a vain utopian sort of imagining? The answer to this question depends upon our view of human nature. Some actually enjoy war — these are the "bellists" described in Chapter 2. Cynics and militarists believe that humans only really understand the language of force. And pro-war protesters such as those in Wasau view military power as essential to national pride. War provides a thrill. I understand the desire to be proud of one's country. And I admit that it is sometimes true that force is a tragic necessity. But I hope that human beings have a desire for goods that do not require violence, an interest in going beyond force, and an ability to identify with the human race beyond one's national or ethnic group. Most human beings — with the exception of a few truly un-rational or psychopathic individuals — are, I think, motivated by a desire to understand both themselves and the world around them. The desire to understand is connected with the ethical point of view insofar as an effort to understand the other is a basic component of compassion. Educational, religious, and political systems can pervert a human being's innate curiosity: hateful and dogmatic ideologies can be fostered by systems of authority. The liberal faith described in the last chapter is founded upon the idea that better education can lead people beyond force, thus preparing the way for more and better democracy. This faith must be strengthened as we work for peace.

PHILOSOPHY AND ZONES OF PEACE

These ideas guide my practice as a philosopher. When I teach, speak, and write I assume that my audience has a desire to know and that they have enough patience and compassion to listen. Indeed, I would claim that most philosophers, educators, and even religious preachers believe that this is true. When Aristotle defined human beings as "rational animals," he articulated this ideal: human beings, unlike other animals, are motivated by reasons and ideas. Moreover, as Kant and his followers taught us, human beings have imaginations that allow us to conceive of new possibilities. When people use their imaginations and allow themselves to be motivated by reasons, they are doing philosophy. When we talk to one another, ask questions, and search for answers, we are doing philosophy. The important point is that when people are doing philosophy, they are not using force. Thus philosophy occurs in and creates a zone of peace. This zone of peace is usually fragile and momentary, but it can provide inspiration for creating more lasting zones of peace in the political world.

The thesis of practical pacifism holds out the possibility that some wars might be justified; the zone of peace created by philosophy is not completely opposed to war. In fact, philosophy may be a prelude to war: philosophical reflection may lead us to the conclusion that a war is justified. However, when we are wondering about the justification of war, we have created a space of questioning that is not itself war. And this zone of peace or space of questioning is quite important for the creation of a more lasting sort of peace. It is too much to claim that if everyone practiced philosophy, war would end. Indeed, philosophy should result in practical action and occasionally the conclusion of a philosophical argument may be that war should be engaged. Nonetheless, if more people engaged in philosophy, there would be far fewer wars and the wars that were fought would be more just.

One of the virtues of philosophy is its commitment to tolerant dialogue.[361] Philosophical dialogue occurs in a space of toleration: one must be willing to refrain from judgment and action long enough to hear and understand the arguments made by one's interlocutors. This is not to say that at the end of the day philosophical dialogue tolerates everything or results in a relativist inability to judge. Rather, when we are engaged in dialogue, our task is to listen so that we might criticize and judge based upon a full understanding of the other. It might be the case that we reach the conclusion that the other is wrong. If we are certain of this, then it might be our task to oppose the other either with words or with force. For the most part, however, human beings do not listen to the other and we quickly jump to the use of force. And, for some reason, we tend to believe that words alone are insufficient to bring about just ends. Part of this shows a lack of patience and a good bit of immodesty: we want the other to be converted immediately to our point of view, while refusing to admit that we ourselves might be, if only a little bit, wrong. But genuine social transformations can take a lifetime or, in the case of profound cultural change, several generations. Moreover, one must admit that one's own perspective might be limited. In other words, one must be willing to transform oneself and one's own culture. Those who advocate the use of force impatiently demand immediate change and immodestly refuse to listen and be moved. Of course, there are some cases when obvious evil must be opposed by force: I am not claiming, for example, that the September 11 terrorists were right and we were wrong. But these sorts of cases are probably more infrequent than our militaristic culture leads us to believe. Moreover, even if we judge that the terrorists were wrong, the question of a proper response to these crimes remains open. Militarism always responds with

---

361. I have developed the views of this section in more detail in "Toleration and the Limits of the Moral Imagination," *Philosophy in the Contemporary World*, 10:2 (Fall-Winter 2003).

vehement self-assertion. Philosophy, by contrast, is a practice of self-examination that tries to imagine alternative courses of action.

Our culture's standard approach to problem solving, conflict resolution, and the administration of justice suffers from problems that can be linked to a certain form of immodesty or arrogance. First, we usually make judgments about others without full knowledge of what these others are thinking or doing. We tend to think we know more about the other than we actually do. Second, we usually do not open our own views to criticism. Often this results from arrogance; but it can also result from a lack of courage. We don't listen to others because we are afraid to admit that we might be wrong or afraid that our arguments and reasons are not as strong as we might have thought. Third, we tend to remain stuck in traditional ways of doing things. The traditional way of administering justice is usually some version of the *lex talionis* — an eye for an eye — that requires the use of violent force. The immodesty is linked to a refusal to reevaluate the way we have always done things. And fourth, when we leap to the use of force, we give up hope that the other could be persuaded by reasons, thus denying his humanity. Again, this leap to force includes arrogance on our part: we often think that we have given others the chance to listen to reason and that the failure to be convinced is their fault and not our own. A bit of self-examination might lead to the conclusion that we have simply not given them compelling arguments. Rather than leaping to force, we might try to understand why it is that our arguments are not compelling for the other with whom we are in dialogue; and we might try to imagine other ways of persuasion, short of violence.

In this discussion, I have used the terms immodesty and arrogance several times to describe a sort of vice. In Greek, this vice is called *hubris*. Hubris is often translated as "pride," but it is pride that is linked to a certain tendency toward violence. Indeed, it can be translated as something like "wanton aggression," which takes pleasure in causing harm. Aristotle tells us that this vice is caused by a lack of self-control (what is called in Greek, *akrasia*, weakness of will). The virtues that help us control this vice are thus self-control and modesty. These are important virtues for philosophy. They are articulated by Socrates when he says that the only thing he knows is that he knows nothing. Socrates and other philosophers are modest about their ability to judge things with certainty; they exercise self-control in resisting the tendency to speak and act without knowledge. In the Platonic scheme of virtues, modesty and self-control are related to temperance or moderation (the Greek word is *sophrosyne*). This is the antidote for hubris. It is well known that hubris is the vice that is suffered in tragedy: Oedipus is motivated by hubris to kill his own father; Medea is motivated by hubris to kill her own children. Hubris is arrogant, violent, self-assertion. Those who suffer from hubris tend to act without self-criticism. The Socratic philosopher, on the other hand, tends to resist such forceful self-assertion by engaging in self-criticism. The Apollonian motto "Know thyself" is thus closely related to the motto, "nothing in excess." Self-control and self-criticism go hand in hand.

An interesting example can be found in the writing of Marcus Aurelius. Marcus was both a Roman emperor and a Stoic sage. He was in a unique position to utilize force. And in fact he was engaged in many wars in distant parts of the empire. His *Meditations* — his spiritual journal — were written while he was engaged in battles on the northern frontier. And yet Marcus writes in his journal to remind himself about the need for self-control, tolerance, modesty, patience, and self-criticism: "If he goes wrong, instruct him kindly and point out what is being overlooked; if you fail, blame yourself or, better, not even yourself."[362] Our duty to other rational beings is to help them to learn what is right and true, just as we would hope that they would do the same for us. Unfortunately, there are misunderstandings and disagreements. But rather than leaping to force, we should recognize that often the misunderstanding is our own fault, or, as Marcus hints, the fault of no one in particular because finite human beings live, as it were, in a world of misunderstanding.

A philosophical term for this idea is "epistemic modesty." We should be modest about what we know for certain. This idea lies at the heart of the theory of practical pacifism. There are some things that we do not and occasionally cannot know, especially when considering political arguments about the need for war. If more of us realized this, we would create zones of peace in which we could work together to create knowledge and mutual understanding.

It is important to realize how important knowledge and skepticism are when thinking about war and peace. Practical pacifism begins from the assumption that we must know with a large degree of certainty that any proposed act of violence or war is justified. Reflection shows that often we do not have strong justification for the use of violence because we lack adequate knowledge about the circumstances of war. If we are not certain that a war is

---

362. Marcus Aurelius, *Meditations* (New York: Everyman's Library, 1992), 10.4, p. 71. I discuss Marcus' idea of tolerance in "Stoic Tolerance," *Res Publica*, 9: 2 (2003).

justified, then our duty is to question and resist until we are sure. Of course, some practical judgment is required and occasionally we must act without certainty. It is rare that we are absolutely certain about anything. A life full of risk and uncertainty requires action based upon less than perfect knowledge. The point is not to use skepticism to produce inaction. Rather, our militarist culture often leads us to believe that force is necessary and justifiable in more cases than is warranted. A bit of self-criticism would lead to the conclusion that often we do not really know whether force is justified. If more people allowed themselves this moment of self-criticism, there would be less violence in the world.

Moreover, there are degrees of certainty within society based upon the division of labor. Acknowledging this creates a healthy brake on the tendency of militarist cultures such as our own. If more of the citizens of militarist democracies were honest about what they really know or don't know about their nations' uses of violence, this brake would work even better.

Philosophy leads in the direction of practical pacifism because, since Socrates, philosophers have been expert at pointing out what it is that we do not know. This puts philosophy into conflict with politics.[363] Politicians make their livings out of making claims about what is true and by convincing others of these "truths" with the skillful use of rhetoric. However, since Socrates, philosophers have pointed out that politicians often do not really know what they are talking about. Rather, the sophisticated use of rhetoric can create the appearance of knowledge. One of the tasks of philosophy is to criticize such rhetoric and to deflate the pretensions of politicians. Of course, this puts philosophers in an antagonistic relation to politicians. And there are risks in this way of behaving: Socrates was eventually executed by the politicians of Athens. Thus the virtue of epistemic modesty is linked to other virtues, including courage. One must be brave enough to admit what one does not know and to pursue self-knowledge wherever this leads. And obviously, one must be courageous when challenging the wisdom of powerful authorities. As an exemplar, Socrates teaches us that we should be afraid of acting unjustly and that we should be afraid of our own ignorance. But we should not fear the pursuit of truth or the requirements of justice.

---

363. This is the thesis of my book, *The Philosopher's Voice* (Albany, NY: State University of New York Press, 2002).

INDIVIDUAL RIGHTS, GROUP IDENTITY, AND HUMANITARIAN INTERVENTION

I began this book with a discussion of why violence and terrorism is bad. My conclusion is that violence violates the autonomy of its victims. I have also argued that war and the inversion of values that occur in wartime similarly undermine the autonomy of individuals. Of course, one might respond by claiming that things are much more complicated in the real world. One might claim that the liberal notion of individuality to which I appeal is part of an imperialist ideology, the ideology of liberal-capitalism, that wants us all to conform to the idea of the autonomous individual conceived as citizen, laborer, consumer. One might also claim that nationalism and patriotism are essential for a sense of belonging. I reject these communitarian counterarguments.

Although the communitarian critique of individualism is important, individualism is the best idea we have. Admittedly, individuality is unstable and individuals living in liberal-capitalist societies suffer from alienation and anomie. But this should not lead us to reject the project of individuality. Rather, it should — in Deweyan fashion — lead us to treat individualism as a problem that requires the continual application of critical intelligence.[364] My primary concern is the question of violence and war. Those who would deny the value of the individual too easily affirm group membership and values like patriotism that historically have been linked to the continuance of violence and war. Individualism — as developed in Emerson or in Mill, for example — is an approach that is deliberately poised against the tyrannical tendencies of social and political organizations. It is individual responsibility and action that will put a brake on militarism. History shows us that large social wholes and political institutions do violence to individuals. If we relinquish the value of individual autonomy, then we have no recourse with which to argue against the tyrannical use of state violence.

I have argued that violence is wrong because it violates autonomy. One might suggest, in opposition to this, that suffering is a more basic and better idea with which to describe violence; i.e., violence causes suffering. But suffering is located in the experience of individuals; and suffering alone is not enough to identify violence. This suffering must also be forced upon the individual against his/her will. This is why the pain caused by the dentist is not a form of violence. Individuals only suffer violence, when suffering is not in fact chosen by them.

---

364. Dewey did just this in *Individualism Old and New* (Prometheus Books, 1999).

And this is why war is usually wrong: it forces individual members of societies to suffer as members of groups, not because of anything that they deserve as individuals. It should be noted that this violation occurs both in forcing individuals to bear arms and in using indiscriminate violence against innocent targets in terrorist acts of violence.

I further deny that nationalism and patriotism are entirely good for us. Yael Tamir has argued to the contrary in her book, *Liberal Nationalism*.[365] Tamir argues both that it is inevitable that we identify with our immediate national group and that this is a good thing. However, in order to resist the tendency of nationalism to devolve toward tribalism and ethnic war, she argues that "liberal nationalism" must occur within the context of a universal scheme of liberal values. She is undoubtedly correct that we do inevitably identify with those who "belong" in some sense to our group. However, the aspiration of a more cosmopolitan form of liberalism is to keep this identification in proper perspective. In general, limited local identities tend to lead to conflict and war and the end of liberal values. Liberals have struggled with this problem — the tension between national identity and cosmopolitanism. One of the problems is that liberals have to allow individuals to define and identify themselves autonomously. If national identity is autonomously chosen by individuals, then national identity should be respected. Another problem is the fear that cosmopolitanism is both vapid and imperialistic. Tamir concludes with a typical remark from this perspective: "A postnational age in which national differences are obliterated and all share in one shallow universal culture, watch soap operas and CNN, eat MacDonalds [sic], drink Coca-Cola, and take the children to the local Disney world, is more nightmare than a utopian vision."[366]

A truly liberal cosmopolitanism is not, however, dedicated to effacing local culture by a process of McDonaldization.[367] Rather, the cosmopolitan view emphasizes the claim that individuals ought to be encouraged to make substantial choices about the good life. Such choices are *not* best facilitated by the spread of markets and advertising. Rather, they are facilitated by critical philosophical education. A liberal cosmopolitan approach is not opposed to local identification, provided that this identification is truly autonomous. However, in today's world, none of us can ignore the fact that there is a global confrontation of *individuals*. This is mediated by cultures; but it is individuals who must make

---

365. Yael Tamir, *Liberal Nationalism* (Princeton University Press, 1993).
366. Tamir, *Liberal Nationalism*, 166-67.
367. Cf. Benjamin Barber, *Jihad vs. McWorld* (Ballantine Books, 1996).

choices about how to deal with each other and with their own cultures. This is not to say that we should adopt a "cosmopolitan smorgasbord" approach to culture, where cultural values can be sampled at leisure by an unencumbered culturally disentangled self — although this may be inevitable. Rather, all individuals should have the opportunity to self-critically affirm their values for good reasons. Some might say that this is imperialistic — as if a commitment to self-critical education and informed choice were imperialistic. I deny this claim. It is imperialistic to force a set of values on another. It is not imperialistic to claim that others should have the opportunity to choose their values for themselves based upon the best evidence and information. Yes, there are some cultures that are opposed to certain forms of education, that seek to prevent members from self-critical education. One might claim that all cultures — even our own — suffer from this tendency to stifle critical education. However, we should recognize that such closed cultures are the true imperialists, organized to preserve a set of values from criticism through the hierarchical organization of social power. Such closed cultures are the most likely to retreat to that pernicious form of nationalism that leads to war. All the liberal cosmopolitan asks is that individuals be given the education and the opportunity to choose a set of values for themselves.[368]

Finally, the liberal cosmopolitan vision makes strong claims about the proper means for developing toward liberal values. Recognition of the interdependence of means and ends is crucial. Liberal values cannot be forced upon people: people cannot be forced to be free. But liberal values can defend themselves; and liberal regimes can use force to defend human rights, provided that they are able to imagine that individuals who suffer under repressive regimes would be willing to endure the risks of the war for their liberation. This should not be seen as a blanket justification of wars of intervention. The burden of proof needs to be quite high. Part of the problem is that individuals should be allowed to help themselves and should not be aided in a patronizing manner. John Stuart Mill's notion of "self-help" remains useful in international politics.[369] Another part of the problem is that we must do our best to respect the autonomy of the innocent individuals who would be harmed by a war of intervention that seeks to defend individual rights. There are trade-offs and

---

368. I am sympathetic, for example, to Martha Nussbaum's "In Defense of Universal Values" in *Women and Human Development: The Capabilities Approach* (Cambridge: Cambridge University Press, 2000).

369. This is discussed in Michael Walzer, *Just and Unjust Wars*, Chapter 6.

difficult decisions to be made in such cases. Since violence is something that is prima facie to be avoided, those who advocate it need to make a very strong case for its necessity and justification. Moreover, since states tend to violate the autonomy of citizens, since violence can be misused by those in power, and since wars tend to become terroristic when not radically constrained by vigorous criticism, we should be skeptical of leaders of liberal regimes who claim that violence is the best or only solution in such cases. This is not to say that we should refrain from intervening in genuine humanitarian crises. Obvious recent cases include Rwanda, Bosnia, and possibly Iraq. But we must be aware that violence used in the name of humanitarian intervention can actually be a hidden form of imperialism and that violence used to defend human rights can also destroy human beings in the process.

CLEAN HANDS AND DIRTY HANDS

One of the objections to the pacifist position is the problem of "clean hands." Pacifists are, it is thought, so concerned with not getting their own hands dirty that they are willing to allow others to suffer even when such suffering could be easily prevented. How dare we not act vigorously to prevent further terror, this argument goes; or how dare we not use military force for humanitarian purposes? The idea is that we should not be reluctant to use violence when this violence will obviously result in a decrease in overall suffering, even if, so the objection goes, the use of violence is ordinarily thought to be bad. The worry is that pacifists are so caught up in an absolutist (usually deontological) argument against violence that they are unwilling to admit that sometimes violence can have good consequences. Occasionally there is a further charge behind the "clean hands" critique of pacifism: there is an idea that pacifists are really cowards, who want to hide their cowardice behind moral principles.

I have dealt with the problem of clean hands in describing my own position as "practical" pacifism. Absolute pacifists are the ones who are most susceptible to the clean hands problem. They may be willing to avoid all use of force even to the point of allowing themselves and their loved ones to be killed rather than to use force to prevent such harm. The practical pacifism I have described in this book is not averse to all uses of force. Force can certainly be used in self-defense and to defend the innocent. But, force is unpredictable and military force often goes beyond the limits of justifiable violence. At best, the use of violence — even in self-defense — is regrettable and tragic. At best one can say that a just war is acceptable but not preferable. This means that it would be better if we could find actions other than war to accomplish our ends. As noted in a previous chapter, the very idea of a "just" war makes it sound as if war is a good thing. The point of view of practical pacifism is that war is always a terrible choice, even if such a choice could be justified. To use violence is always to "dirty" one's hands.

The problem of dirty hands is a political problem. Political action, in general, seems to create conditions in which we will have to do things — like use force — that, while justifiable, are also regrettable. In an important article on this topic, Michael Walzer has claimed that most politicians face the problem of dirty hands because the very idea of running for office usually creates situations in which one's integrity will be compromised. Politicians must often do things that are morally suspect in order to consolidate power; and they must often do things once they have power that are less than morally acceptable. The case of using military force is obvious. A politician's first duty is to defend his people from enemy invasion. However, such a defense will often go beyond the bounds of what is strictly speaking, morally acceptable. And in my analysis, even if the use of force is morally acceptable, it is still unfortunate and regrettable. Thus, if a politician is doing his duty, he will do something that is wrong. This is a paradox. Indeed, Walzer says, "Here is the moral politician: it is by his dirty hands that we know him."[370] Those in power face genuine dilemmas, which is why political power is often the subject of tragedy. In Sophocles' *Antigone*, for example, Antigone must choose between her political commitments and her familial commitments, which are in this case also political, since her family is the ruling family. Whichever choice she makes, she will have to reject the requirements of the other set of goods. The point of tragedy is that there is no way to resolve the dilemma or reconcile the tension. We must choose. But whatever we choose, we will sacrifice some good.

Walzer goes so far as to say that we want politicians to feel guilty when they violate moral rules in order to bring about the greatest good for their constituents. Thus, politicians will always suffer from some sort of bad faith — and maybe so will all mortals. Antigone goes so far as to kill herself as a result of her dilemma. It is possible that the guilt and bad faith of political action may not be redeemable, although Walzer holds out the possibility that some larger

---

370. Michael Walzer, "Dirty Hands," *Philosophy and Public Affairs*, 2:2 (Winter 1973), 168.

religious scheme could provide the vantage point from which the politicians "necessary evils" could be redeemed. What is significant about this problem is that in a democracy, the implication is that all of us have dirty hands to some extent: if we are responsible for those we have elected and for their actions, we are responsible, in part, for the deeds — including the misdeeds — of our leaders. If this is right, then we should feel guilty when our politicians lead us into unjust wars: "we" chose these leaders and let them lead us into war, even if we did not vote for them. Of course this guilt is indirect. And it seems unjust because it links individual responsibility to collective acts. Nonetheless, such collective guilt is important because it can be mobilized into political action and resistance to war.

It is true that pacifists are concerned with their own clean hands, and that this is a problem. This discussion of guilt is meant to show that no one's hands are entirely clean in a democracy that unjustly uses force. The problem of clean hands can return when we realize that the decision not to use force can occasionally result in more suffering than the decision to use force. In the case of humanitarian intervention, for example, to refrain from acting could lead to more suffering and death. This is why absolute pacifisms are often connected to religious belief, to the idea that undeserved suffering and death can be redeemed in another world. The practical pacifism defended in these pages does not begin from the hope of redemption. Rather, we must act in this complicated world as best we can. Although practical pacifism hopes for the best, the tragic fact is that the world in which we live is precarious and our lives and hopes are fragile.

The problem of dirty hands points us to the conclusion that what we want is as much certainty as possible with as little risk of doing wrong as possible. This is why the practical pacifist will argue with, criticize, and question those in power. One of the implications of this approach is that our hands will be as "clean" as possible if we do our best to ensure that we are making the right decisions about using force. Thus the questioning and resistance of pacifist citizens of democracies is intended to help establish certainty so that politicians and citizens can be reasonably sure that they are making the right decisions. Absolute certainty is rare, when we are talking about the use of force. And it may turn out that we have decided wrongly. However, the process of philosophical dispute and active questioning in pursuit of truth is essential for ensuring that our hands are as clean as they can be.

"MEN WITHOUT CHESTS"?

Two final problems with pacifism must be dealt with before we conclude. First, the contrast between war and peace may be ideological. We citizens of the United States like to imagine that we are at peace. However, it might be the case that our peace is founded upon war. September 11 provides us with insight into the underside of our peaceful reality. After the attacks, critics on the political left were glad to point out that the United States had created enemies throughout the world by using imperial power to exploit the global working class. From the right, a cynical, Hobbesian analysis of political reality reminded us that peace is always founded upon power. Thus, from both perspectives the peace enjoyed by citizens of the United States is based upon a certain ignorance about the conditions of war that make this peace possible. From the right, one might claim that when pacifists rejected the war on terror, they made this claim from within the shelter provided by the force of arms. From the left, one might claim that pacifists, who condemned the terrorists, were really engaged in an ideological support of the imperialist status quo. In the real world, objectors from both sides might say that violence is politically necessary and nonviolence is the delusion of those who are not on the front lines of the global struggle for power.

The second problem is that our love of peace may represent a pathetic form of life — the form of life of Nietzsche's last man. Francis Fukuyama worried about this problem back when it seemed that the triumph of liberal values was ushering in "the end of history." Peace lovers seem to be, in Fukuyama's (and Nietzsche's) terms, "men without chests."[371] That is, the love of peace can be a hollow and cowardly love of quiet and repose. This might come at the expense of any deeper commitment to values which demand courage and sacrifice. When pacifists claim that peace should be preserved, this claim might be a form of cowardice of those who are unwilling to fight for their values.

To reply to the first objection, we must recognize that the accusation of ideology cuts both ways. Those who claim that war is the prevalent state of human affairs and that peace is provided by power make this claim from within a world-view that normalizes war. Critics from both the left and the right can condemn pacifism. This shows us the pervasive idea that violence is politically necessary. On the left, this violence is the violence of the political uprising; on

---

371. Francis Fukuyama, *The End of History and the Last Man* (New York: The Free Press, 1992), Chapter 28.

the right, it is the violence of military force. In both cases there is a commitment to the idea that force is the only language of politics. The pacifist rejects this view for at least three reasons. First, the pacifist claims that it is simply not true that human beings are essentially war-like. Second, the pacifist claims that nonviolent alternatives can be practically effective to bring about social change. And third, the pacifist worries that belief in the idea of the necessity of force is what leads to war in the first place. For peace to prevail, we need to move beyond the basic assumption that politics is based upon brute force.

At issue here is the question of the burden of proof. The realist (whether on the right or on the left) assumes that reality is war and demands that the pacifist prove that it is not. The pacifist assumes that reality is not war and demands that the militarist should prove that it is. The basic assumptions of these different approaches lead to different methodological approaches. The resolution to this dilemma is pragmatic. We must experiment to see which assumption is correct. But a genuine experiment in nonviolence will always be hindered by the prevalent violent background assumptions of our culture. Pacifism has not yet been allowed to flourish, in part because the interests of the ruling elite are bound up with the assumptions of militarism. In other words, no pacifist experiment can get off the ground until the power of the ruling militarist point of view is weakened. The difficulty of pacifism is that the ruling military ideals must not be appropriated by those who would argue against them. The strategy of terrorists and rebels is to fight military power with military power. But this approach only strengthens our faith in military power while producing misery all around. As Gandhi showed us, the solution is experiments in nonviolent political action.

To reply to the second objection, we must consider the nature of human flourishing. Bellists claim that struggle and war are good for us because they bring out our strength and courage. This can be seen in the Nietzschean idea of the importance of struggle, power, and self-overcoming. But the pacifist claims the opposite, i.e., that the truly good things in life are the goods found in peace. And the pacifist must emphasize that one can struggle and engage in self-overcoming without committing violence. The natural and cultural worlds provide opportunities for meaningful struggles that do not include the struggles of violence. One of our problems is that we still hold on to the ancient cultural values in which war is seen as a natural part of human experience; but conditions have changed and it is time to reject these old stories and create new ones of our own.

CONCLUSION

There are many things that provide human beings with satisfaction and happiness. Our perspectives vary depending upon geography, biography, and cultural context; but most agree that one of the highest goods for human beings is the pursuit of truth. This pursuit is only possible within the context of peace. As mentioned before, philosophy creates a zone of peace. This zone of peace is important for human flourishing because it is only in this zone that we can come into contact — via dialogical encounters with others — with the truth about what is good for us. It is possible that the philosophical argument may result in the claim that war can be justified in some cases, although this conclusion will be rare. Rather, once the philosophical zone of peace has been created, what will probably be discovered is that human existence and the social and natural worlds are so amazingly complicated that we don't have time for war. This is not the weakness of "men without chests." Rather it would be the triumph of human beings as rational animals.

Philosophy is the art of wondering; and wondering is a fragile art. It requires peace, courage, and other virtues. It is the highest art for human beings. It is something that we all do when we allow ourselves to think. And it is the great hope for the future of mankind. If each generation were to wonder about war with more and more of a skeptical eye, perhaps one day a generation would be born that would view the war system as an incomprehensible remnant of a sad and gladly gone history. To create this future, we need more and better education about the horrors of war, the advantages of peace, and alternative means of achieving our goals. We need the courage to question the militaristic system, which currently passes for commonsense. Finally, a good dose of Socratic skepticism is required toward those in power. We must demand that the powerful prove to us the moral necessity of the military system that continues to spend vast amounts of human creative power in preparation for war. The image of Socrates is inspiring and sobering. Socrates stood up to his government; but he was executed for his efforts. Such are the risks of questioning the status quo and envisioning a new way of life. These risks would not be so great if each one of us as individuals took upon ourselves the responsibility to question and resist the militarist system in which we live.

INDEX

A

Abraham (father of Isaac) 195, 196
Addams, Jane 5, 10, 12, 14, 15, 50, 53
Afghanistan 1, 20, 22, 113, 121, 123, 141, 147, 149, 162, 165, 227
Al-Qaeda 178
Anarchism 85
Annan, Kofi 6, 14
Aquinas, Thomas 74, 78
Augustine 73, 78

B

Bellism 55
Bin Laden, Osama 198
Bonobos 44
Buddhism 62, 71
Bush, George W. (President) 29, 121, 146, 148, 149, 154, 156, 158, 160, 161, 165, 167, 169, 178, 184, 200, 201

C

Chomsky, Noam 16, 17, 20, 21, 24, 113, 115, 157, 170, 172, 173, 180, 188
Christianity 8, 10, 18, 41, 47, 49, 58, 60, 61, 62, 63, 64, 65, 67, 68, 69, 70, 73, 75, 78, 92, 103, 124, 133, 140, 141, 145, 146, 187, 188, 192, 194, 195, 196, 200, 202, 203, 211
Civil Disobedience 13, 21, 67, 92, 100
Conspiracy theories 166, 168
Cynicism 207, 208, 210, 212

D

Dalai Lama 22, 71, 225
Democracy 6, 12, 115, 157, 168, 172, 184, 197, 206, 215, 218, 221, 225
Dewey, John 10, 13, 14, 19, 53, 106, 107, 132, 157, 171, 172, 205, 206, 207, 208, 209, 210, 214,
215, 218, 220, 221, 234
Double Effect (doctrine of) 81, 96, 116, 118
Doyle, Michael 5, 53, 76, 134, 141, 153, 174, 211, 217

E

Emerson, Ralph Waldo 5, 6, 7, 10, 11, 12, 14, 21, 85, 171, 219, 234
Epistemology 19, 85, 97, 128, 132, 138, 182, 191, 203, 218
Eschatology 177, 188, 190, 191, 192, 193, 194
Ethics 10, 27, 28, 32, 33, 34, 35, 36, 42, 60, 65, 67, 69, 70, 71, 72, 78, 79, 81, 86, 88, 92, 96, 100, 105, 110, 111, 116, 121, 124, 137, 156, 191, 192, 193, 194, 195, 196, 197, 198, 200, 215, 225, 229

F

Fallibilism 31-36, 60, 201, 222, 223
Fear 69, 183, 195, 225
Freud, Sigmund 39, 90, 91, 103, 124, 208, 209
Fukuyama, Francis 142, 240

G

Gandhi, Mohandas K. 8, 9, 10, 12, 15, 22, 50, 57, 63, 64, 65, 66, 67, 68, 71, 72, 92, 93, 241
Girard, Rene 48, 189, 196
Glover, Jonathan 7, 51, 86, 98, 110, 115, 117, 147, 148, 160, 207, 208
God 18, 32, 36, 47, 48, 49, 59, 60, 61, 62, 63, 64, 65, 66, 68, 69, 72, 73, 86, 87, 92, 103, 122, 137, 177, 184, 192, 193, 194, 195, 196, 197, 199, 200, 202, 213, 216
Gulf War (1991) 115, 160, 161, 174

H

Hatred 179, 182, 183, 196

Printed in the United States
21748LVS00004B/211-219

9 780875 862903